JOURNAL OF

Medieval Military History

Volume VIII

The journal's hallmark of a broad chronological, geographic, and thematic coverage of the subject is underlined in this volume. It begins with an examination of the the brief but fascinating career of an armed league of (mostly) commoners who fought to suppress mercenary bands and to impose a reign of peace in southern France in 1182–84. This is followed by a thorough re-examination of Matilda of Tuscany's defeat of Henry IV in 1090–97. Two pieces on Hispanic topics – a substantial analysis of the remarkable military career of Jaime I 'the Conqueror' of Aragon (r. 1208–76), and a case study of the campaigns of a single Spanish king, Enrique II of Castile (r. 1366–79), contributing to the active debate over the role of open battle in medieval strategy – come next. Shorter essays deal with the size of the Mongol armies that threatened Europe in the mid-thirteenth century, and with a surprising literary description, dating to 1210–20, of a knight employing the advanced surgical technique of thoracentesis. Further contributions correct the common misunderstanding of the nature of deeds of arms *à outrance* in the fifteenth century, and dissect the relevance of the 'infantry revolution' and 'artillery revolution' to the French successes at the end of the Hundred Years War. The final note explores what etymology can reveal about the origins of the trebuchet.

JOURNAL OF MEDIEVAL MILITARY HISTORY

Editors

Clifford J. Rogers
Kelly DeVries
John France

ISSN 1477–545X

The Journal, an annual publication of **De re militari: The Society for Medieval Military History**, covers medieval warfare in the broadest possible terms, both chronologically and thematically. It aims to encompass topics ranging from traditional studies of the strategic and tactical conduct of war, to explorations of the martial aspects of chivalric culture and *mentalité*, examinations of the development of military technology, and prosopographical treatments of the composition of medieval armies. Editions of previously unpublished documents of significance to the field are included. The Journal also seeks to foster debate on key disputed aspects of medieval military history.

The editors welcome submissions to the Journal, which should be formatted in accordance with the style-sheet provided on De re militari's website (www.deremilitari.org), and sent electronically to the editor specified there.

JOURNAL OF

Medieval Military History

Volume VIII

Edited by

CLIFFORD J. ROGERS

KELLY DeVRIES

JOHN FRANCE

THE BOYDELL PRESS

First published 2010
The Boydell Press, Woodbridge

Transferred to digital printing

ISBN 978–1–84383–596–7

The Boydell Press is an imprint of Boydell & Brewer Ltd
PO Box 9, Woodbridge, Suffolk IP12 3DF, UK
and of Boydell & Brewer Inc.
668 Mount Hope Ave, Rochester, NY 14604, USA
website: www.boydellandbrewer.com

A CIP catalogue record for this book is available
from the British Library

The publisher has no responsibility for the continued existence or accuracy of
URLs for external or third-party internet websites referred to in this book,
and does not guarantee that any content on such websites is,
or will remain, accurate or appropriate.

This publication is printed on acid-free paper

Contents

1

People against Mercenaries: The Capuchins in Southern Gaul

John France

The Capuchins were a sworn confraternity whose members took up arms in order to impose the peace in the violently disordered world of southern Gaul in the years 1182–84. In doing this they acted under the authority of Canon 27 of the Third Lateran Council of 1179, and took upon themselves something of the character of crusaders. Their movement originated amongst the townspeople of Le Puy in the Auvergne, and although it embraced all classes of society and enjoyed the approbation of bishops and clergy, it was clearly popular rather than aristocratic in nature. For a time it was remarkably successful. Ultimately the Capuchins found themselves confronting the great powers of the area and were crushed by troops in the service of the great men whose quarrels were the ultimate cause of the political disorder which plagued southern Gaul. The circumstances both of their success and their failure tell us something of military reality in twelfth-century Europe.

Our vision of medieval warfare in the twelfth century is dominated by the upper classes. The men on horseback, knights and great lords, claimed to be the rightful arms-bearers and protectors of society. They portray themselves on seals and in pictures, mounted, in full armor, often bearing swords, because the military role was central to their sense of identity. They even adapted their religious beliefs to suit their way of life.[1] Most of the chroniclers of the age, when they talk about war, focus on their deeds as warriors. And they certainly were the leading element in all the armies of the period. They were more than simply cavalrymen: the mounted knight as a weapons-system has been overstated, as Matthew Bennett and Stephen Morillo have pointed out.[2] But nobles and knights came from the better-off in society and had the leisure to train for war, and, therefore to develop their physique and technique to a very high level. Ordericus Vitalis reports the deaths of two of the Giroie family while practising for war – one killed by a carelessly tossed javelin and the other from broken ribs when

[1] Richard W. Kaeuper, *Holy Warriors: The Religious Ideology of Chivalry* (Philadelphia, 2009).
[2] Matthew Bennett, "The Myth of the Supremacy of Knightly Cavalry," in Matthew J. Strickland, ed., *Armies, Chivalry and Warfare* (Stamford, 1998); Stephen Morillo, "The 'Age of Cavalry' Revisited," in Donald J. Kagay and L. J. Andrew Villalon, eds., *The Circle of War in the Middle Ages* (Woodbridge, 1999), pp. 45–59.

he was thrown onto stone steps during a friendly wrestling-match![3] At the battle
of the Standard in 1138 Ordericus commented on how formidable they were
as footsoldiers, stiffening the ranks of the English infantry so that "mounted
knights could by no means continue against knights in armour who fought on
foot, close together in immovable formation."[4] At the battle of Worringen in
1288 a sergeant advised the army to kill the enemy nobles first of all: "As each
man comes to any noble, let him not turn aside until he has slain him. For, were
their army so great that it stretched from here to Cologne, They will lose the
battle if their nobles are killed."[5]

Yet these men were not the majority in the armies of the day. Chroniclers
describe forces as made up of *milites et pedites*, and the latter were clearly far
more numerous than the former in almost all cases. Furthermore, even amongst
the cavalry noblemen and knights were a shrinking group. As the twelfth century
wore on nobles became ever more exclusive and the wealthier knights were
increasingly regarded as being aristocrats, so that while *milites* in the eleventh
century can usually be translated as "cavalry," by the end of the twelfth the
cavalry was made up of nobles, knights and others.[6] The word *servientes* appears
in our sources, usually translated "sergeants," meaning non-noble soldiers, and
it is clear that sometimes they acted as horsemen. Gilbert of Mons was chan-
cellor of the count of Hainaut and he is very careful to distinguish this group
from the knights. They were usually, but not always, less well-equipped, and we
can assume this is because they were drawn from people of limited means.[7] But
they were clearly of great value and they seem to become commoner with the
passing of time. Some at least seem to have been professionals of war and this
means that they merge into another group numerous in twelfth-century armies,
the mercenaries.

We usually think of mercenaries in the twelfth century as being footsoldiers,
and many of them were. But there is evidence that others fought on horseback
and could compete on equal terms with the greatest. At Dol in 1174 Henry II
(1154–89) of England sent a mercenary force which destroyed the Breton rebels
at the battle of Dol.[8] Mercadier, Richard of England's great mercenary leader,

3 Ordericus Vitalis, *Historia Aecclesiastica*, ed. Marjorie Chibnall, 6 vols. (Oxford, 1969–79),
   2:23–31. Hereafter cited as OV.
4 OV, 6:350–51.
5 Jan van Heelu, *Rijmkronijk*, translated in J. F. Verbruggen, *The Art of Warfare in Western Europe
   during the Middle Ages*, trans. Sumner Willard and Mrs. R. W. Southern (Woodbridge, 1997),
   p. 267.
6 David Crouch, *The Birth of Nobility: Constructing Aristocracy in England and France 900–1300*
   (Harlow, 2005).
7 For example: Gilbert of Mons, *Chronique*, ed. Léon Vanderkindere (Brussels, 1904), pp. 171,
   197; trans. Laura Napran, *Chronicle of Hainaut* (Woodbridge, 2005), pp. 95 and 108. The
   terms *servientes* or *stratores* are very fluid. Some clearly had landholdings, but others were
   very humble people indeed. For a discussion see John France, *Western Warfare in the Age of
   the Crusades 1000–1300* (London, 1990), pp. 64–66.
8 John D. Hosler, *Henry II: A Medieval Soldier at War, 1147–1189* (Leiden, 2007), p. 144.

seems to have been a person of some status.[9] Such formidable competence allied
to an ambiguous status may go some way to explaining the aristocratic William
the Marshal's bitter dislike of Mercadier whom he in many ways resembles – as
being one who rose in the service of kings by military ability.[10] But most mercenaries were footsoldiers. We know very little about where and how infantry
were recruited. Many were undoubtedly the servants of greater men and knights
raised from amongst the more adventurous peasants on their estates. Henry II
at the start of his reign attempted to impose on his magnates infantry quotas
comparable to their obligation as tenants to produce knights, but this failed.
Ultimately he was noted for his employment of mercenaries.[11] Their great virtue
was that, as long as they were paid, they were willing soldiers and they formed
an important element in almost all European armies.[12]

These, then, are the *dramatis personae* of medieval warfare. They are a
familiar cavalcade. The mounted knights clad in iron helm and chain-mail and
equipped with shield, lance and sword; the infantry in padded jackets, perhaps
with iron helmets, wielding spears for the close-order battle, and bows, sometimes crossbows, which were useful in the field and at sieges. But these forces
existed in a wider society which in a military sense we tend to ignore and regard
as essentially demilitarized. Indeed a famous passage in the Annals of St Bertin
has long been interpreted as a crucial moment when the mass of the population
in Gaul were excluded from the bearing of arms:

> The Danes ravaged the places beyond the Scheldt. Some of the common people living
> between the Seine and the Loire formed a sworn association amongst themselves and
> fought bravely against the Danes on the Seine. But because their association had been
> made without due consideration, they were easily slain by our more powerful people.[13]

---

[9] Mercadier was never ennobled but he was given substantial lands and permitted to make a very advantageous marriage, which suggests that he was by no means of very humble origins: H. Géraud, "Les routiers au xiie siècle," and "Mercadier. Les routiers au xii siècle," *Bibliothèque de l'Ecole des Chartes* 3 (1841–42), 125–47, 417–43.

[10] David Crouch, "William Marshal and the Mercenariat," in John France, ed., *The Mercenary Identity in the Middle Age* (Leiden, 2008), pp. 15–32.

[11] At the Northampton Court of 1164 Henry II experimented with a system of infantry recruit-ment based on the magnates raising them in parallel with their obligation to produce knights, but this was not a success and was quickly abandoned: Michael Prestwich, *Armies and Warfare in the Middle Ages: The English Experience* (New Haven, 1996), pp. 120–21, 148–50.

[12] Important general surveys of mercenaries in this period remain H. Grundmann, "Rotten und Brabazonen, Söldner-heere in 12. Jahrhundert," *Deutches Archiv für die Erforschung des Mittelalters* 5 (1942), 419–92; J. Boussard, "Les mercenaires au xiie siècle. Henri II Plante-genet et les origines de l'armée de métier," *Bibliothèque de l'Ecole des Chartes* 106 (1945–6), 189–224; J. Boussard, "Services féodaux, milices et mercenaires aux X et XI siècles," in *Ordinamenti militari in Occidenti nell'Alto Medioevo: Settimane di Studio del Centro Italiano di Studi sull'Alto Medioevo XV, Spoleto 30 March – 5 April 1967* (Spoleto,1968), pp. 131–68; J. Schlight, *Monarchs and Mercenaries* (Bridgeport,1968); Stephen D. B. Brown, "The Merce-nary and his Master: Military Service and Monetary Reward in the Eleventh and Twelfth Century," *History* 74 (1989), 20–38; France, ed., *Mercenary Identity*.

[13] *Annals of St Bertin*, ed. Janet Nelson (Manchester, 1991), s.a. 859, p. 89.

The mass of the population is indeed portrayed as passive in a military sense, and even in consequence, some have thought, enjoyed a certain immunity from war's terrors because of this exclusion.[14] But in fact the mass of the population regularly suffered from the attentions of warriors. In medieval circumstances battle was relatively rare. This was because both parties had to want to hazard all on a collision in the open field, not a common eventuality. Commanders knew that, in the words of Vegetius: "It is preferable to subdue an enemy by famine, raids and terror, than in battle where fortune tends to have more influence than bravery."[15]

And they understood all too well the risks to their own lives. Their armies were very imperfect instruments with poor command structures and this increased the hazards of battle immensely. Moreover a defeated enemy could take refuge in fortified towns and castles, so that a victory might merely lead to a siege with all its problems of supply and organization.[16] In these circumstances the best means of waging war was to ravage an enemy's lands. This undermined the will of his supporters, damaged his economic base and provided attacking soldiers with food and loot. This was war which could pay for itself, always an attractive notion. Of course it was not very pleasant for the "civilian" population. William the Conqueror's biographer famously praised him for his methods of war:

> He [William the Bastard, duke of Normandy] sowed terror in the land by his frequent and lengthy invasions; he devastated vineyards, fields and estates; he seized neighbouring strongpoints and where advisable put garrisons in them; in short he incessantly inflicted innumerable calamities upon the land.[17]

And William notoriously devastated northern England in a way which even contemporaries found shocking. But these were not unusual acts. William de Breteuil in his feud in Normandy in 1089–92 with the Goël family funded his struggle by extorting ransoms from the country people.[18] In 1185 Baldwin of Hainaut devastated some 110 villages belonging to his enemy, Jacques of Avesnes, as an act of revenge.[19] This was how war was fought – at the expense of the mass of the population.

In southern Gaul this kind of devastation reached critical levels towards

---

[14] For example see Matthew Strickland, *War and Chivalry: The Conduct and Perception of War in England and Normandy 1066–1217* (Cambridge, 1996).

[15] Vegetius, *Epitome of Military Science*, trans. N. P. Milner (Liverpool, 1993), p. 108.

[16] On the nature of medieval armies see France, *Western Warfare*, 39–52. For the discussion amongst historians on the importance or otherwise of evading battle see Clifford J. Rogers, "The 'Vegetian Science of Warfare' in the Middle Ages" and Stephen Morillo, "Battle Seeking: The Contexts and Limits of Vegetian Strategy," both in *The Journal of Medieval Military History* 1 (2002), 1–20, 21–42.

[17] Trans. John Gillingham, in "William the Bastard at War," in *Studies in History presented to R. Allen Brown*, ed. Christopher Harper-Bill, Christopher J. Holdsworth and Janet L. Nelson (Woodbridge,1986), p. 148. There is a more recent translation: William of Poitiers, *Gesta Guillelmi*, ed. and trans. R. H. C. Davis and Marjorie Chibnall (New York, 1998).

[18] OV, 4:287–96.

[19] Gilbert of Mons, *Chronique*, p. 182; *Chronicle*, p. 97.

1180. The area suffered from political fragmentation, and though strong political authorities intruded into the area, their actual power was limited. The Plantagenet, Henry II, as duke of Aquitaine, had laid claim to the county of Toulouse as early as 1156, but this was rejected by the counts of Toulouse. There followed Henry's great expedition against Toulouse in 1159 and what has been called "The Forty Years War," really an intermittent series of conflicts, which dragged on until 1196. Henry's son, Richard, as duke of Aquitaine, was especially concerned with the claim to Toulouse after he had gained possession of the duchy by 1174. Inevitably, the kings of France took an interest in this dispute, and usually supported the counts of Toulouse. This conflict, therefore, became enmeshed in the wider Angevin-Capetian rivalry which in the 1180s would severely affect the region of Berry, where Bourges was an important French royal centre.[20] Moreover, the barons of Aquitaine did not enjoy the stern rule of their Angevin masters, and there were serious rebellions against Henry II and Richard in 1168, 1173–74, 1176, 1178/9, 1182/3, 1188, 1192 and 1193, that of 1183 being strikingly important and far-reaching because of the participation of Henry II's eldest son, Henry the Young King.[21] But there was also another war in the same area. The kings of Aragon wanted to assert their claim to Provence, the lands east of the Rhône, and other parts of the south, against the counts of Toulouse. This resulted in a series of wars embroiling Provence, the Auvergne and the Languedoc which smouldered on in parallel with the Angevin-Capetian conflicts, particularly after 1166. It is hardly surprising that the kings of Aragon and the Angevins were commonly allies during the twelfth century.[22] The consequences of all this violence are described by Stephen, abbot of St.-Geneviève of Paris, who was in the entourage of the Papal Legate, Cardinal Henri de Marcy:

> I followed the bishop of Albano though mountains and valleys, through vast wastelands and the savagery of robbers and the very image of death, through burnt villages and the ruins of houses where there was no security and nothing which did not threaten peace and life itself.[23]

[20] For the wider context see John Gillingham, *The Angevin Empire* (London, 2001). On the war see Jane P. Martindale, " 'An Unfinished Business': Angevin Politics and the Siege of Toulouse, 1159," *Anglo-Norman Studies* 23 (2000), 115–54; Richard Benjamin, "A Forty Years War: Toulouse and the Plantagenets, 1156–96," *Historical Research* 61 (1988), 270–85. This author died in an accident and his supervisor, Professor John Gillingham, brought this work to press. Bourges had been purchased by Philip I (1060–1108) in 1101, on which see Jean Dunbabin, *France in the Making 843–1180* (Oxford, 1985), p. 219.

[21] André Debord, *La société laïque dans les pays de la Charente, X^e–XIIe siècles* (Paris, 1984), pp. 382–402.

[22] Charles Higounet, "La rivalité des maisons de Toulouse et de Barcelone pour la prépondérance médiévale," in Charles-Edmond Perrin, ed., *Mélanges d'histoire du moyen âge dédiés à la mémoire de Louis Halphen* (Paris, 1951), pp. 313–22.

[23] "Sequor Albanum episcopum per montes et valles, per vastas solitudines, per praedonum rabiem et mortis imaginem, per incendi villarum et ruinas domorum, ubi nihil tutum, nihil quod non minetur saluti et non insidietur vitae." Quoted in Yves M.-J. Congar, "Henri de Marcy, abbé de Clairvaux, Cardinal-Évêque d'Albano et Légat Pontifical," *Studia Anselmiana* 43 (1958), 39.

At the root of these disasters were the wars of the kings of France, England and Aragon and the counts of Toulouse, together with their friends and supporters. Contemporaries were well aware that it was the great who started wars and prosecuted them with little regard to innocent victims. Geoffroy de Breuil de Vigeois was a monk of St.-Martial at Limoges who later became abbot of Vigeois (1170–84), to the south-east of Limoges in the modern département of Corrèze. In his chronicle he records that in a single day in the spring of 1177 some nobles of the Limousin, led by Aimar, Viscount of Limoges, massacred 2,000 people of both sexes in a drive towards Brive.[24] But condemning such grandees and their great vassals was, to say the least, impolitic. Contemporaries, therefore, blamed their instruments, the mercenaries. These professional soldiers were used by all the great kings, but they were regarded with contempt and disdain by their employers and with fear by the Church and all others who were their victims.[25] The Church disliked all violence but drew a clear line between those who served kings as vassals and were, therefore, defenders of the social order, and men who only fought for money and were regarded as deeply sinful.[26]

The grave troubles in southern Gaul explain why the vast majority of the twenty-six French bishops who attended the Third Lateran Council in 1179 were from southern Gaul. Alexander III (1159–81), now firmly in unchallenged possession of the Holy See, was determined to establish proper order in Christian society.[27] The concerns of the southern bishops were powerfully amplified by Henri de Marcy, abbot of Clairvaux (1176–79) and later Cardinal Legate to the area. He had written to the pope before the council, urging him to launch a crusade against the heresy which was rampant in the south. Indeed, at some time during the years 1174–77 the Cathar Council of Saint-Félix-de-Caraman (now Saint-Félix-Lauragais) had openly challenged the Roman church with the creation of four Cathar bishops for Albi, Agen, Carcassonne and Toulouse.[28]

Of course Stephen may well have exaggerated the devastation to highlight his own devotion, but it is unlikely that he invented it.

[24] Geoffroy de Vigeois, *Chronica*, in vol. 2 of Philippe Labbe, *Novae Bibliothecae manuscriptorum et librorum rerum Aquitanicarum*, 2 vols. (Paris, 1657), p. 323.

[25] Hosler, *Henry II*, pp. 119–24, discusses Henry's employment of mercenaries while for aristocratic attitudes see Crouch, "William Marshal and the Mercenariat."

[26] After Hastings all the soldiers of the Norman army had to perform penance for homicide, but it was much heavier for the mercenaries than for Duke William's own men, on which see H. E. J. Cowdrey, "Bishop Ermenford of Sion and the Penitential Ordinance Following the Battle of Hastings," *Journal of Ecclesiastical History* 20 (1969), 225–42.

[27] On the Council see Raymonde Foreville, "La place de Latran III dans l'histoire conciliaire du xii siècle," in J. Longère, ed., *Communications présentées à la table ronde du CNRS 26 avril 1980* (Paris, 1982), pp. 11–31.

[28] Congar, "Henri de Marcy," pp. 12–19; Beverly Mayne Kienzle, *Cistercians, Heresy and Crusade in Occitania, 1145–1229: Preaching in the Lord's Vineyard* (Woodbridge, 2001), pp. 109–34. Rather curiously this work ignores the Capuchins; Bernard Guillemain, "L'épiscopat français à Latran III," in J. Longère, ed., *Le Troisième Concile de Latran (1179)* (Paris, 1982), pp. 23–32. Amongst the French bishops present who will be mentioned in this article were Guillaume de Toucy, Bishop of Auxerre (1167–81) (*Gesta Episcoporum Autissiodorensium*, in L. M. Duru,

Canon 27 of the Third Lateran Council in 1179 anathematized the heretics of Gascony, the Albigeois and the Toulousaine, and, in the very same breath condemned those called "Brabantionibus et Aragonensibus, Navariis, Bascolis, Coterellis et Triaverdinis" who destroyed churches and the countryside, the poor and the innocent without any distinction of sex or status. Anyone who employed such mercenary soldiers would have their names published in churches and be liable to excommunication. Those who associated with either the heretics or the mercenary bands would also be liable to excommunication. Anyone who acted against these outlaws, providing they were "following the council of holy bishops and priests," would receive "a remission of two years penance and will be placed under the protection of the Church just like those who undertake the journey to Jerusalem."[29]

"Mercenary" (*mercenarius*) is rather a rare word in the Latin sources of the high Middle Ages, and always used pejoratively, because it clearly had heavy overtones of Christ's words in which he contrasts the mere hireling (*mercenarius*) who flees at the first sign of trouble for his flock, with himself, the "Good Shepherd."[30] It was not used in Canon 27. Geoffroy was writing his chronicle in the Limousin in the 1180s at the heart of the area troubled by these soldiers, and he recorded the terrible sufferings they inflicted. He uses the term *mercenarios* of churchmen corrupted by rich living, before going on almost immediately to list the soldiers who afflicted the Aquitaine as "Primo Basucli, postmodum Teuthonici Flandrenses et, ut rustice loquar, Brabansons, Hannuyers, Asperes, Pailer, Navar, Turlau, Vales, Roma, Cotarel, Catalans, Aragones."[31] A thirteenth-century chronicler who provided valuable information on the subject of this paper referred to the mercenaries as: "Ruthariorum, Arragonensium, Basculorum, Brabancionum et aliorum conducticiorum."[32] For the most part such words derive from the supposed origins of these professional soldiers. Brabançons (men of Brabant) is the commonest word used for mercenaries in the twelfth century, but the range of terms used in these sources reflects

---

Bibliothèque historique de l'Yonne, 2 vols. (Auxerre and Paris, 1850–63), 1:428) and Pons d'Arsace, Archbishop of Narbonne (1162–82), on whom see below, p. 000; the earlier date of 1167 for the Council of Saint-Félix-de-Caraman is not now favored, on which see Claire Taylor, *Heresy in Medieval France: Dualism in Aquitaine and the Agenais, 1000–1249* (Woodbridge, 2005), pp. 172–73.

29 Charles Joseph Hefele, *Histoire des Conciles*, ed. and trans. H. Leclerq, 9 vols. (Hildesheim, 1973), 5.2:1106–08.

30 Vulgate: Iohannes 10.12–14.

31 Geoffroy de Vigeois, *Chronica*, p. 328. Geoffroy's Latin is very difficult and the P. Labbe edition is not very satisfactory. However, it is the only full text of the Chronicle, though extracts from it appear in *Recueil des Historiens des Gaules et de la France*, ed. Léopold Delisle, 24 vols. (Paris, 1869–1904), 10:267–9, 11:288, 12:421–51, 18:211–23 and MGH SS 26:199–203. There is a study by Pierre Botineau, "Chronique de Geoffroi de Breuil, prieur de Vigeois," unpublished doctoral thesis, École des Chartes (Paris, 1964), but I have not been able to obtain a copy of this.

32 Anonymous of Laon, *Chronicon Universale Anonymi Laudunensis (1154–1219)*, ed. Alexander Cartellieri and Wolf Stechele (Leipzig and Paris, 1929), p. 37.

the diverse origins of those who troubled them, recruited by rulers from several areas.

Roger of Howden was an important historian who had served as a royal clerk under Henry II and later went on crusade with Richard I (1189–99).[33] He must have come into close contact with the military household of the English kings, and had a sharp perception of the kinds of soldiers with whom he was dealing.[34] He always uses the term *Brabanceni* and is careful to distinguish them from others in the service of King Henry.[35] *Aragonensibus*, *Navariis*, *Bascolis* and *Hannuyers* are, respectively, those from Aragon, Navarre, the Basque lands and Hainaut. *Turlau* could refer to Le Puy-Turlau (Périgord) or Turlau near the town of Curemonte (Corrèze) but these seem unlikely, while *Vales* and *Roma* are obscure. *Asperes* poses difficulties. Geoffroy de Vigeois includes them in a list of people from the Netherlands, but goes on to mention Aragonese and others in the same breath. Asperen, in what is now Holland, is a possible place of origin, but so is Vallée d'Aspe (Pyrénées Atlantiques, région du Béarn). Alternatively this may be derived from Latin *asper* (rough) (which perhaps could be rendered in English as "ruffians") or an allusion to the *asperiolus*, a coin. Other obvious generic terms are *Rutharii* – derived from *Rupta* or *Ruta*, meaning men of the companies, analogous to *routiers* – *conducticii* and *coterelles*, and all could be translated as gangsters or cut-throats in English.[36] *Triaverdinis*, used in the list given by Canon 27, is a very rare word which Ducange thinks may be connected with *Trialemello* meaning thrice-armored. Geoffroy de Vigeois explicitly reserves *Palearii* (rough sleepers) for a large group of diverse origins who were sent to the Limousin by Philip II Augustus, King of France (1180–1223), to assist those who supported the rebellion of his eldest son, Henry "the Young King," against Henry II in 1183. Interestingly, Geoffroy reports that the young king was afraid his father would hire these mercenaries away from him by paying them more.[37] In his list of mercenaries Geoffroy gives pride of place to the Basques (*Basculi*), and this is paralleled in *The Miracles of Our Lady of Rocamadour*, which report a number of stories connected with mercenaries,

---

33 David Corner, "Howden," in *Dictionary of National Biography* (Oxford, 2005–), http://www.oxforddnb.com/articles/

34 The classic study of the military household is that of J. O. Prestwich, "The Military Household of the Norman Kings," *English Historical Review* 96 (1981), 1–35. It should be said that we have no comparable study of the household under the Angevins though the work of S. D. Church, *The Household Knights of King John* (Cambridge, 1999) is very valuable.

35 Roger of Howden, *Chronica*, ed. William Stubbs, 4 vols. (London, 1868–71), 2:47, 51, 55, 64–5.

36 I have used Charles du Fresne Du Cange, *Glossarium ad scriptores mediae et infimae Latinitatis*, 3 vols. (Paris, 1678); J. F. Niermeyer and C. Van der Kieft, *Mediae Latinitatis Lexicon Minus*, 2 vols. (Leiden, 2002) and other dictionaries. I would like to thank Nicolas Prouteau of the University of Toulouse who consulted Ernest Langlois, *Table des noms propres de toute nature compris dans les chansons de geste* (Paris, 1904) and introduced me to www.gencom.org which is so valuable for topographic and village names before the French Revolution.

37 Geoffroy de Vigeois, *Chronica*, p. 334. *Palearii* is connected with *paleare* meaning a stack of straw: Niermeyer and Van der Kieft, *Mediae Latinitatis Lexicon Minus*, 2:983.

at first always referring to Basques, but later changing to Brabançons.[38] This change may reflect the increasingly firm action taken by the Angevins, for they were great hirers of Brabançons, as Howden makes clear. Amongst the stories about mercenaries, the Rocamadour miracles report that Mende, attacked by Basques and Brabançons, was saved after its inhabitants prayed to Our Lady of Rocamadour, who caused part of the wall to fall on the attackers, frightening them off. This collection was created after 1172 and the stories indicate the long-term presence of the mercenaries in the area.[39] This extraordinary range of terms reflects the fact that southern and central Gaul was the theater for several conflicts whose protagonists recruited in different areas. These conflagrations came to a head in the early 1180s. Even Howden, who must, as a servant of Henry II, have been inured to the horrors of war, comments on the ruthless devastation of the area by mercenaries.[40]

A combination of circumstances raised these wars to a new pitch towards 1180. The Emperor Frederick Barbarossa (1152–90) had ambitions west of the Saône-Rhône corridor, and in 1166 it was probably his mercenaries (Brabançons) who supported Count William of Chalon in his attack on Cluny, which resulted in a massacre of the town militia. Shortly after this, Louis VII and Barbarossa concluded a treaty outlawing mercenaries in their lands, but excluding those permanently retained by a lord or married to local women.[41] Although the treaty between Frederick and Louis VII ended this particular confrontation, mercenaries employed by the emperor must have continued to move down the Saône-Rhône corridor to the western passes into Italy which Frederick often used, and after the treaty of Venice of 1177 they would have found themselves out of work as the Italian wars fizzled out. Alfonso II (1162–96) of Aragon was particularly vigorous in pursuing the claims of his house in southern Gaul against the house of Toulouse. In 1180 his brother, the count of Provence, was assassinated, and

---

[38] Marcus Bull, ed., *The Miracles of Our Lady of Rocamadour* (Woodbridge, 1999) refers to Basques (pp. 104–05, 134), to Basques and Brabançons (p. 184), and Brabançons only (pp. 191, 192–3).

[39] Bull, *Miracles of Rocamadour*, pp. 104–05, 134, 184, 191, 192–3. I would like to thank Marcus Bull for drawing my attention to this aspect of the *Miracles*.

[40] Howden, *Chronica*, 2:277; on this chronicler's knowledge of the Aquitaine see John Gillingham, "Events and Opinions: Norman and English Views of Aquitaine, c. 1152–c. 1204," in Marcus Bull and Catherine Léglu, eds., *The World of Eleanor of Aquitaine: Literature and Society in Southern France between the Eleventh and Thirteenth Centuries* (Woodbridge, 2005), pp. 71–81.

[41] Edmond Martène and Ursin Durand, *Veterum scriptorum et monumentorum historicorum, dogmaticorum, moralium; amplissima collectio*, 9 vols. (Paris, 1724–33), 2:880–81, and also MGH Diplomata 10/3.No. 575, 46–7; Marcel Pacaut, *Louis VII et son royaume* (Paris, 1964), pp. 88–90; Giles Constable, "The Abbot and Townsmen of Cluny in the Twelfth Century," in David Abulafia, Michael J. Franklin and Miri Rubin, eds., *Church and City 1000–1500: Essays in Honour of Christopher Brooke* (Cambridge, 1992), pp. 161–63, reprinted in Giles Constable, *Cluny from the Tenth to the Twelfth Centuries* (Aldershot, 2000), and see Brown, "Military Service and Monetary Reward," p. 29.

this led to a close alliance with Henry II in 1181 and a new phase of war.[42] The rebellion of Henry II's son, Henry the Young King, in 1183 triggered a particularly violent convulsion in the Limousin as the lords of the area took the opportunity to rise against Henry II and his son, Duke Richard. The death of Henry the Young King on 11 June 1183 did not end the rebellion led by Aimar of Limoges and Archambaud de Comborn. The rebels were supported by the king of France and the count of Toulouse, and savage fighting ravaged the area.

These horrors had prompted the condemnation of mercenaries issued at the Third Lateran Council in 1179, but the Council went further than mere condemnation. Canon 27 offered to those who took active steps to attack the heretics and mercenaries something of the status of crusaders: "a remission of two years penance and [placement] under the protection of the Church just like those who undertake the journey to Jerusalem."[43] The mention of Jerusalem cannot have been accidental. In this way action against the enemies of Christendom in southern Gaul was given enormous prestige and appeal. The architect of Canon 27 was Henri de Marcy, who had become firmly convinced of the need for a crusade against the heretics.[44] By 1181 he was Cardinal of Albano and a Papal Legate, and in that year led the "Crusade against Lavaur," which violently eliminated a major heretic center 30 kilometers north of Toulouse, where Count Roger of Béziers, his wife, and numerous heretics had taken refuge. The surrender of this place was attributed by the *Chronicle of Clairvaux* to a miracle. By the terms of the surrender all the heretics renounced their errors, though it seems that most soon lapsed.[45] In September 1181 Henri de Marcy, in his capacity as Papal Legate to southern Gaul, attended a council at Le Puy, very shortly after his triumph in the "Crusade of Lavaur." He subsequently summoned Councils at Bazas on 24 November and Limoges on 28 February 1182.[46] Since his legacy was specifically intended to purify the Church and to mitigate the evils which the area was suffering, and since he was the architect of Canon 27 of Third Lateran, it is not hard to imagine that he urged these assemblies to take militant steps, for that was the whole tenor of his preaching mission in southern Gaul. Canon 27 was an astonishing decree for it in effect created a crusade against heretics and mercenaries, but did not specify who could call it. Those who took such action could only do so "following the council of holy bishops and priests." This radical step reflected the breakdown of society and its institutions in southern Gaul at this time.

---

[42] Geoffroy de Vigeois, *Chronica*, p. 326; Higounet, "Rivalité des maisons de Toulouse et de Barcelone," p. 386.

[43] See above, p. 7, n. 29.

[44] Kienzle, *Cistercians, Heresy and Crusade in Occitania*, pp. 121–24, 127.

[45] Geoffroy de Vigeois, *Chronica*, 326; Howden, *Chronica*, 2:160–66; Congar, "Henri de Marcy," pp. 35–38.

[46] Claude de Vic and Jean Vaissette, *Histoire Générale de Languedoc*, 15 vols. (Toulouse, 1872–92), 8:341–44, 371–73; Hefele, *Histoire des Conciles*, 5:2.112.

Canon 27 urges a crusade against heretics and mercenaries, yet the significance and distinctiveness of this has not been recognized by modern historians.
This is because the Capuchin movement has been seen in the light of an older
tradition of peace-making which was important in southern Gaul at the time,
and which itself is often connected with the crusading movement. The Peace
and Truce of God has attracted much attention, both as something of importance
in itself and because many have thought it played an important role in preparing
men's minds for the appeal made at Clermont in 1095. This view was firmly
endorsed by Erdmann, Delaruelle and Duby, to name simply the most important,
and through them it passed into the common currency of crusader writing.[47] The
only writer to have contested this view is Marcus Bull, who sharply doubts the
impact of this movement on the arms-bearing laity by the end of the eleventh
century.[48] The bishops of southern Gaul instituted The Peace of God in the later
tenth century to combat the violence and disorder arising from the eclipse of
royal power and the subsequent competition between rival local magnates.[49] At
the Council of Le Puy in 975 Bishop Guy (c.975–93) had attempted to extract
an oath from the arms-bearers of the region to respect the peace. This began the
"Peace of God," which for over half a century attempted to impose a degree of
stability in central and southern Gaul and even beyond. We tend to think of it
simply as a form of moral pressure upon the arms-bearers, not least because of
the vivid picture painted by Rodulfus Glaber who was writing in the 1030s at
the height of the movement. He portrays a Peace Council as a kind of fervent
camp-meeting, at which relics were exposed, miracles performed and sermons
preached, at the culmination of which the bishops demanded an oath to observe
the peace:

> Such enthusiasm was generated that all the bishops raised their croziers to the heavens,
> and all cried out with one voice to God, their hands extended: "Peace! Peace! Peace!"
> This was the sign of their perpetual covenant with God. It was understood that after
> five years all should repeat this wonderful celebration in order to confirm the peace.[50]

But while the moral pressure of the excited masses was important, it was accompanied by the threat of force. Bishop Guy was able to call upon his relatives,
the counts of Brioude and Gévaudan, to help him threaten the recalcitrant.[51]

[47] Carl Erdman, *Origins of the Idea of the Crusade*, trans. Marshall W. Baldwin and Walter Goffart
(Princeton, 1977), chap II, pp. 57–94; Etienne Delaruelle, "Essai sur la formation de l'idée de
Croisade," *Bulletin de literature ecclésiastique* 45 (1944), 37–42; Georges Duby, "Laity and the
Peace of God," in *The Chivalrous Society*, trans. Cynthia Postan (London, 1977), pp. 124–31.

[48] Marcus Bull, *Knightly Piety and the Lay Response to the First Crusade: The Limousin and
Gascony c.970–c.1130* (Oxford, 1993), chap. 1, pp. 21–69.

[49] On the movement in general see Roger Bonnaud-Delamare, "Fondement des institutions de
paix au xi siècle," in *Mélanges d'Histoire dédiés à la mémoire de Louis Halphen* (Paris, 1951),
pp. 19–26.

[50] Rodulfus Glaber, *Historiarum Libri Quinque*, in *Opera*, ed. John France (Oxford, 1989), 4:16,
pp. 196–97.

[51] H. E. J. Cowdrey, "The Peace and Truce of God in the Eleventh Century," *Past and Present* 46
(1970), 42–67.

Aimo de Bourbon, Archbishop of Bourges (1031–71), carried this to its logical
conclusion by embodying a militia of peasants and some nobles which enjoyed
a degree of military success before this attempt to create an army of the Church
fell foul of local aristocratic faction and was destroyed in 1038.[52]

The Truce of God (*Treuga Dei*) originated at the Council of Elne in 1027 and
became important after the Council of Arles in 1041. It was a rather different
concept which from its inception neither sought nor received the same mass
enthusiasm. Instead of seeking to protect people, it tried to limit the violence
of the powerful by forbidding fighting between Thursday and Monday in
memory of the Crucifixion and in veneration of the Sabbath. At the same time
those who promulgated it proclaimed that it was evil for any Christian to kill
another. Implicitly this encouraged the arms-bearers to vent their violence upon
non-Christians, though the immediate purpose was probably to reinforce their
message of peace.[53] The movement survived as a result of agreements between
bishops and local magnates, and indeed spread as a useful instrument in the
hands of secular lords, producing the *Landfrieden* in Germany.[54] It may have lost
some of its vigor in the course of the eleventh century, but Thomas Bisson has
argued that it was revived by Urban II (1088–99) as a means of ensuring security
for the lands of absent crusaders, especially in the troubled south of Gaul.[55] Bull
does not think there was a "deep-seated ideological linkage" with the expedition proposed in 1095 at Clermont, and suggests that Urban was simply using
it as a device to reassure potential crusaders.[56] Nevertheless, Bisson produces
convincing evidence that in southern Gaul its vitality continued. In 1140 a
Synod at Auch was demanding peace-oaths and in 1155 Louis VII of France
(1137–80) proclaimed the "General Peace of the Whole Realm" shortly after
a journey through the south to Compostella in 1155. Local peace agreements
between bishops and magnates are quite frequent in Narbonne (1149–74) where
the Templars were involved, confirmed by popes as late as 1190. They are also
found at Elne (1156), and Tarascon (1226), where the agreements allowed for
the raising of money and a peace-militia. In 1163 the count of Toulouse and
the bishop of Albi made a peace proclamation after concluding an agreement
with the viscount of Béziers. There were other agreements at Toulouse in 1163,
Comminges in 1170 (where a peace-tax received papal confirmation), Rodez in

---

52 Thomas Head, "Andrew of Fleury's Account of the Peace League of Bourges," in Thomas Head
    and Richard Landes, eds., *The Peace of God: Social Violence and Religious Response in France
    around the Year 1000* (Ithaca, NY, 1992), pp. 219–38.
53 Thomas Head and Richard Landes, "Introduction," in Head and Landes, eds., *The Peace of
    God*, pp. 7–9. Cowdrey, "Peace and Truce of God," p. 44.
54 Aryeh Grabois, "De la trêve de Dieu à la paix du roi: Étude sur la transformation du mouve-
    ment de la paix au XII siècle," in P. Gallais et Y-J. Riou, eds., *Mélanges offerts a René Crozet
    à l'occasion de son soixante-dixième anniversaire par ses amis, ses collègues, ses élèves et les
    membres du C.É.S.C.M*, 2 vols. (Poitiers, 1966), 1:585–96.
55 Thomas Bisson, "The Organized Peace in Southern France and Catalonia ca. 1140–1223,"
    American Historical Review 82 (1977), 295.
56 Bull, *Knightly Piety*, pp. 58–59.

1169–70, Rouergue in 1169, Béziers in 1170, Rousillon in 1173, Albi in 1190, the Bordelais under Richard I in the years 1189–95 and Montpellier in 1215. Clearly agreements between the high nobility and the upper ranks of the Church were important efforts to stabilize society in southern Gaul, leading Bisson to comment: "the old condominia of higher clergy and baronage, ... as we are now learning, had survived the age of ecclesiastical reform."[57]

The effectiveness of such declarations is another matter. It is possible, but far from certain, that it was a coalition of this kind which gathered an army and crushed a group of Richard's mercenaries in 1177.[58] Moral influences of this kind backed by the likelihood of force presumably had some restraining power provided they were backed by a broad consensus of aristocrats and senior clergy. However, the crisis of the mercenaries in the very early 1180s did not evoke any such response. Some of the lords of the area were clearly involved with the mercenaries, as witness Geoffroy de Vigeois's story about Ebles VII de Charenton at Dun-le-Roi near Bourges, which will be discussed later.[59] Unemployed mercenaries and their families needed places to stay and markets, and this offered opportunities for lords. More simply, the local nobility were caught up in the rivalries of the great and forced to take sides. No consensus with the bishops could, therefore, arise. These divisions also go some way to explain the short life of the Capuchin movement which, despite its effectiveness and enormous spread, seems to have vanished by 1184.

Faced with this situation the bishops of the south at the Third Lateran sought an alternative, and under the leadership of Henri de Marcy found it in the notion of a crusade. Probably the hope may have been to enlist a sufficient force to overawe the quarreling forces in the area. In a sense this happened, but in a novel way, for the effect of Canon 27 was to create an armed fraternity originating at Le Puy in 1182, and founded in a wave of popular enthusiasm under the auspices of the Virgin, striving by armed might to impose peace. They were called Capuchins (*capuciati*) because they wore a distinctive hood (*capucium* or *caputium*) and cloak bearing a badge of the Virgin and Child.

Geoffroy de Vigeois wrote his account of the Capuchins very shortly before his death and it has a sense of immediacy. According to Geoffroy, a poor man of Le Puy, a carpenter called Peter Durandus, was inspired by a vision of the Virgin to approach the bishop of Le Puy, Peter IV of Solignac (1159–89), urging him to preach an oath of peace. The bishop was at first dismissive of this pious and humble man, but as the movement grew and organized itself, he was moved to support it. All who agreed to take the oath were required, apparently at the bidding of the Virgin, to wear a white hood (*caputium*) blazoned with her image

---

57 Bisson, "The Organized Peace in Southern France and Catalonia," p. 311.
58 These continuations of the Peace Movement are noted by Frederic L. Cheyette, *Ermengarde of Narbonne and the World of the Troubadours* (Ithaca, NY, 2001), p. 283.
59 See below, p. 20.

and the words "Agnus Dei qui tollis peccata Mundi, dona nobis pacem."[60] He goes on to make it clear that this was a substantial movement, and his account implies that the Capuchins were already a considerable force before the death of "the Young King" on 11 June 1183, suggesting they originated in 1182–83. Robert of Torigni (c.1110–86), Abbot of Mont-St.-Michel from 1154, wrote a *Chronicon* in which he failed to mention the carpenter's name, but confirms that a carpenter had a vision of the Virgin who presented him with an icon inscribed with the *Agnus Dei*. He was to report this to the bishop and bid him preach the peace, and the sign of its adherents would be a white hood and the icon of Our Lady. Robert stresses that the movement was joined by clergy and people of all classes and succeeded in destroying the enemies of the peace.[61]

Rigord was the author of a life of Philip Augustus, completed in 1196 then revised by 1200. He died in 1209. He emphasizes that the problems of the area arose from the quarrel between Aragon and Toulouse (thereby disassociating the king of France from these difficulties), and asserts that God sent aid not through any great person but Durand, a poor man of Le Puy who, shortly before the Assumption, had a vision of Christ who presented him with the picture of the Virgin and its inscription, which became the emblem of the movement. On the feast of the Assumption, Bishop Peter and a great assembly of the princes and people of the area listened to an exhortation by Durand, and all were moved to take an oath to maintain the peace and to wear a white scapular set with the holy icon of the Virgin as signs of adherence to this strict fraternity.[62] Gervase of Canterbury was a Benedictine monk and chronicler (c.1145–c.1210) who started his *Chronica* about 1188, covering the period from 1100 to his own time. He stresses the ravages of the *Brabaceni* and says that an un-named carpenter of Le Puy had a vision of the Virgin who bade him preach the peace. He was at first reluctant, but eventually approached the bishop, who was impressed. Bishop Peter of Solignac then spoke secretly to twelve prominent good men of Le Puy who agreed to support the fraternity which then spread like wildfire, enlisting clergy and laity, rich and poor, who wore the hood bearing a leaden seal of the Virgin.[63]

[60] Geoffroy de Vigeois, *Chronica*, pp. 338–39: "O Lamb of God, who takest away the sins of the world: grant us peace" (trans. *The English Missal for the Laity* [London, 1958], p. 325) is a prayer said in the Canon of the Mass between the consecration of the Host and the Communion. It would, therefore, have been very well known to the laity as well as the clergy; D. Kennelly, "Medieval Towns and the Peace of God," *Medievalia et Humanistica* 15 (1963), 35–53, notes that the seal of Narbonne bore this same device and inscription, but this dates from 1218.

[61] Robert of Torigni, *Chronicon*, in Richard Howlett, ed., *Chronicles of the Reigns of Stephen, Henry II and Richard I*, 4 vols. (London, 1884–89), 2:309.

[62] Rigord, *Histoire de Philippe Auguste*, ed. Elisabeth Carpentier, Georges Pon and Yves Chauvin (Paris, 2006), Book 1, ch. 25, pp. 168–69. The older edition is that of H. François Delaborde, ed., *Gesta Philippi Augusti Christianissimi Francorum Regis*, in *Oeuvres de Rigord et de Guillaume le Breton*, 2 vols. (Paris, 1882–85).

[63] Gervase of Canterbury, *Chronica*, in William Stubbs, ed., *The Historical Works of Gervase of Canterbury*, 2 vols. (London, 1879–80), 1:300–302, trans. Joseph Stevenson, *The Church Historians of England*, vol. 5, part 1 (London, 1879), p. 304.

All these are broadly sympathetic accounts of the Capuchins. A different viewpoint is offered by Robert of Auxerre (1156–1212), who began his universal chronicle before 1202, for he wrote it at the bidding of his abbot, Milo of Trainel (1155–1202), though we do not know when he wrote the passage about the Capuchins. He is a very hostile witness and says the peace was first proclaimed by "a man [never named] of humble birth and little fortune," while Eustace of Auxerre, writing after 1206, makes no mention of a carpenter, but makes clear that the movement has its origins amongst humble people whom he accuses of subverting the social order.[64] Guiot de Provins wrote a satire, *La Bible*, sometime after 1206. He had certainly been in the south, because about 1194 he joined the abbey of Cluny, but we know that in 1184 he was living in the north. Guiot offers a few hostile comments on Durand the Carpenter who, he claims, swindled his Capuchin followers of 200,000 livres. The comments are so limited that it is difficult to know what to make of them, except to say that he clearly disdained the Capuchins as humble men and regarded them as subversive.[65] The Anonymous of Laon was almost certainly a Premonstratensian whose *Chronicon Universale Anonymi Laudunensis* was probably completed about 1218. He is bitterly hostile to the Capuchins, and presents a very pejorative version of their origins. According to him Durandus was a simple man who was deceived by a greedy canon of Le Puy. This cleric was concerned lest the depredations of the mercenaries cause the cancellation of the splendid and luxurious gathering of the local nobility held every August, which was so important to the economy of the town. Therefore the canon concocted a false vision and convinced Durandus. The Anonymous admits that this inspired the people of Aquitaine, Gascony and Provence to turn against the mercenaries, but, like Robert and Eustace, he accuses the Capuchins of being social revolutionaries, saying that they terrified the lords of the area.[66]

In view of the very widespread notice taken of the Capuchins there can be little doubt that this was a substantial and important movement. Gervase of Canterbury and Robert of Torigni were remote from the Capuchins, but they lived within the Angevin "Empire" which embraced much of southern Gaul. The Anonymous of Laon was so deeply interested in Angevin affairs that his chronicle is a useful source for English history. However, the Auxerre writers provide testimony that by 1183 the Capuchins were active in that diocese, which is only 100 miles south of Paris, while Rigord, who came from Alais, tells us that they imposed the peace on the whole of *Gothia*, meaning Languedoc and much of Provence. A charter of Bernard, lord of Anduze, to the church of Sommières (Gard) was given in 1183: "when Philip reigned as king of the

---

64 Robert of Auxerre, *Chronicon*, MHG SS 26.247 and Delisle, *Recueil*, 18:706; Eustace, "Life of Bishop Hugh of Noyers (1183–1206)," in Duru, *Gesta Episcoporum Autissiodorensium*, pp. 445–46.
65 Guiot de Provins, *La Bible*, in J. Orr, ed., *Les oeuvres de Guiot de Provins. Poète lyrique et satirique* (Manchester, 1915), lines 1927–35.
66 Anonymous of Laon, *Chronicon Universale*, pp. 37–40, 58.

French and William of Uzès was bishop of Nîmes (1183–1207), the same year in which the peace of the Blessed Mary was spread."[67]

The sources display very different attitudes to the Capuchins, but leave little doubt that this was a popular movement which originated at Le Puy in the Auvergne with a carpenter called Durandus and spread across south and central Gaul in reaction to the mercenary plague.

But to call it a popular movement is not the same as saying that it was revolutionary and a threat to the social order. The Capuchins were working entirely within the framework of Canon 27 of the Third Lateran Council of 1179. This urged people to act against the scourge of the mercenaries "following the council of holy bishops and priests." The Capuchin founder, Durand, appears to have followed this pattern very precisely. According to Geoffroy de Vigeois, Robert of Torigni, Rigord, and Gervase of Canterbury he approached the bishop of Le Puy and the fraternity was supported by that dignitary. Even the Anonymous of Laon accepts that the Church helped and supported the movement. Furthermore, they were following the example of Henri de Marcy and his "Crusade against Lavaur."[68] Others bishops were working in the same direction. Amongst the southern bishops present at Third Lateran was Guillaume de Toucy, Bishop of Auxerre, under whose rule the Capuchins became established in that diocese. Another was Pons d'Arsace, Archbishop of Narbonne (1162–82). In 1179 he promulgated its decrees at a local council, but in an even sharper form. He made quite explicit the connection between heretics and the mercenaries who protected them and condemned various major figures, including the vicomte of Béziers.[69] The Capuchins emerged in this troubled and excited world of the south with the support of the Church – indeed it is hard to imagine how they could have spread so widely in so short a time without such official help.

The character of the movement as crusading and military has been obscured by the charge of being revolutionary, which has been accepted and amplified by most of the modern historians who have chosen to write about it.[70] The evidence

---

[67] Vic and Vaissette, *Histoire Générale de Languedoc*, 8:355. This document was noted by Auguste Fayard, "De Ruessium à Saint-Paulien," *Cahiers de la Haute-Loire* (1976), 118.

[68] Vic and Vaissette, *Histoire Générale de Languedoc*, 8:341–44, 371–3; Hefele, *Histoire des Conciles*, 5:2.112.

[69] Hefele, *Histoire des Conciles*, 5:2.112.

[70] Achille Luchaire, first produced "Un essai de révolution sociale sous Philippe Auguste," *Grande Revue* (1900), pp. 327–28, but later expanded his ideas in *La société française au temps de Philippe-Auguste*, 2nd ed. (Paris, 1909), trans. Edward Benjamin Krehbiel as *Social France at the Time of Philip Augustus* (London, 1912). A further edition was produced by Harper & Row in New York in 1967. The manuscript of the book was found in Luchaire's papers after his death in 1908 and edited for publication by Louis Halphen. Cheyette, *Ermengarde*, pp. 283–85 treats briefly of the Capuchins, accepting that they were seen as "a conspiracy against the social order." Robert Fossier, "Remarques sur l'étude des 'commotions' sociales au XIe et XIIe siècles," *Cahiers de Civilisation Médiévale* 16 (1973), 50, was doubtful about the charge of subverting the social order but never developed his ideas which were firmly opposed by Jean Perrel, "Une révolution populaire au Moyen-Age. Le mouvement des Capuchonnés du Puy 1182–84," *Cahiers de la Haute-Loire* (1977), 61–79. Some scepticism on this subject was

offered in support of this contention by the sources is at best very vague. The Anonymous of Laon says the magnates were threatened and terrorized by the Capuchins. Some accounts are very strange. Robert of Auxerre says that the peace was first proclaimed in the year 1183 by "a man [never named] of humble birth and little fortune" but adds that it was the magnates of the region, "Arverniae proceres in mutua pacis foedera coniurarunt," who attacked the Brabançons who had so long infested the area, killing about 3,000 and ending their reign of terror. In the following year, 1184, he reports that the sect of those who are called Capuchins (*Capuciatos*), founded in the previous year at Le Puy, multiplied in the kingdom of France, but was destroyed by the powerful whose dominion over them they had insolently denied.[71] Eustace of Auxerre wrote the life of Bishop Hugh of Auxerre (1183–1206), and when he comes to the Capuchins immediately tells us that: "at this time there arose in France a truly horrible and dangerous presumption which began to drag all the poor people into rebellion against their superiors and the extermination of their power."

He never mentions the mercenaries, though admits that at first the Capuchins had good intentions – which are never specified. He asserts that as the Capuchins spread to Berry, Burgundy and the Auxerrois its members simply sought to subvert the social order:

> There was no longer fear or respect for superiors. All strove to acquire liberty, saying that it belonged to them from the time of Adam and Eve, from the very day of creation. They did not understand that serfdom is the punishment of sin! The result was that there was no longer any distinction between the great and the small, but a fatal confusion tending to ruin the institutions which rule us all, through the will of God and the agency of the powers of this earth.[72]

As a result, Bishop Hugh took his army to the Capuchin centre of Gy and suppressed the movement, taking away their hoods and ordering that the offending peasants, in all seasons and whatever the weather, should always go bare-headed, though he remitted this sentence at the request of his uncle, Guy of Noyers, Bishop of Sens (1176–93).[73] This seems a very mild punishment for such subversion, and the contrast with Eustace's strong language is interesting

In fact the evidence suggests that the Capuchins were not at all a revolutionary movement. Both Robert of Torigni and Rigord insist that the Capuchins united all classes of society, the rich and the poor.[74] Rigord portrays them as a

expressed by Fayard, "De Ruessium à Saint-Paulien," pp. 43–127, but this was buried in a general consideration of the history of the Le Puy diocese. Georges Duby, *The Three Orders: Feudal Society Imagined*, trans. Arthur Goldhammer of a French original of 1978 (Chicago, 1980), pp. 327–36, produced a modern and very popular restatement of Luchaire.

71 Robert of Auxerre, MHG SS 26.247 and Delisle, *Recueil*, 18:706.
72 Luchaire, *Social France*, p. 17.
73 Eustace, "Life of Bishop Hugh of Noyers (1183–1206)," in Duru, *Gesta Episcoporum Autissiodorensium*, pp. 445–46. Hugh's predecessor, Bishop Guillaume de Toucy (1167–81), was the brother of Bishop Guy of Sens and, therefore, Hugh's uncle.
74 Robert of Torigni, 2:309.

great fraternity with a strict discipline. He tells us that if one of the Capuchins killed the brother of another, the victim's family was obliged to receive the killer and give him food.[75] This appears to reflect an insistence that the claims of the fraternity transcended even family obligation. Gervase of Canterbury says that nobody who had taken the oath was permitted to leave, and that all were required to rally in arms when called upon to do so.[76] But the Anonymous of Laon, for all his hostility to the movement, seems to have had access to an actual list of the regulations of the Capuchins which he records:

1. No gamblers were permitted to be members of the *fraternitates*.
2. Members were not to wear rich or ostentatious clothing.
3. They were not to carry knives (perhaps meaning concealed weapons).
4. They were not allowed to enter taverns.
5. They were prohibited from swearing false oaths.
6. They were prohibited from lewd swearing.[77]
7. They had to attend special masses and feasts dressed in their hoods.

Priests, monks and women could take the oath, but they were segregated and not expected to bear arms. The puritan nature of these regulations suggests an anxiety that the fraternity be seen as respectable in a very conventional sense, and the prohibition of wearing rich clothes indicates that some of the membership had substantial means. Moreover, joining the Capuchins involved paying an annual fee; according to Geoffroy de Vigeois, 6 *denarii*, payable at each Pentecost. The Anonymous of Laon says the fee was 12 *denarii* and that within two months the organization had collected an enormous sum, 400,000 pounds![78] The Anonymous's figures are clearly hugely inflated, but this appears to have been a well-financed organization which could hardly have been supported by the poor alone. Of course, the rural poor may well have offered support, but few of them could have afforded the military equipment and the petty pomp of the special masses and processions.[79]

---

[75] Duby, *Three Orders*, p. 330 remarks on the social inclusiveness of the movement; Rigord, *Histoire*, p. 40.
[76] Gervase of Canterbury, *Chronica*, p. 301.
[77] This provision is couched in very obscure Latin: "ab umbelico inferius nullum membrum in Deo, vel in eius pia matre, sive in aliquot sanctorum vel sanctarum eius nominari, prohibuit sancta Dei mater fieri omnino." I am grateful to my colleague, Ifor W. Rowlands, who puzzled over this with me and also noted that at about this time Daniel of Beccles, in the first English courtesy book, the *Urbanus*, prohibited swearing by the parts of the bodies of holy persons. On this see Robert Bartlett, *England under the Norman and Angevin Kings, 1075–1225* (Oxford, 2000), pp. 579, 582–88, citing *Urbanus Magnus Danielis Becclesiensis*, ed. J. Gilbart Smyly (Dublin, 1939), pp. 49–50; and also John Gillingham, "From *Civilitas* to Civility: Codes of Manners in Medieval and Early Modern England," *Transactions of the Royal Historical Society* 6th ser., 12 (2002), 267–89.
[78] Anonymous of Laon, *Chronicon Universale*, pp. 38–39; Geoffroy de Vigeois, *Chronica*, p. 339.
[79] At least in the Charente there is no evidence at this time of lords imposing new burdens upon their peasants, thereby provoking resistance. This does not seem to have happened until the early thirteenth century: Debord, *Société laïque*, pp. 403–16, 429–49.

Southern Gaul had some important cities and ports, notably Toulouse, Carcassonne, Marseilles and Narbonne, and beyond these it was a prosperous area with a reasonably rich agriculture. Comfortable people, perhaps often townsfolk like Durandus himself, whose livings were threatened by mercenary disorders, probably formed the backbone of the Capuchin movement. We know that such men were armed because Henry II, by his Assizes of Le Mans of 1181, ordered that throughout his continental lands his subjects should equip themselves with weapons. A man worth 100 *livres angevin* was required to have a horse and all the weapons proper to a knight. Those possessed of 40, 30 or 25 *livres* should be able to produce an aubergel (a lighter variant of the hauberk), iron helmet, lance and sword, while poorer men needed to have an aketon, iron helmet, lance and sword or at least a bow and arrows. The broad categories of the Assizes of Le Mans obscure from us what kind of men were expected to have precisely what weapons, but the language suggests that even the very poorest could find a bow and arrows. For his English lands Henry later issued the Assize of Arms of 1181 which is much more elaborate. It imposed upon the Justices the task of drawing up lists of all with a worth over 16 marks and ensuring that they conformed properly. The purpose of these assizes was probably to ensure that substantial numbers of people, quite apart from the knights and nobles, were enrolled in defence of stability and order.[80] But Henry could not have issued them if people did not very often have such arms. The bitter experience of war, the enthusiasm of the Capuchins, and the support of the Church, made people willing to use them. The very widespread existence of these weapons made the Capuchins possible. And the accusation of undermining the social order has diverted attention from the fact that the Capuchins were for a time, and in certain circumstances, very effective.

This, at first, might seem counter-intuitive. Mercenaries were professional soldiers, hardly to be put down by mere civilians. But we tend to approach them in the light of the highly organized bodies, like the Grand Catalan Company and the various groups which plagued Italy in the age of Sir John Hawkwood. But in the twelfth century mercenaries seem to have been recruited as individuals rather than as organized companies, and away from the command structures of organized forces they were very fallible.[81] In August 1173 some of Henry II's Brabançons were defeated by local peasants at St.-Jaques-de-Beuvron and in 1176 another group was destroyed at St.-Mégrin, while in 1177 local forces wiped out mercenaries sent by Richard to ravage the Limousin.[82] These events,

---

80 Roger of Howden, *Chronica*, 2:253 and 260–63. Hosler, *Henry II*, pp. 113–19 has comments on the Assizes.
81 Ramon Muntaner, *Chronicle*, trans. Henrietta Goodenough, 2 vols. (London, 1920); Michael Mallett, *Mercenaries and their Masters: Warfare in Renaissance Italy* (London, 1974), pp. 6–24, sees companies emerging only towards the end of the thirteenth century. William Caffero, *John Hawkwood: An English Mercenary in Fourteenth-Century Italy* (Baltimore, 2006); France, *Western Warfare*, pp. 68–76.
82 France, *Western Warfare*, pp. 74–75 and n. 28.

all close to the Aquitaine, may well have encouraged the formation of the Capuchins.

The Auvergne was undoubtedly the heart of the Capuchin movement. According to Geoffroy de Vigeois, the Capuchins began by attacking Neufchâtel where the mercenaries were commanded by the famous Mercadier.[83] Geoffroy de Vigeois reveals them to have been very active in the Limousin and even further to the north. He reports that an especially violent group of mercenaries of mixed origin, the *Paleari*, were driven from the Auvergne by the Capuchins. They fled into the Berry where they were attacked by "the soldiers who are called Peacemakers, those who had sworn an oath to enforce the peace" ("militibus qui Paciferi appellantur, eo quod pacem facere iurauissent"). At Dun-le-Roi near Bourges the Capuchins killed the mercenaries and burned their corpses. Geoffroy says that Ebles VII de Charenton, lord of Dun-le-Roi, and other lords were involved in this, and that the number of dead was estimated at 10,525. The Capuchins recovered the great booty which the mercenaries had stolen from churches.[84] The Anonymous of Laon seems to confirm this story. He reports that the *Rutharii* fled the Auvergne towards Burgundy, and sought shelter with one *Nabo de Carenci* (perhaps the same Ebles VII). The *iuratos de Arvernis* arrived in force and demanded that Nabo expel them from his town on pain of being himself attacked. He agreed, but pretended to the mercenaries that he would attack the Capuchins. The mercenaries with their wives and families marched out but, unsupported by the treacherous lord, were massacred to the number of 17,000.[85] Some twenty days later, according to Geoffroy, a mercenary leader bearing the name of a famous Turkish soldier Kerbogah (*Curbaranus*), was hanged with 500 of his followers near Millau in the Rouergue and shortly thereafter another, Raymond the Brown, was killed at Neufchâtel. Geoffroy says that this Kerbogah had been in the service of Aimar of Limoges, in association with *Saucius* and another called *Guarcifer*, during the rebellion against Henry II triggered by "the Young King." The Anonymous confirms the death of Kerbogah but says 9,000 perished with him and adds that his head was sent to Le Puy.[86]

But it was one thing for them to attack and destroy unemployed mercenaries at Dun-le-Roi and Millau. It was quite another for them to attack mercenaries

---

[83] Geoffroy de Vigeois, *Chronica*, p. 339.
[84] Geoffroy de Vigeois, *Chronica*, p. 338.
[85] Anonymous of Laon, *Chronicon Universale*, p. 40.
[86] Because of his name, it has been suggested by John S. Moore, "Who was 'Mahumet'? Arabs in Angevin England," *Prosopon* 11 (2000), n. 31, that Kerbogah was a Saracen, but this seems unlikely. If he had been a Saracen this would surely have been noted. I think it more likely that he was a leader who had taken on or been given the name of the legendary Muslim leader, defeated at Antioch during the First Crusade, as a tribute to the terror he inspired. For Kerbogah on the First Crusade and his entry into western myth, see John France, *Victory in the East: A Military History of the First Crusade* (Cambridge, 1994), pp. 269–96. F. M. Powicke, *The Loss of Normandy 1189–1204*, 2nd ed. (Manchester, 1961), p. 284, drawing on the Norman pipe rolls, remarks that "there is good evidence that he (Richard I) had brought a band of Saracens to fight for him."

in the service of a great lord, and this was the undoing of the Capuchin movement. Geoffroy de Vigeois shows himself to have been directly involved in the terrible events of Mercadier's raid against Comborn of October 1183. The death of Henry "the Young King" on 11 June had not ended the rebellion of the Aquitanian lords led by Aimar of Limoges and Archambaud de Comborn. The rebels were supported by the king of France, and savage fighting ravaged the area. Mercadier, doubtless in the service of Richard, targeted the lands of Archambaud de Comborn. Geoffroy was celebrating the feast of St. Pardulf (13 October) in the very midst of this area when the raid occurred and was obviously an eyewitness to its horrors. There was much destruction and the mercenaries ruthlessly demanded ransoms from the people of the villages. In particular, Mercadier and his companions, Constantine of Born and Radulf of Castellnau, extorted 650 *solidi* from the monks for the safety of Pompadour. However, when it seemed that the Capuchins (*iuratos Arverniae*) were going to attack them, the mercenary forces under Mercadier melted away.[87] But the Capuchins never actually fought Mercadier, because they were diverted by the "evil counsel" of a local knight, *Guilelmus de Chameleyra*. Geoffrey goes on to say that this was very unfortunate because the Capuchins now made common cause with the rebels. He never explains how or why this came about, and the Latin in this passage is very difficult, but the overall importance of the passage, which has not been noted by other writers, is quite clear.[88] The Capuchins were becoming caught up in political conflict, and on this occasion probably siding with the rebels against Richard I. It may be that this caused the nobles who had hitherto been associated with them to leave, but the sources provide no proof of this.

Under the year 1198 the Anonymous of Laon tells us that Mercadier succeeded Louvart (*Lupacius*) as Richard's commander of mercenaries. As an aside, he adds the detail that Louvart had surprised and destroyed the Capuchins at the "Portes de Berthe," thus putting down the movement.[89] This event is not dated by the Anonymous, but Robert of Auxerre, although he never mentions the "Portes de Berthe," does say that the Capuchins were crushed in 1184.[90] This places their destruction in the context of the fighting of 1183–84. It seems probable that the Capuchins' siding with the rebels against Richard I led to their defeat. This event is presented by the Anonymous of Laon as the crushing of a threat to the social order, but the reality was that they had become involved in the quarrels of the

---

87 Geoffroy de Vigeois, *Chronica*, pp. 340–1.

88 The Latin in this passage of Geoffroy de Vigeois, *Chronica*, pp. 340–41, is very difficult. It reads: "Dominica mane recesserunt timentes iuratos Arverniae qui venire disponebant, nisi Gillelmus de Chameleyra miles differri consilio faceret pravo: quod factum in tantos poenituit ut Ademarum Lemovicensem sacramenti sui efficerent participem, sicut avunculum illius Archambaldum fecerant pridem."

89 Anonymous of Laon, *Chronicon Universale*, p. 58; on Mercadier in general and his relations with Richard I see John Gillingham, *Richard I* (New Haven, 1999) and see above, n. 00. The location of the "Portes de Berthe" is unknown.

90 See above, p. 17, n. 71.

great. Mercenary companies like that of Louvart, under strong leadership and in the context of real armies, were very formidable, and they took their revenge accordingly.

The affair of the Capuchins demonstrates that we should not allow the prominence of the lords and knights and the presence of mercenaries to obscure the fact that medieval society was an armed society. There was enormous military potential because of this, particularly when substantial men took arms. In 1217 the crusading army of Simon de Montfort tried to seize Toulouse by a sudden coup, but it was repelled by the citizens who then formed the backbone of a garrison which successfully endured a long siege.[91] The fact that under some conditions they were able to defeat mercenaries should not surprise us. They were evidently organized and had some nobles in their ranks. By contrast, the mercenaries seem to have been caught by surprise and disorganized and, at least at Dun-le-Roi, were encumbered by their families. Above all, they were detached from the organization and leadership which participation in a greater force provided. In the end the Capuchins were defeated because they became involved in the rivalries of the great, and the mercenaries, as part of their forces, took their vengeance and destroyed them. The Capuchins and their enemies, the mercenaries, both needed the leadership and organization which only the highest ranks of society had the knowledge, will and prestige to provide.

The military importance of the Capuchin movement has been concealed by the emphasis on their supposed revolutionary nature. Popular movements always excited suspicion amongst churchmen and the leaders of society. The "People's Crusade" is a case in point, particularly in the account of Guibert de Nogent.[92] The real reason why the writers of the early thirteenth century were deeply hostile to the Capuchins was that they shared this suspicion, and also that they regarded the movement as a failure. Their preoccupation was with heresy: not only had the Capuchins not tackled this, but by the time of Innocent III (1198–1216) it was evident that the very milieu from which they came was one in which heresy flourished. Moreover, the Church had moved on to a highly centralized call for a crusade, supervised by the papacy, and the spontaneous associations of the Third Lateran Council must have seemed hopelessly out of date, and, indeed, positively harmful and dangerous to the established order which was now so threatened. This should not be allowed to hide the facts that the Capuchins were acting in accordance with the wishes of the Third Lateran Council, had something of the status of crusaders, and, for a time at least, formed a pretty effective fighting force.

[91] France, *Western Warfare*, p. 111.
[92] Guibert de Nogent, *The Deeds of God through the Franks*, trans. Robert Levine (Woodbridge, 1997), pp. 47–52, is disdainful of the "Peasants' Crusade."

2

The Last Italian Expedition of Henry IV:
Re-reading the *Vita Mathildis* of Donizone of Canossa

Valerie Eads

It is well over a century since the second and last Italian expedition of Emperor Henry IV was the subject of a dedicated study.[1] The gap is notable since the Italian policy of Henry IV was once studied intensively under the rubric of the Investiture Controversy. The neglect of the military aspects of that policy is even more striking since Henry IV was known to be "tireless in war" and "quick to resort to arms" in a generation that did not lack aggressive military leaders. William of Malmesbury's estimate that Henry IV undertook some sixty-two military actions could as easily be an underestimate as an exaggeration.[2]

Henry IV's first recorded military action is an expedition to Hungary undertaken on behalf of his brother-in-law Salomon in 1063, when he was thirteen years old. Assuming that the young king's presence was symbolic and that this was a learning experience, there was plenty of opportunity to put such learning to use in later years. Once he was old enough to be allowed to rule independently, Henry IV, like Charlemagne, campaigned almost every year.[3]

*

Despite this record of sustained bellicosity, Henry IV's military career remains largely unstudied. The Saxon wars of 1073–75 and 1077–80 have been briefly and selectively discussed, but until the end of the twentieth century the Italian expeditions merited only a single brief mention in a survey of medieval

---

1 Richard Hildenhagen, *Heinrich IV. von 1090–1092* (Potsdam, 1876); Christian Volkmar, *Der dritte Römerzug Heinrichs IV.* (Magdeburg, 1876). In Donizone's account, Henry IV's second Italian expedition is the third *adventus*, counting the journey to Canossa in 1077 as the first; Volkmar, and more recently Ian Robinson (cited n. 3 below), continue the practice.

2 "Heinricus militiae laboribus infatigabilis," Bruno of Magdeburg [Merseburg], *Liber de bello saxonico*, ed. G. H. Pertz, MGH Scriptores 5 (Hanover, 1844), p. 379; "... ad arma prompte concurrere, ut qui sexagies et bis atie collocata dimicarit," William of Malmesbury, *Gesta regum anglorum: The History of the English Kings*, vol. 1, ed. and trans. R. A. B. Mynors, R. M. Thomson and M. Winterbottom (Oxford, 1998) book 3, chap. 289.2, p. 522.

3 Ian Robinson, *Henry IV of Germany* (Cambridge, 1999) is followed for the outline of Henry's life and military career. See Appendix, pp. 61–68 below.

warfare.[4] Although neglected, Henry IV's Italian expeditions are not unknown or obscure and are treated in the standard compendia of Gerold Meyer von Knonau and Alfred Overmann.[5]

One reason for the lack of interest in Henry IV's military career in general and the Italian expeditions in particular is the types of actions that were undertaken, or rather not undertaken. There were few battles and, worse, no decisive battle. The battle at Homburg on the Unstrut River (1075), for example, ended the first phase of the Saxon rebellion, but the reaction to the king's excommunication the following year showed that his position was not secure despite the victory in the field. In the battle on the Elster River (1080) his rival, the anti-king Rudolf of Rheinfelden, was killed, but Henry had abandoned the field thus tarnishing the victory. It was the lack of internal unity among his opponents, not the outcome of the battle, that led to a delay of ten months until another anti-king, Hermann of Salm, was elected. Sometimes troops were mustered, but there was no subsequent engagement. Sieges were settled by negotiation or bribery rather than by assault, and they often failed, patterns especially notable in the Italian expeditions. Henry often achieved his objective by these means, but what was traditionally seen as the hallmark of military success, the decisive battle, is missing.

Second, Henry's principal opponent in both of the Italian expeditions was a woman, Matilda of Tuscany, not something that recommended itself to military historians of earlier generations. And, while the Italian expedition of 1081–84 could be characterized as successful – Pope Gregory VII was driven from Rome, and Henry received the long-delayed imperial coronation from his chosen pope, Clement III – the long expedition of 1090–97 failed. In 1097, Urban II, not Clement III, was pope in Rome, and Matilda of Tuscany still controlled her vast Italian patrimony.

A third difficulty is the sources. The sequence of events of the expedition of 1081–84 can be teased from many sources such as letters, charters, polemics and the papal register in addition to narratives. But the main – often the only – source for the actions of the 1090–97 expedition is Donizone, a monk of St. Apollonio at Canossa, Matilda's biographer and a source on which historians are reluctant to rely.

4   Hans Delbrück, *History of the Art of War within the Framework of Political History* 3 *The Middle Ages*, trans. Walter J. Renfroe, Jr. (1923; trans. Westport, CT, 1982), pp. 131–45; more recently John Gillingham, "An Age of Expansion, c. 1020–1204," in *Medieval Warfare: A History*, ed. Maurice Keen (Oxford, 1999), pp. 73–76, notes the prominence of pitched battles in the Saxon wars; Bruno of Magdeburg, *Liber de bello saxonico*, n. 2 above, is the main source for these actions. John Beeler, *Warfare in Feudal Europe 730–1200* (Ithaca, 1971), pp. 205–06.
5   Gerold Meyer von Knonau, *Jahrbücher des deutschen Reiches unter Heinrich IV. und Heinrich V.*, 4 (Leipzig, 1903); Alfred Overmann, *Gräfin Mathilde von Tuscien: Ihrer Besitzungen, Geschichte ihres Gutes von 1115–1230 und ihre Regesten* (Innsbruck, 1895; repr. Frankfurt am Main, 1965); Paul Sander, *Der Kampf Heinrichs IV. und Gregors VII. von den zweiten Exkommunikation des Königs bis zu seiner Kaiserkrönung (März 1080 – März 1084)* (Berlin, 1893) is still useful for the first Italian expedition.

Obviously much has changed in the century and more since Overmann and Meyer von Knonau collated the available sources. A veritable mountain of studies treating northern Italy during the latter part of the eleventh century has been published as have standard editions of the charters of Henry IV and of his kinswoman and nemesis Matilda of Tuscany.[6] Scholars now regularly analyze the sieges and maneuvers that constituted the day-to-day conduct of war, and sources once considered beyond the pale of reliability have been shown to be useful if carefully handled.[7] The role of women in warfare, once marginal at best, has earned a modest place in general treatments of medieval warfare although gender theory and literary figures still command more scholarly interest than campaign analysis.[8] In 2000, the doctoral dissertations of Valerie Eads and David Hay concentrated in different ways on the military career of Matilda of Tuscany and perforce on that of her great opponent, Henry IV.[9] Both noted the dearth of studies of the later years of her life, especially the military aspect, and called for further efforts in this direction. Matilda of Tuscany died in 1115 with her vast Italian patrimony intact despite imperial deposition, the lack of an heir and the rise of the communes. To understand how this came about requires that she be regarded an opposing general and not dismissed as an amazonian anomaly or an image. The time would seem right for a reconsideration of Donizone's description of Henry IV's last Italian expedition.

Donizone's poem has been studied since the dawn of modern medieval studies with editions going back to the seventeenth century. The manuscript tradition is not complex as the work was not widely copied, and the extant copies are

---

6   *Die Urkunden Heinrichs IV.*, ed. Dietrich von Gladiss and Alfred Gawlik, MGH Diplomata 6:1–3 (Weimar and Hanover, 1941, 1959, 1978) [hereafter *Urkunden Heinrichs IV.*]; *Die Urkunden und Briefe der Markgräfin Mathilde von Tuszien*, ed. Elke Goez and Werner Goez, MGH Diplomata, Laienfürsten 2 (Hanover, 1998) [hereafter *Urkunden Mathilde*].

7   For a good example of dealing with recalcitrant texts, John France, "War and Sanctity: Saints' Lives as Sources for Early Medieval Warfare," *Journal of Medieval Military History* 3 (2005), 14–22.

8   Helen Nicholson, *Medieval Warfare: The Theory and Practice of War in Europe, 300–1500* (New York, 2003), pp. 60–64; Clifford J. Rogers, *Soldiers' Lives through History: The Middle Ages* (Westport, CT, 2007), pp. 16–18; for a review of the literature see Valerie Eads, "Means, Motive, Opportunity: Medieval Women and the Recourse to Arms," paper read at 20th Barnard Medieval & Renaissance Conference, War and Peace in the Middle Ages & Renaissance, 2 December 2006. Available online at http://www.bobrowen.com/valerieeads/medievalwomen-inwar.html

9   Valerie Eads, "Mighty in War: The Role of Matilda of Tuscany in the War between Pope Gregory VII and Emperor Henry IV" (Ph.D. dissertation, City University of New York, 2000), presents a detailed analysis of Matilda's conduct of the war of 1081–84 with references to the events of 1090–97, pp. 201–03; David Hay, "The Campaigns of Countess Matilda of Canossa (1046–1115): An Analysis of the History and Social Significance of a Woman's Military Leadership" (Ph.D. dissertation, University of Toronto, 2000), pp. 59–98, focuses on contemporary perceptions of Matilda's position as a war leader throughout her life. References in this article to David J. Hay, *The Military Leadership of Matilda of Canossa, 1046–1115* (Manchester, 2008) are based on a pre-publication excerpt, pp. 117–59, made available online http://deremilitari.org/resources/articles/hay.html

in relatively good condition.[10] Donizone's approach to his subject, his language and prosody are less straightforward. He produced his poem for presentation to Matilda. It was therefore limited to events and descriptions of those events that he thought would be at least acceptable to her. It was written in the form of a heroic poem and, Donizone's editors uniformly agree, it was written badly.

Leibniz excused his emendations of an undamaged text on the grounds that otherwise many things in the work of this semi-barbarous and very difficult writer had no meaning.[11] Muratori downgraded Donizone to full Iron Age barbarity because of his unskilled and disordered style, destitute of all poetic *colore*. In Muratori's view the poet-monk's only virtues were his sincerity and obvious affection for his subject.[12] What drove Muratori to shouting apparently amused Ludwig Bethmann who described Donizone's uncultured discourse as employing a rough heroic meter and "words often extraordinarily in manner transposing."[13]

Donizone's awkward prosody is not the only difficulty. The monk is the only source and he might have been forgiven his tortured syntax and pretense to a greater knowledge of Greek than he had,[14] but he also demonstrates ignorance or disregard of facts well-known from more reliable sources. Donizone misdates the death of Gregory VII and neglects to mention that Matilda of Tuscany ever went to Rome, or that she ever had a husband, much less two of them. Since Matilda's second husband is directly involved in these events, the problems are potentially substantial. The sober Bernold of St. Blasien to whom Donizone is often compared could properly present an account despite his Gregorian leanings, which were at least as strong as those of Donizone.[15]

---

[10] Donizone, *Vita Mathildis celeberrimae principis Italiae: Carmine scripta a Donizone presbytero*, ed. Luigi Simeoni, *Rerum Italicarum Scriptores nuova edizione* 5.2. (Bologna, 1930–40; repr. Turin, 1973) is the standard edition [hereafter *Vita Mathildis*; other editions will be cited by editor]. A history of the editions and the manuscript tradition is given in the Introduction, pp. vi–xxiii. See also *Matilde e Canossa: il poema di Donizone*, ed. and trans. Ugo Bellocchi and Giovanni Marzi, Deputazione de storia patria per le antiche provincie Modenesi, Monumenta 24 (Modena, 1970), pp. 25 ff. *Vita di Matilde di Canossa*, trans. Paolo Golinelli (Milan, 1987) has extensive notes. Translations of Donizone in this article are my own.

[11] Gottfried Wilhelm von Leibniz, "Introductio," *Scriptores Rerum Brunsvicensium* 1, no. 40. The Introduction is not paginated. The text of the *Vita Mathildis* is pp. 629–88.

[12] Ludovico Antonio Muratori, "Praefatio," *Vita Mathildis Comitissae*, Rerum Italicarum Scriptores 5 (Milan, 1724), p. 337. "Rudi sane, atque incomposito stilo, & Poësi omni poëtico colore destituta, rem ille suam peregit, ut proculdubio barbarum Scriptorem, ac ferreum, continuo clames. Verum quod illi inelegantia stili defuit, veritatis amor, & quaedam sinceritatis imago satis supplevit."

[13] The meter is "satis rudi" because the hexameters sometimes have five or seven feet; also, "vocibus saepe mirum in modum transpositis," *Donizonis vita Mathildis*, ed. Ludovico Bethmann, MGH Scriptores 12 (Hanover, 1856), p. 348.

[14] "Graecisque pro more illius saeculi cum affectatione quadam insertis." Bethmann, *Donizonis vita Mathildis*, p. 348; Luigi Simeoni, "La *Vita Mathildis* di Donizone et il suo valore storicho-critiche," *Atti e memorie della Deputazione de storia patria per le antiche provincie Modenesi*, ser. 7, vol. 4 (1927), 24.

[15] Hildenhagen, for example, cites Donizone only as a last resort when the brief notices in preferred

It is easy enough to see what Donizone failed to do; he did not write classical hexameters. More recent editors have given a somewhat kinder opinion of Donizone's poem, pointing out that the flaws in his classical style reflect newer trends in medieval Latin prosody in which he is much more at home. Superimposing the rhymes and assonances of the new accentuated forms on the quantitative structure of classical poetry gave rise to some "remarkable forms."[16] More recently, the *Vita Mathildis* has been studied as an example of commemorative *vitae* without discussion of its poetic peculiarities.[17] Most editors, however, agree that when Donizone rhetorically declared that he lacked the skill to do the great work he had undertaken, he was being no more than truthful.

Despite these reservations, historians must use Donizone's poem, *faute de mieux*, but often with disclaimers and cautions about his unreliability.[18] Bernold's remarks are brief and were written at some distance; his account of Italian events is as limited as it is accurate. What cannot be faulted in Donizone is his firsthand knowledge. Although Matilda spent little time at Canossa and was not Donizone's source, the expedition of 1090–97 took place in his lifetime, and he was an eyewitness to some of the events.[19] As valuable as this knowledge is, it can cause as many difficulties as the monk's poetic experiments because he takes for granted an equal knowledge on the part of his audience. Reading Donizone requires filling in a great deal of background before his reports of specific events can be analyzed. The *Vita Mathildis* is as selective and biased as most medieval *vitae* and written in what can be considered an experimental style. Is it also, in its own way, accurate?

In Donizone's account, in the 1090–97 expedition Henry IV's approach was both systematic and – at least initially – effective. After arriving in Italy in April 1090, the emperor moved methodically against Matilda's positions, pushing her back city by city and castle by castle into the mountains. By the end of the 1091 campaign season, Henry was in almost complete control of the territory north

---

sources fail. Donizone's "Tertius est mensus, foliis florebat et herbis" (sic) is compared unfavorably to Bernold of St. Blasien's plainer statement, "Heinrico in anno in Langobardiam ingresso," (sic) even though Donizone gives more detailed information. *Heinrich IV.*, p. 16, n. 4. *Vita Mathildis*, 2.4, line 453, p. 71; Bernold of St. Blasien, *Chronicon*, ed. Georg Heinrich Pertz, MGH Scriptores 5 (Hanover, 1844; repr. Stuttgart, 1995) s.a. 1090, p. 450; Simeoni summarizes Donizone's errors, "La *Vita Mathildis*," p. 39.

16 Bellocchi and Marzi, *Matilde e Canossa*, p. 36; Gina Fasoli, "Rileggendo la 'Vita Mathildis' di Donizone," *Studi Matildici: Atti e memorie dell II Convegno di studi matildici, Modena – Reggio Emilia, 1–2–3 maggio 1970*, ed. Giordano Bertuzzi (Modena, 1971) [hereafter *Studi Matildici II*], pp. 15–39.

17 Thomas N. Bisson, "Princely Nobility in an Age of Ambition (*c.* 1050–1150)," in *Nobles and Nobility: Concepts, Origins, Transformations*, ed. Anne J. Duggan (Woodbridge, Suffolk, 2000), pp. 101–13.

18 "The material treated by him in the poem is historical, but we cannot say the same of the purpose of the author." Simeoni, "La *Vita Mathildis*," p. 35; see also pp. 26–28.

19 Paolo Golinelli, "Donizone," *Dizionario biografico degli Italiani*, 41 (1992), 200–3 as well as the introductions of Simeoni, Bellochi and Marzi and Golinelli, cited n. 10 above; Fasoli, "Rileggendo," pp. 17–19.

of the Po. Momentum slowed after he crossed the river in 1092. The siege of Monteveglio failed, and a council convened in Carpineti by Matilda decided to continue the resistance, but Henry was still in a far stronger position. Then, in October, near the castle of Canossa, the weather, the terrain and Matilda's vigilance inflicted on him a defeat from which his prestige never recovered. Henry was forced to withdraw back across the Po, shadowed by Matilda's troops. From then on his support dwindled. First his son, Conrad, and then the empress Praxedis, his second wife, turned against him. The emperor was cut off in Italy with limited forces at his disposal, unable to influence events either in Germany or at Rome.[20] In 1097, he negotiated a return to Germany where he remained until his death, still actively campaigning. The outline is clear enough, but the details, the reasons why movements were made or actions succeeded or failed, have yet to be filled in.

The first point not mentioned by Donizone is that sometime in 1089 a marriage took place that united two of Henry IV's most determined and long-standing opponents, Matilda herself, then about forty-three years old and a widow for thirteen years, and Welf IV, the father of the groom, Welf V, who was at most eighteen years old.[21] The elder Welf had been a power in German politics throughout Henry's reign. His support was invaluable in the king's victory in the Saxon rebellion of 1073–75, but he later turned against Henry. In 1077, he took part in the election of Rudolf of Rheinfelden as anti-king and was deprived of the duchy of Bavaria. In the struggle between Henry IV and Gregory VII he was an ally of the papacy even before his deposition. Gregory VII's plans saw him as a potential military ally of Matilda of Tuscany.[22] After Rudolph's death, Welf IV would have been the pope's choice to replace him as king, but the strong opposition of the Saxon magnates prevented this and led to the election

---

[20] *Vita Mathildis*, 2.4–7, pp. 70–79, for the events of 1090–92; the separation of Henry and Praxedis, 2.8, pp. 79–81; the siege of Nogara, 2.9, pp. 81–82; and Conrad's turning from his father, 2.11, pp. 83–84; after this Henry disappears from the story until his death in Germany, 2.15, pp. 89–90. Donizone's chronology is, as usual, confused.

[21] Elke Goez, "Welf V. und Mathilde von Canossa," in *Welf IV. Schlüsselfigur einer Wendezeit. Regional und Europäische Perspektiven*, ed. Dieter R. Bauer and Matthias Becker (Munich, 2004), pp. 360–87, with the sources cited there; Hansmartin Schwarzmaier, "'Dominus totius domus comitisse Mathildis:' Die Welfen und Italien im 12. Jahrhundert," in *Festschrift für Eduard Hlawitschka zum 65. Geburtstag*, ed. Karl R. Schnith and Roland Pauler (Kallmünz, 1993), pp. 296–301; Meyer von Knonau, *Jahrbücher Heinrich IV.* 4, pp. 273–74; Overmann, *Gräfin Mathilde*, pp. 155–61.

[22] *Das Register Gregors VII.*, ed. Erich Caspar, MGH Epistolae selectae 2.2 (Berlin, 1923) 9.3, p. 574. A complete translation is available. *The Register of Pope Gregory VII (1073–1085)*, trans. H. E. J. Cowdrey (Oxford, 2002). The pope's letter of March 1081 to his supporters, Bishop Altmann of Passau and Abbot William of Hirsau, tells them to remind Welf of promises made in 1077 "when his *beneficium* was granted to him after his father's death"; his Italian father, Azzo II of Este, was very much alive although about eighty-five years old when this letter was written; Azzo's other sons, Welf IV's half-brothers Fulco and Hugo, also have a role in these events. On Welf IV's claims in Italy, see Katrin Baaken, "Herzog Welf VI. und seine Zeit," in *Welf VI.*, ed. Rainer Jehl (Sigmaringen, 1995), pp. 17–19.

of a compromise candidate. After Henry returned from Italy in 1084 one of his first actions was to retake Augsburg; earlier that year Welf IV had taken the city and installed a Gregorian bishop. Henry was successful, but four years later the city was back in Welf's hands. It was Welf IV and not Hermann of Salm who defeated Henry IV at Pleichfeld on 11 August 1086, but once again the rebels were unable to take advantage of their victory; by the summer of 1088 Hermann had departed from Saxony, and the Saxon princes were seeking reconciliation with the emperor. This left only the south German princes, chief among them Welf IV, still in open rebellion.[23]

The expedition of 1081–84 achieved its immediate goal, the installation of Clement III as pope, but the emperor was well aware that there was unfinished business in Italy. Pope Clement's position in Rome was not secure. A Gregorian successor, Victor III, was elected in 1086 although he was able to make only a token stay at Rome before his death the following year. On 12 March 1088 a second Gregorian successor, Urban II, was elected at Terracina and entered Rome later in the year. During the next few years, the rival popes alternated residency in Rome.[24]

A failure of the papacy of Clement III could call into question the validity of Henry's imperial coronation. Things were much as they had been in 1080. The emperor needed to go into Italy; in order to do that, he needed first to resolve his quarrels with the lay and ecclesiastical magnates of Germany. He also needed to deal with Matilda who, despite having been deprived of her possessions for her actions in 1081–84, was still in control of the Italian patrimony, a power base that she had wielded effectively during the war.[25] The emperor's efforts at reconciliation with the German magnates had been progressing, but the marriage alliance with Matilda of Tuscany made any settlement with the powerful Welf family impossible.[26]

In 1077 the Welfs and their allies had control of the eastern Alpine passes including the important main route into Italy, the Brenner Pass. Henry with his wife and small son was forced to risk a winter crossing of the Mt. Cenis, a much higher western pass, in order to enter Italy. After the success of that venture, he took measures to secure the eastern routes before the 1081 expedition, and had further strengthened them thereafter. Since 1077 the march of Verona and the duchy of Carinthia were in the hands of Henry's supporter and kinsman,

23 Robinson, *Henry IV*, pp. 173, 209–10, 239–40, 260–62, 268–69, 274; on Pleichfeld see also Delbrück and Gillingham, cited in n. 4 above.

24 Clement III had already left Rome by spring 1088, but returned the following year and held a spring synod in St. Peter's only to have Urban II re-enter the city on 3 July. Before the end of the year, Clement III had departed the city once again although the departure was not permanent; he returned by spring 1091 when he occupied the Castel Sant'Angelo. Meyer von Knonau, *Jahrbücher Heinrich IV* 4, 193–95, 202–03, 265–71, 337.

25 Valerie Eads, "The Geography of Power: Matilda of Tuscany and the Strategy of Active Defense," in *Crusaders, Condottiere and Cannon*, ed. Donald J. Kagay and L. J. Andrew Villalon (Leiden, 2003), pp. 355–86.

26 Robinson, *Henry IV*, pp. 280–81; similarly, Hay, *The Military Leadership*, pp. 125–27.

Liutold of Eppenstein; Swabia was in the hands of his son-in-law, Frederick of Büren, from 1079; and Henry himself had continued to hold Bavaria since the deposition of Welf IV. Liutold's brother Udalric became patriarch of Aquileia in 1086; a third brother, Henry, held Istria and Carniola while yet another brother, Hermann, was anti-bishop of Passau.[27] Liutold's death in May, 1090, did not disrupt the expedition.

None of this interested Donizone, for whom the struggle for the papacy was paramount. Henry resumed his attack on the Church by attacking Matilda and recommencing the confrontation that had not been resolved in 1084.

> Since King Henry became a radical enemy of Holy Church and of the kind lady Matilda, in any place where it was possible for him he took away her lands, committing himself completely that anywhere she had (lands) he would have them. (2.4, 439–42)
>
> [Rex ut Heinricus factus gravis est inimicus
> Aecclesiae sanctae, dominaeque Mathildis amandae,
> In quocumque loco poterat sibi tollere, toto
> Nixu tollebat terras ubicumque tenebat,]

Ignoring the five years between the two events, Donizone writes that after taking all of her maternal inheritance in the Lorraine, where only the large and well-supplied castle of Briey held out against him, Henry moved into Italy.[28] He arrived at Verona in April 1090, and quickly moved against Matilda's positions in a systematic manner. The first objective was Mantua, effectively her capital, where her family had been counts since the time of her great-grandfather, Adalberto-Azzo.[29] Donizone describes an active siege. Henry made frequent attacks which were driven back by the defenders' sorties. But, despite being garrisoned and supplied by Matilda, who stayed in the mountains, Mantua surrendered in April of 1091.[30] Although Donizone cannot disguise the fact that the city held out for eleven months, he devotes an entire chapter of his poem to a scolding of Mantua delivered by the personified castle of Canossa.[31] Conquest could have been honorable, the castle says, but Mantua surrendered. The city compares unfavorably to Troy which held out for ten long years against a much greater

---

[27] Robinson, *Henry IV*, pp. 166, 183, 259. The bishops of Verona were imperial appointees. For a succinct discussion of the close relationship of Verona and the Empire and of the reasons that the city so resolutely supported Henry IV, see Carlo Guido Mor, "Dalla caduta dell'impero al comune," in *Verona e il suo territorio* 2 (Verona, 1964), pp. 143–49.

[28] *Vita Mathildis*, 2.4, 443–47, p. 71; for Matilda's possessions in the Lorraine, Overmann, *Gräfin Mathilde*, pp. 37–39, with a fuller discussion pp. 193–210, 237–38. These actions were taken in 1085, after Henry's return from the first Italian expedition. In 1086, he granted property that had previously belonged to Matilda to two churches in Speyer. *Urkunden Heinrichs IV*, nos. 379, 385, pp. 505, 510–11.

[29] Overmann, *Gräfin Mathilde*, p. 15; Vito Fumagalli, *Le origini di una grande dinastia feudale, Adalberto-Atto di Canossa*, Bibliothek des deutschen historischen Institut in Rom 35 (Tübingen, 1971), p. 34.

[30] *Vita Mathildis*, 2.4, 458–60, 469–82, p. 71.

[31] *Vita Mathildis*, 2.5, 491–549, pp. 72–74.

opponent, a feat justly celebrated by Mantua's great poet, Virgil. The stately grandeur of Matilda's Easter courts is contrasted with the drunken brawls now hosted by the German schismatics within the city. The city is admonished to recall Matilda and regain its former honor and dignity.

The "Objurgatio ac detestatio" must be considered in context. Donizone wrote his poem at the end of Matilda's life, twenty-five years after these events took place. As Simeoni eloquently demonstrated, the goal was to persuade Matilda to be buried at Canossa, as most of her ancestors were.[32] Her mother, Beatrice of Lorraine, died in Pisa and was buried there.[33] Pisa had an important role in Matilda's policy and stood by her when other cities did not.[34] Donizone was no doubt aware of this. He chides Pisa for not adequately mourning Beatrice, but his eloquence, his wrath, is aimed at Mantua where Matilda's assassinated father, Bonifacio, was buried. Mantua is totally unworthy of such an honor. The case is made by Canossa speaking in its own voice, boasting of its strength and ability to resist long sieges, thus recalling a point already made in the first half of his poem.[35]

During the troubled 950s and 960s when Berengar of Ivrea and his son Adalbert competed with Otto I for supremacy in northern Italy, the castle withstood sieges, one lasting more than three years.[36] The rise of Matilda's family began with backing the winner in that conflict, Otto.[37] Although Donizone's narrative presents the usual problems, such as establishing chronology, it introduces a number of recurrent themes. One is the strength and impregnability of Canossa.

> Gnashing his teeth with rage he [Berengar] immediately gathered troops and came to Canossa intending to destroy it entirely. "I am rock; not wood. Azzo abides up here; skilled and wise men are inside with him. King Berengar, attack with weapons as much as you wish, but you may die before you can break our defenses. Neither ram nor fox nor any machine would be able to reach to our heights." (1.1, 231–38)

> [Iratus, frendens, coadunans ilico gentes,
> Venit Canossam, putat illam frangere cunctam.
> "Sum petra, non lignum, manet Atto desuper intus,

---

[32] "With this clear demonstration of his macabre hope, which must have caused poor Mathilde goose bumps – as she was already 69 years old and in poor health ... he closed the first book ..." Simeoni, "La *Vita Mathildis*," pp. 30–32.

[33] *Vita Mathildis*, 1.20, 1360 ff., pp. 52–53.

[34] H. E. J. Cowdrey, "The Mahdia Campaign of 1087," *The English Historical Review* 92 (1977), 1–29.

[35] *Vita Mathildis*, 1.8, 597–748, pp. 27–31.

[36] *Vita Mathildis*, 1.1, 231 ff., p. 15. Although the siege itself is elsewhere attested, Donizone's chronology presents difficulties. Clearly, Berengar did not remain outside Canossa for three years while conducting a war with Otto, but someone else could have maintained the siege while Berengar conducted other actions. The death of Otto's son Liudolf in 957 is attested, but he died of fever, not in battle as Donizone describes. For a discussion of Donizone's sources for this period see Simeoni, "La *Vita Mathildis*," pp. 38–42, 52–55; Fumagalli, *Le origini*, pp. 80–83, is comprehensive.

[37] Fumagalli, *Le origini*, pp. 4 ff.

Secum prudentes homines sunt et sapientes;
Rex Berengeri, quantum vis percute telis,
Ante perire potes, quam nostram rumpere molem.
Non aries, vulpis, neque machina prevalit ullis
Ictibus, excelsis nostris pertingere tectis."]

Besieging a castle is not presented as a passive undertaking. It involves gathering intelligence, devising stratagems, and the use of signals and short-range maneuvers in the area of the main objective, actions that recur in the second book of the poem.

After Berengar was taken to Germany as a prisoner by Otto I, Adalbert claimed the crown and renewed the siege of Canossa which he maintained "for two Lents and three months more." This time Otto's son Liudolf came to Azzo's aid. When King Adalbert heard that Liudolf had arrived at Verona he sounded his horn and withdrew to Baiso.[38] The castle of Baiso is located a bit over 14 kilometers to the southeast of Canossa, at an elevation of 642 meters, comparable to Canossa's elevation of 576 meters, placing it on the second or central line of the defensive system at Matilda's disposal.[39] The defensive system of the lords of Canossa will be discussed in greater detail below.

*

Presumably, Adalbert moved through the mountains to avoid a confrontation with Liudolf who was approaching from the plain. Donizone doesn't continue his story beyond this point. His goal is not to describe the conduct of war, but to demonstrate the strength and constancy of Canossa. In the tenth century

[38] *Vita Mathildis*, 1.1, 310–20, pp. 16–17. On the use of horns and trumpets for signaling see *Vegetius: Epitome of Military Science*, trans. N. P. Milner (Liverpool, 1993), 2.22, 3.5, pp. 55–56, 69–71; J. F. Verbruggen, *The Art of Warfare in Western Europe during the Middle Ages*, 2nd ed. rev., ed. and trans. Sumner Willard and Mrs. R. W. Southern (Woodbridge, Suffolk, 1997), pp. 84–85; for a fuller discussion of aural signals, see also Aldo A. Settia, "'Quando con trombe e quando con campane:' segnali militari nella città dell'Italia commmunale," *Archivio storico Italiano* 164:4 (2006), 603–23; Philippe Contamine, "La musique militaire dans le fonctionnement des armées: l'example français (v. 1300 – v. 1550)," in *From Crécy to Mohacs: Warfare in the Late Middle Ages (1346–1526)*, XXIInd Colloquium of the International Commission of Military History, published by the Heeresgeschichtliches Museum (Vienna, 1997), pp. 93–106; accessible online at http://www.deremilitari.org/resources/articles/crecymohacs.htm

[39] The most current list and map of Matilda's holdings is Thoman Groß, *Lothar III. und die Mathildischen Güter* (Frankfurt am Main, 1990), pp. 148 ff.; the numerous maps included in Vito Fumagalli, "Economia, società ed instituzioni nei secoli XI–XII nel territorio modenese," in *Lanfranco e Wiligelmo. Il Duomo di Modena* (Modena, 1984), pp. 37–65, are helpful for an appreciation of the number, type, and extent of the known holdings of Matilda's family. There is little information about the earlier history of Baiso. Andrea Castagnetti, *L'organizzazione del territorio rurale nel Medioevo: circoscrizione ecclesiastiche e civili nella "Langobardia" e nella "Romania,"* 2nd ed. (Bologna, 1982), p. 118. The mention of this castle may be an acknowledgement of Raymond of Baiso, who appears as a witness to a number of Matilda's charters, but none dating before 1099, *Urkunden Mathilde, ad indicem*. Rocco Morretta, "L'Apparato difensivo dei signori di Canossa nell'Appennino Reggiano," *Atti e memorie della Deputazione di storia patria per le antiche provincie modenesi*, ser. 9, vol. 4 (1965), 489–500.

Canossa served Azzo well, and in the eleventh, unlike Mantua, Canossa came through for Matilda.

Donizone reports that during the siege Henry took the obvious step of securing Matilda's positions outside Mantua. The castles of Ripalta (upriver) and Gubernolo (downriver) also surrendered. Henry had thus effectively taken control of transport and trade along the Mincio.[40] After Mantua surrendered to a generous bribe of imperial privileges, Matilda's supporters escaped by boat.[41] Donizone clearly expected that anyone reading his description would be familiar with Mantua and felt no need to describe the layout of the city. In Matilda's time Mantua occupied only about twelve hectares (29.65 acres) on the highest part of a large island in the Mincio. It was protected by walls about two meters thick and ten meters high, slightly over a kilometer in length, and also by a ditch about three meters deep.[42] Henry clearly preferred the surrender of an intact city to the damage and outrage that could result from attempting to capture or annihilate Matilda's garrison. Bernold of St. Blasien also comments briefly on the siege of Mantua and by observing gender conventions manages to blame the defeat on Welf rather than Matilda who left the city in his hands.[43] As Donizone also reports that Matilda was not in Mantua but remained in the mountains,[44] most scholars accept that Welf led the defense of the city.[45] If so, he delayed Henry at Mantua for nearly a year during which, Donizone reports, Matilda repaired her defenses and gathered intelligence.

Henry's campaign continued successfully for the rest of 1091. According to Donizone he held almost all of the positions on the north side of the Po with the

---

[40] Although it is not known when or under what circumstances the castle surrendered, Henry issued a confirmation charter "apud castrum Riualte" on 26 June 1090. *Urkunden Heinrichs IV.* 414, pp. 551–53. Gina Fasoli, "Navigazione fluviale – porti e navi sul Po," in *La navigazione mediterranea nell'alto medioevo*, Settimane di studio del Centro di studi sull'alto medioevo (Spoleto, 1978), pp. 565–607. The maps following the article are especially informative about the extent of the riverine trade routes throughout Matilda's territory. The Mincio was navigable for its entire course from Lake Garda to the Po, p. 587.

[41] *Urkunden Heinrichs IV.*, no. 421, pp. 563–64; *Vita Mathildis* 2.4, 480–82.

[42] Ercolano Marani, "Topografia e urbanistica di Mantova al tempo de Sant'Anselmo," pp. 211–15, and map, p. 227, is especially informative; see also Vito Fumagalli, "Mantova al tempo di Matilde di Canossa," pp. 159–67, both in *Sant'Anselmo, Mantova e la Lotta per le Investiture, Atti del convegno internazionale di studi (Mantova, 23–24–25 Maggio, 1986)*, ed. Paolo Golinelli (Bologna, 1987); Gina Fasoli, "La realtà cittadina nei territori canossiani," *Studi Matildici: Atti e memorie del III convegno di studi matildici, Modena – Reggio Emilia, 7–8–9 ottobre 1977* (Modena, 1978) [hereafter *Studi Matildici III*], pp. 57–61.

[43] Bernold, *Chronicon*, s.a. 1091, p. 451. "Eo tempore Mantuani, diuturna obsidione a Henrico rege iam per annum constricti, a domino suo Welfone duce discesserunt et se et civitatem suam suo devastatori tradiderunt." Similarly, *Annales Augustani*, s.a. 1091, ed. G. H. Pertz, MGH Scriptores 3 (Hanover, 1839; repr. Stuttgart, 1987), p. 133: "Mantuani longa obsidione coacti, emisso ducis Welfi filio urbem tradunt imperatori."

[44] "Keeping to the mountains, she looks down upon all enemies." Both the literal and figurative meanings of *despicit* are undoubtedly intended. *Vita Mathildis*, 2.7, line 460, p. 71.

[45] Meyer von Knonau, *Jahrbücher Heinrich IV.* 4, p. 333, n. 2; *Vita Mathildis*, p. 72, note to line 481; Golinelli, *Vita di Matilde*, p. 143, n. 83; Hay, *Military Leadership*, p. 128.

exceptions of Piadena on the west bank of the Oglio, about 32 kilometers west of Mantua, and Nogara on the Tartaro, 21 kilometers east of Mantua.[46] He also took the large castle (*arx magna*) of Minervia.

> In this same summer indeed *Minervia* is taken; he took it at length with hunger, and not with any weapons; (2.6, 559–60)
>
> [Hac et in aestate capitur Minervia sane;
> Hancve fame cępit nonnullis denique telis;]

Donizone does not say how long the castle was under siege or why it could not be resupplied. His narrative focuses on Matilda who could still move freely south of the Po in the regions of Modena and Reggio gathering intelligence. She was constantly aware of Henry's movements.

> [Matilda] went serenely through the countryside of Reggio and Modena, and strengthened her own castles, absolutely in no way losing hope of overcoming the king. In this way she very often found out his habits and routes so that she always knew where the evil man went and how many soldiers he had. (2.6, 563–68)
>
> [Quae per Regensem comitatum seu Motinensem
> Ibat laetanter, proprias firmabat et arces,
> Nullatenus certe desperans vincere regem.
> Mores atque vias illius sepius ipsa
> Reperiebat ita, quod semper quo malus ibat
> Noverat, athletas et quantos ipse tenebat.]

This awareness led to one of the few field battles, near *Tres Comitatus*, usually rendered in its Venetian dialect form as Tricontai. Tricontai is not a castle or a town, but the region where the three *comitatus* of Verona, Vicenza and Padua meet.[47] Donizone reports that after the successful operation at *Minervia* Henry crossed the Adige with a small following. Matilda became aware of this movement and sent a force of more than one thousand men with orders to intercept him and force him to battle in the field.[48] Henry apparently had his own information-gathering capabilities, and things did not go well. He evaded

---

[46] Both of these castles had been in the possession of Matilda's family since the time of her father Bonifacio although the terms of possession were complex. Overmann, *Gräfin Mathilde*, pp. 19–20, 24; Aldo A. Settia, *Castelli e villagi nell'Italia padana: popolamente, potere e sicurezza fra IX e XIII secolo* (Naples, 1984) is a bible of fortifications, *ad indicem*; Castagnetti, *L'organizzazione*, pp. 201–02. Henry IV's last military action in Italy was a failed attempt to take Nogara in 1095. *Vita Mathildis*, 2.9, pp. 81–82.

[47] Some scholars refer to Tricontai as a village. *Vita Mathildis*, ibid.; Angelo Ferretti, *Canossa: Studi e richerche*, 2nd ed. (Florence, 1884), p. 107; Golinelli, *Vita di Matilde*, p. 169; Hay, *Military Leadership*, p. 132. Donizone calls it a "pagus," *Vita Mathildis*, 2.6, line 585, p. 75; contemporary charters of the Este family use "locus" and "terra." See n. 62, below.

[48] Donizone is not the only source for Matilda's ability to gather intelligence. She apparently had sources of information within the emperor's household. *Das Register Gregors VII.*, 9.11 (May 1081), pp. 588–89.

Matilda's troops for eight days while recalling his own, who had presumably been dismissed.

> Now that the great castle of *Minervia* was a captive, the king departed across the river Adige in winter without any princes and at that time not supported by *milites*. The wise countess, of course, learned this; she swiftly ordered brave men, more than one thousand in number, to fight against the enemy, to thus pursue the contest in the field. So, they crossed the fords, the waters of the Po and of the Adige; the crafty king evaded them for eight days, delaying and recalling his own troops.[49]

> [Nam postquam magna fuit arx Minervia capta,
> Tempore rex hiemis Athesis trans flumen abivit,
> Principibus vacuus tunc militibus neque fultus.
> Hoc didicit nempe prudens Comitissa, repente
> Mille viros fortes numero plus iussit ad hostem
> Pergere bellandum, campi certamine tantum.
> Cumque Padi latices, Athesis, [nec] non vada sissent,
> Insidiis plenus rex, ipsos octo diebus
> Vitavit, tardans proprias revocando phalanges.]

A traitor was able to persuade Matilda's troops that Henry had no stomach for battle and that he could not rejoin his troops. The result was a significant defeat for Matilda's troops who were caught unprepared and unarmed when Henry's army suddenly appeared. Many were captured. Donizone names Manfred, son of Albert – the fabulously wealthy viscount of Mantua in the days of Matilda's father Bonifacio – as one of those taken prisoner. Manfred, who survived his captivity, was presumably among the defenders who fled after the surrender of Mantua, but nothing is known about his role in either action.[50] Donizone also names the traitor, Hugo del Mansi, but cannot add that the execrated Hugo was an in-law, a half-brother of Welf IV, since Welf is not part of his story. His focus is on Matilda, the prudent commander who speaks gently to those returning in defeat, with due regard for the morale of troops who, she makes clear, will have to face the same enemy again. That Matilda, like Canossa, is firm in adversity is the point here. Henry's objective, the reasons why a battle took place at Tricontai, is simply irrelevant.

---

49 *Vita Mathildis*, 2.6, 569–77, p. 74. The word "nec," which appears in all the earlier editions, is missing from Simeoni's, the standard, edition but is clearly present in the facsimile. Donizone di Canossa, *Vita der Mathilde von Canossa, Vat.lat. 4922: entstanden 1115*, Codices e Vaticanis selecti 62 (Zürich, 1984) fol. 63r. Line 575 is obscure even when corrected. Golinelli, *Vita di Matilde*, p. 87, translates this line as "Because the waters of the Po and of the Adige did not allow them to ford," which would account for the delay even without Hugo's treachery. Simeoni, however, notes that they had already crossed: *Vita Mathildis*, 2.6, 569–77, p. 74. Donizone's account emphasizes Hugo's betrayal, not the difficulty of crossing the rivers. I am here construing *sissent* as a compound of *eo* with the prefix truncated (*s-issent*); similarly, Bethmann, *Donizonis Vita Mathildis*, note, p. 391; cp. *Epitome Polironese* 11, in *Vita Mathildis*, p. 122.
50 *Vita Mathildis* on Albert, 1.13, 993–1022, pp. 40–41; on *Tres Comitatus*, 2.6, 569–99, pp. 74–75; Meyer von Knonau, *Jahrbücher Heinrich IV.* 4, p. 346 is concise.

*

It is possible to fill in some of the "irrelevant" details. Donizone relates only that Mantua surrendered in April, and Henry celebrated Easter there. Sometime afterward (*in aestate*) he took the castle of *Minervia*; later in the year (*tempore hiemis*) he crossed the Adige, and then conducted a successful action at *Tres Comitatus*. Where is *Minervia*?[51] This doubtless was obvious to Donizone, but scholars have proposed four possible locations. The first candidate is Manerbio, 54 kilometers northwest of Mantua.[52] A second possibility is Manerba del Garda on the southwest shore of Lake Garda, which boasts a *rocca*, but there is no record that Matilda held these places or that either one was a "large castle."[53] A third possibility is Minerbe located about four kilometers east of the Adige and suggestively close to Tricontai. The Ganaceto, a family allied to Matilda's, had extensive holdings there,[54] but there is, again, no evidence of a castle at Minerbe, and if Henry was already east of the Adige, he would not have crossed the river to get to Tricontai. A final candidate is another uncertain location, *Manerva*, held by one of Matilda's distant relations, Count Hubert, son of Count Arduin of Parma, who can be shown acting with Matilda on a number of occasions.[55]

---

[51] Overmann, *Gräfin Mathilde* and Settia, *Castelli e villagi* do not discuss *Minervia*; Aldo A. Settia, "Castelli e villaggi nelle terre canossiane tra X e XIII secoli," *Studi Matildici III*, p. 305, and Groß, *Lothar III.*, p. 208, add nothing concerning the location of *Minervia* although both update Overmann on many points.

[52] Golinelli, *Vita di Mathilde*, note 92, p. 143, supports the location on the plain, as does Muratori, p. 371, n. 91.

[53] Simeoni prefers the location near Lake Garda, *Vita Mathildis*, notes to 2.6, 559–60, p. 74. The *rocca* was finally destroyed in the eighteenth century to keep bandits from using it. On the archeology of Rocca di Manerba, which has been occupied since Neolithic times, see http://www.arch-ant.bham.ac.uk/research/rocca.htm

[54] Muratori notes this location as a possibility, but decides in favor of Manerbio: *Vita Mathildis comitissae*, n. 91, p. 371; Castagnetti, *L'organizzazzione*, p. 196.

[55] Reinhold Schumann, *Authority and the Commune, Parma, 833–1133* (Parma, 1973) proposes that *Manerva* was "not far from Mantua between Mincio and Adige," pp. 317–18. The relevant documents, Count Hubert's donations to San Benedetto Polirone, do not specify the location of "*roka Manerva*." Pietro Torelli, ed., *Regesto Mantovano: le carte degli archivi Gonzaga et di stato in Mantovana e dei monasteri mantovani soppressi*, 1 (Rome, 1914), pp. 80–82. The donated land is in *Medula* (Medole) 29 kilometers northwest of Mantua, i.e., well west of the Mincio. Johann Grässe et al., *Orbis Latinus: Lexikon lateinischer geographischer Namen des Mittelalters und der Neuzeit*, 2 (Braunschweig, 1972), p. 536. Pierpaolo Bonacini describes Hubert as the defender of the castle of "Manerba" without discussion of its location: "Il monasterio di S. Benedetto Polirone: formazione del patrimonio fondario e rapporti con l'aristocrazia italica nei secoli XI e XII," *Archivio storico Italiano* 158.4 (2000), pp. 644–45, with references to more recent editions of the relevant documents. For Matilda's extended family see Fernando Fabbi, "Le famiglie reggiane e parmensi che hanno in comune l'origine con la contessa Matilde," *Studi Matildici: Atti e memorie del convegno di studi matildici, Modena e Reggio Emilia, 1963* (Modena, 1964), pp. 19–53, esp. 41–47; M. G. Bertolini, "Note di genealogia e di storia canossiana," *I ceti dirigenti in Toscana nell'età precomunale* (Pisa, 1981), pp. 111–49.

The emperor's charters support the first two locations both of which are near Brescia where Matilda's family had held comital rights since the time of her grandfather, Tedaldo. Henry issued a charter at Bassano (*actum Bassan*), only a short distance from Manerbio, on 5 May, less than a month after the surrender of Mantua. Another, undated, charter was issued at Botticino (*in comitate Brixiense, curte Buticini*) which is somewhat closer to Manerba del Garda.[56] These charters suggest that, having secured Mantua, Henry next moved to gain control of the region around Brescia, the northwest quadrant of Matilda's territory, that is, north of the Po and west of Mantua. As a river port, Brescia was an important source of income to whoever controlled it.[57]

The emperor was in Verona in August when Welf IV and other magnates came from Germany to reopen talks. Whether because they demanded terms he could not meet or because Henry felt no need to negotiate the effort came to nothing. The emperor also issued charters in Verona in September.[58] After Verona his location is unknown until the successful operation at *Tres Comitatus*. *Minervia* could have fallen any time between May and August, and, assuming that Henry commanded the siege himself, the battle could have occurred any time after late September.

The region east of the Adige was important to Henry IV for a number of reasons. First, he had a great deal of support there. Bishops Milo of Padua and Hezilo of Vicenza appear in the charter issued at Bassano in May.[59] Possibly, their troops took part in the successful action at *Minervia* and departed afterward. In January 1091, shortly before his successful re-entry into Rome, Pope Clement III came to Padua to meet with the emperor.[60] Henry may have intended to undertake a late-year campaign with fresh, or at least resupplied, troops from the same sources; he may also have considered himself secure enough to travel the relatively short distances between Verona and Vicenza or Padua (44 kilometers and 67 kilometers respectively) with a minimal escort, but the most direct route between these cities does not pass through Tricontai.[61]

---

56 *Urkunden Heinrichs IV.*, nos. 418–419, pp. 556. The charters for this period present a number of problems. Some lack dates and others places of issue. Henry issued a number of charters dealing with affairs at Mantua, although the dates and places of issue are not certain. Overmann, *Gräfin Mathilde*, p. 4.

57 Fasoli, "Navigazione fluviale," pp. 574–75, and esp. p. 569, n. 12, with the additional works cited.

58 Robinson, *Henry IV*, p. 282. Of two charters dated 2 September and 21 September, the first was issued in Verona, while the latter can "probably" be assigned to that location. *Urkunden Heinrichs IV.*, nos. 424, 426, pp. 569–72.

59 Note 56, above.

60 Meyer von Knonau, *Jahrbücher Heinrichs IV.*, 4, 336–37.

61 This would be similar to Henry's preparations before the battle on the Elster River in 1080: Bruno of Magdeburg, n. 2 above; Schumann, *Authority and the Commune*, finds that Henry was in fact going to Vicenza, p. 318, n. 6; the cited source, *Epitome Polironese*, 11, does not specify a destination, but the supposition is reasonable. For the text of the *Epitome Polironese* see *Vita Mathildis*, p. 122.

A further reason for Henry's interest in the area is the strong presence there of the family that came to be known as the Este, now Matilda's kin by marriage. The toponym *Tres Comitatus* appears in charters issued by Marquis Azzo II and his son Fulco including a donation of 1100 in which Fulco described himself as living in Montagnana, about 13 kilometers east of the Adige and the Legnago crossing.[62] In 1091, Marquis Azzo was in his nineties and presumably less active than before. Like his eldest son, Welf IV, Azzo had both supported and opposed Henry IV in his struggles with the papacy. The marquis was present at the meeting between Henry IV and Gregory VII at Canossa in 1077, and supported Henry's efforts to be freed from excommunication. Shortly afterward, Henry confirmed the considerable inheritance of Azzo's younger sons, Fulco and Hugo.[63] In the following confrontation with the pope, Azzo's support of Gregory, or lack of support for Henry, caused one of the king's polemicists to label the marquis "most iniquitous" and "impious."[64] Fulco somehow earned Henry's anger, and was released from the imperial ban in 1097 by Henry's rebellious son Conrad.[65] Hugo had apparently been expected to take over the inheritance of his mother, Garsenda of Maine (hence he is called Hugo del Mansi), but was unable to establish himself in France.[66] It is not clear when he returned to Italy, but Fulco is unlikely to have been eager to share the Italian patrimony.[67] Their sister Adelasia is among the very few women whose name can be associated with Matilda's circle. She is reported as one of the beneficiaries of the miracles that occurred at the tomb of Matilda's spiritual adviser, Anselm of Lucca, after his death in 1086.[68] What any of the siblings may have thought about Welf IV's reappearance in Italian affairs is obviously conjectural, but since at least some of Azzo's holdings had come with his marriage to Welf IV's mother, Kunigunde, the daughter of Welf II, the situation was potentially volatile.[69] Hugo's position after his return to Italy is unclear, as is the reason for his presence among Matilda's troops. There was presumably some degree of communication and cooperation between Matilda and her husband's family although this does not explain why it was left to Matilda to deal with Henry in what could be regarded

---

[62] Muratori, *Vita Mathildis comitissae*, p. 371, n. 95; the relevant documents are found in idem, *Delle antichità estensi ed italiane*, 1 (Modena, 1717), pp. 313–15; similarly, Simeoni, note to line 585, *Vita Mathildis*, p. 75.

[63] *Urkunden Heinrichs IV*, no. 289, pp. 377–79. The list includes Montagnana.

[64] *Petri Crassi defensio Heinrici IV. Regis*, ed. L. de Heinemann, MGH Libelli de lite 1 (Hanover, 1891), p. 434. The considerable issue of Azzo's age is passed over.

[65] *Urkunden Heinrichs IV*, Conrad, no. 2, pp. 672–73.

[66] *Vita Mathildis*, note to line 586, p. 75.

[67] An agreement was reached between Fulco and Hugo in 1095, after which Hugo disappears from the sources, Muratori, *Delle antichità estensi*, 1, pp. 272–74. The identification of Hugo has been challenged by Katrin Baaken who finds evidence that he was not in Italy at this time, E. Goez, "Welf V.," p. 371, n. 69.

[68] *Vita S. Anselmi Lucensis episcopi a Bardone scripsit*, ed. Roger Wilmans, MGH Scriptores 12 (Hanover, 1856), chap. 69, p. 32.

[69] Katrin Baaken, "Herzog Welf VI.," pp. 17–19; see also Gregory VII's letter of March 1081, cited n. 22 above.

as the Este back yard. The obvious conclusion is that she was better able to do so.

There is no information about the role of Welf V in any of the actions described by Donizone, including the operation that ended at Tricontai. Given his father's lifelong military activism, he may well have gained some field experience at a young age, but there is no evidence of it. There is likewise no evidence that any significant number of troops came with him from Germany.[70] That a very young and relatively inexperienced man would have been given actual command of Matilda's army is highly improbable, but he would surely have been given some position and supplied with advisors and, at least initially, an interpreter. Viscount Manfred may have been one of them. The presumably unintentionally amusing comments of Bernold of St. Blasien suggest an active role in the field for Welf leaving Matilda to formulate strategy and, perhaps, further from the fighting and the danger of death or capture.[71] Whether acting as an advisor to his nephew, as a liaison or as a guide, Hugo may have seen an opportunity to improve his position by alerting Henry, whose second Italian expedition had so far gone very well. Donizone, of course, does not speculate as to Hugo's motives or explain why he was able to influence the actions of Matilda's troops. Naming the traitor is as close as Donizone comes to acknowledging the existence of Matilda's second husband. He assumes that anyone reading his work will know to whom Hugo del Mansi was related as well as who resided near *Tres Comitatus* across the Adige.

The multiple references to river crossings suggest other things that Donizone expects his audience to be aware of, the roads and the rivers.[72] The Adige is a swift-flowing river with a long history of flooding and difficult crossings.[73] Gregory the Great and Paul the Deacon report an extremely destructive flood in 589 that miraculously spared the church of St. Zeno in Verona.[74] It was at

---

[70] Goez, "Welf V.," pp. 363–64.

[71] "In Italiam nobilissima dux Mathildis ... Welfoni duci filio Welfonis ducis coniugo copulatur ... ut tanto virilius sanctae Romanae aeclesiae contra excommunicatos posset subvenire." *Chronicon*, s.a. 1089, p. 449.

[72] The following discussion owes much to the collegial generosity of the Centro di Studi sui Castelli di Montagnana, Italy, and Euratlas-Nüssli, Yverdon, Switzerland.

[73] In 312 Constantine needed to secure the north before moving on to Rome. Verona was held against him, and in order to properly invest the city Constantine had to find a way to cross the Adige above Verona which he was able to do only after a number of attempts. A crossing below the city was apparently out of the question. Edward Gibbon, *The History of the Decline and Fall of the Roman Empire*, 1 (New York, 1841), p. 236; "Panegyric of Constantine Augustus," in *In Praise of Later Roman Emperors: The* Panegyrici Latini, ed. and trans. R. A. B. Mynors, C. E. V. Nixon and Barbara Saylor Rogers (Berkeley, 1994), pp. 307–08; Latin text pp. 598–99.

[74] Gregory the Great, *Dialogues*, trans. Odo John Zimmerman (New York, 1959) book 3, chap. 19, p. 150, a discussion of miracles; Paul the Deacon supplies a date (17 October 589) for the flood and mentions that part of the city wall was destroyed, *Pauli Historia Langobardorum*, MGH SS in usum scholarum 48 (Hanover, 1987) book 2, chap. 23, p. 128. Among the available translations is Paul the Deacon, *History of the Langobards*, trans. William Dudley Foulke (Philadelphia, 1907; repr. 1974), p. 127.

this time that Este (*Ateste*) ceased to function as a river port when the Adige (*Athesis*) changed its course.[75] Donizone does not mention any exceptional restlessness of the river in 1091, but would expect his readers to know that the Adige was a potentially dangerous river with a limited number of crossings. The routes of the Roman roads (the Via Annia or the Via Aemilia Altinate) west of Padua and the location of the bridges of the Adige are matters of some discussion. The possible crossings include Legnago, Begosso, Castagnaro and Lendinara, from north to south.[76] Of these, Legnago is closest to Tricontai, but the town was firmly in the hands of the bishop of Verona, an imperial appointee.[77] Given that Nogara, loyal to Matilda and able to resist Henry, was only 19 kilometers to the west, the Legnago crossing was a potential point of conflict, but not a place where an army of more than a thousand could expect to cross unnoticed. There would be no element of surprise, no need for a betrayal, and Henry could simply withdraw if he was outnumbered.

Even without a major flood, which Donizone would surely have mentioned, the roads near the rivers were unusable for part of the year.[78] In addition to large tracts of marshland there were also heavily wooded areas such as that recalled by the modern place name Boschi Sant'Anna.[79] The weather is also a factor. October is the rainiest month of the year meaning that the rivers are higher in the latter part of the year; the fogs are heaviest in December and January. Donizone gives only the general statement that this operation took place in winter as opposed to summer, but factoring in woods, marshes, rain or fog makes it understandable that Matilda thought her troops could move undetected or that Henry IV could avoid detection for several days. Henry was no stranger to fighting under such conditions.[80]

Donizone can be maddeningly vague about details, but he is clear enough about the larger picture. Henry wanted to take all of Matilda's lands; in other words, he needed to cut off her revenues so that she no longer had the means to wage war. He was successful in taking her capital, Mantua, and had also successfully secured the northwest quadrant of her territory, the county of Brescia. Ferrara, like Brescia, was a countship held by Matilda's family since

[75] Gérard Rippe, *Padoue et son contado: Xe–XIIIe siècle. Société et pouvoirs* (Rome, 2003), p. 44.

[76] Touring Club Italiano, *Strade dell'Italia romana* (Milan, 2004), pp. 150–54, is most current. Any of these locations is credibly close to Tricontai.

[77] Castagnetti, *L'organizzazione*, p. 201.

[78] For a discussion of geography, weather, the changing courses of the rivers over the centuries, and the Este holdings, the "Préliminaires" in Rippe, *Padoue*, are informative: pp. 37–48, 65–70, 123–28.

[79] Rippe, *Padoue*, pp. 55 ff. Boschi Sant'Anna is clearly indicated as a wooded area in a surviving fifteenth-century map. Silvana Anna Bianchi, "La viabilità terrestre in territorio veronese fra norme teoriche e realizzazione pratiche (secoli XII–XV)," in *Per terre e per acque: vie di comunicazione nel Veneto dal Medioevo alla prima età moderno*, ed. Donato Gallo and Flaviano Rossetto (Padua and Monselice, 2003), pp. 203–38, map, p. 207.

[80] Cp. The account of the battle on the Elster River (1080). Bruno of Magdeburg, *Liber de bello*, pp. 380–81; Delbrück, *History of the Art of War*, 3:138–40.

the time of Tedaldo.[81] Ferrara itself is south of the Po, but had interests across the river. The northeast sector of Matilda's holdings, that is, north of the Po and east of the Mincio, had to be secured to deny her the revenues deriving from the trade along the Po and its tributaries east of Mantua.[82]

Archbishop Guibert of Ravenna was elected pope at the synod of Brixen in June 1080, and Matilda last issued a charter in Ferrara in November 1080 a short time after troops she had mustered for Pope Gregory's intended campaign against Guibert were defeated at Volta Mantovana.[83] Ferrara was a suffragan of Ravenna, and the archbishop's suffragans remained uniformly loyal to him as Pope Clement III.[84] That Matilda could not exercise authority in the city does not mean that she had no access to resources in the Ferrarese. Matilda's family and those families allied with the Canossans – the Baggiovara, the Ganaceto and the Calaone – had substantial holdings in the region between the Po and the Adige. The Canossan holdings were concentrated between the Po and the Tartaro, a navigable river between the Po and the Adige that passes through Nogara. Two additional fortified sites were located east of Nogara, Cerea on the Menago and Anghiara (Angiari) on the west bank of the Adige.[85] Donizone does not mention the other rivers, much less discuss the trade that moved along them. Earlier in the poem he noted that Matilda held the road of the Po, and that apparently is all he thought necessary.[86] For Henry, moving into the area between the Po and Adige was a step toward gaining control of the Po, but it was not something to attempt without first securing the crossings of the Adige. Failing this, the emperor would be vulnerable on both sides with Matilda still able to send troops across the Po and her husband's family in control of at least some of the crossings of the Adige. The Este may well have feared finding themselves besieged.

It would be expecting a great deal more chronological precision than Donizone demonstrates to insist that since he refers to the area north of the Po as being under Henry's control before he relates the battle at *Tres Comitatus* this is the order of events. The battle clearly took place north of the Po, and if the entire area except Nogara were already under Henry's control it is unlikely that

---

81 Overmann, *Gräfin Mathilde*, pp. 4, 21–23.

82 Luigi Bellini, *Le saline dell'antico delta padano*, Deputazione provinciale ferrarese di storia patria, Atti e memorie, n.s. 24 (1962), pp. 169–271, while focusing on the salt trade includes a detailed discussion of the Po trade route within the larger picture in northern Italy; Andrea Castagnetti, *Società e politica a Ferrara dall'età postcarolingia alla signoria estense (Sec. X–XIII)* (Bologna, 1985), pp. 39–55.

83 *Urkunden Mathilde*, no. 32, pp. 114–16.

84 Ingrid Heidrich, *Ravenna unter Erzbischof Wibert (1073–1100)* (Sigmaringen, 1984), pp. 107–18; Matilda's successful reestablishment of her authority in Ferrara in 1101 shortly after Clement III's death is outside the scope of this article: *Vita Mathildis*, 2.13, 930–40, p. 87.

85 Castagnetti, *L'organizzazione*, pp. 183–202. The Ganaceto are associated with both Minerbe and Trecenta (located between the Po and the Adige); the Baggiovara with Ostiglia, location of the fords of the Po. Ibid., p. 196. If or when Matilda lost control of Cerea or Anghiara in not known. Fumagalli, "Economia, società," p. 53 (note 39, above).

86 "Ipsa Padi stratam tenet," *Vita Mathildis*, 2.3, line 335a, p. 67. Donizone is here discussing the time before the battle at Sorbara (1084).

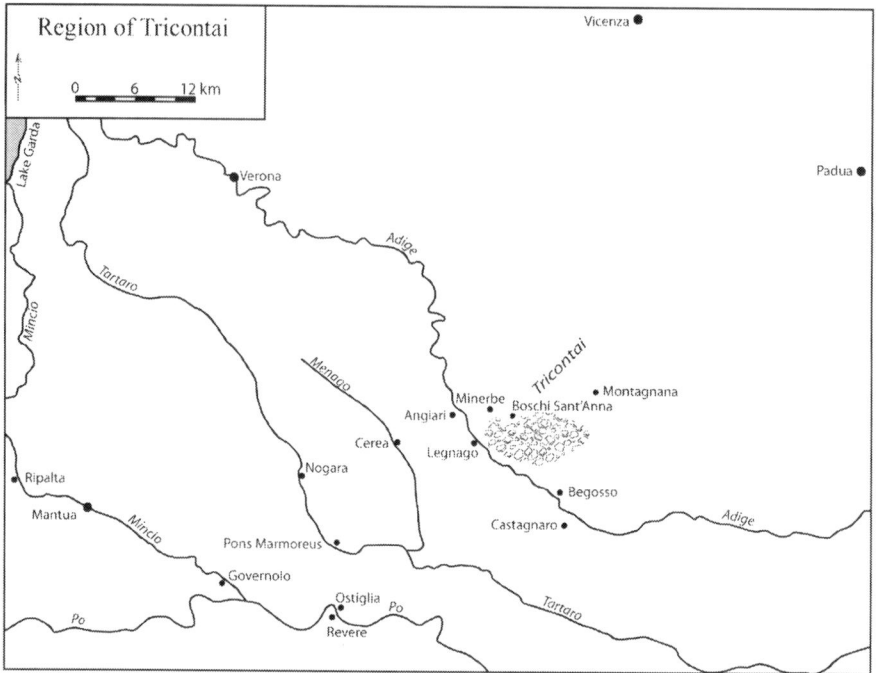

Region of Tricontai

0   6   12 km

an army sent by Matilda could have crossed the region unopposed. The implication is that as of late September Matilda still held the fords of the Po at Ostglia-
Revere and had control of the river traffic along the Po and Tartaro.[87] Although
Donizone ignores the Tartaro, it was of great interest to Matilda's father, Bonifacio, who never neglected an opportunity to expand the area under his control.
Some of these attempts brought him into conflict with the counts and bishops
of Verona who could easily see that his acquisition of such points as Cerea was
leading to the Adige, and successfully opposed his moves to gain control of that
important artery. Marquis Bonifacio also reopened a canal between Ostiglia and
Pons Marmoreus (Ponte Molino), connecting the Po and the Tartaro.[88] These
facts suggest a line of march for Matilda's troops by way of Ostiglia and *Pons
Marmoreus* and then to the crossing of the Adige. The more usual route by way
of Ostiglia, Nogara and Legnago would be ruled out by the need for secrecy and
the fact that the bishop of Verona held Legnago. Given the time of year, any of
the crossings may not have been usable although clearly some were passable
since Matilda's troops were able to reach Tricontai.

---

[87] Revere probably came to the family through Bonifacio's first wife, Richildis. Overmann, *Gräfin
      Mathilde*, p. 17; M. G. Bertolini, "Bonifacio di Toscana," *Dizionario biografico degli Italiani*,
      12 (Rome, 1970), p. 97; Castagnetti, *L'organizzazione*, pp. 108–10.
[88] Mor, "Dalla caduta dell'imperio," cited n. 27 above, pp. 148–49.

Henry was preparing to move into the region between the Po and the Adige to take control of it from Matilda. The preparations had to include securing the crossings of the Adige, something that could hardly be done without the knowledge of the family that dominated the area and who turned to their powerful neighbor and kinswoman. If Matilda's forces crossed the Po at Ostiglia-Revere and then turned east to cross the Adige at one of the points downriver from Legnago, they would have approached from the south through the wooded area with the objective of cutting Henry off from retreat and forcing him to battle while outnumbered. If the Legnago crossing was not feasible due to the October rains and subsequent high water, Henry could be caught between Matilda's forces and the Adige. The possibility of support from Nogara only 19 kilometers west of Legnago, cannot be ruled out. Matilda's intelligence had alerted her to an opportunity to attack when her enemy was at a great disadvantage.[89]

Whether the initiative came from Hugo, as Donizone's narrative strongly suggests, or whether Henry IV had shown himself at least equal to Matilda in knowing what was going on in the enemy's household can probably not be determined, but the possibility must be considered. Welf IV's return and his claims in Italy must have disconcerted his younger half-brothers. Fulco, who had the most to lose, apparently followed his father in supporting Matilda and the reform popes, while Hugo had nothing to lose and potentially everything to gain by backing Henry, who seemed likely to prevail. The possibility that the emperor set a trap when he moved into Este territory with a conspicuously small following is not even hinted at by Donizone, but if there was dissension among Azzo's sons it is likely that Henry was aware of the situation and he may have made the first overture. In any case, by the time Donizone was writing, Hugo was no longer present and could take the full blame for backing the wrong side.

*

Matilda's effort to pre-empt Henry's move toward the Po and the Ferrarese by quick and decisive action failed. After this success Henry was, as Donizone writes, in almost complete control of Matilda's territory north of the Po. The following year he moved against the strongholds in the southeast quadrant.

The tide of the war turned in 1092, as Matilda had all but predicted in her speech to her troops after Tricontai. The year started successfully enough for Henry who continued the fight against Matilda's troops through the winter. The winter campaign apparently went well because the emperor held his Christmas and Easter courts in Mantua and then crossed the Po in June with a large following of both Italians and Germans. First he secured the strong points on the plain (*loca campestria nobiliora*), which Donizone does not identify, but which probably included such Canossan holdings as Guastalla and Luzzara north of Reggio which effectively gave Matilda control of the south bank of the Po between the

---

[89] Hay finds that Matilda was shifting from a strategy of battle avoidance to battle-seeking and thus taking a considerable risk, *Military Leadership*, p. 132.

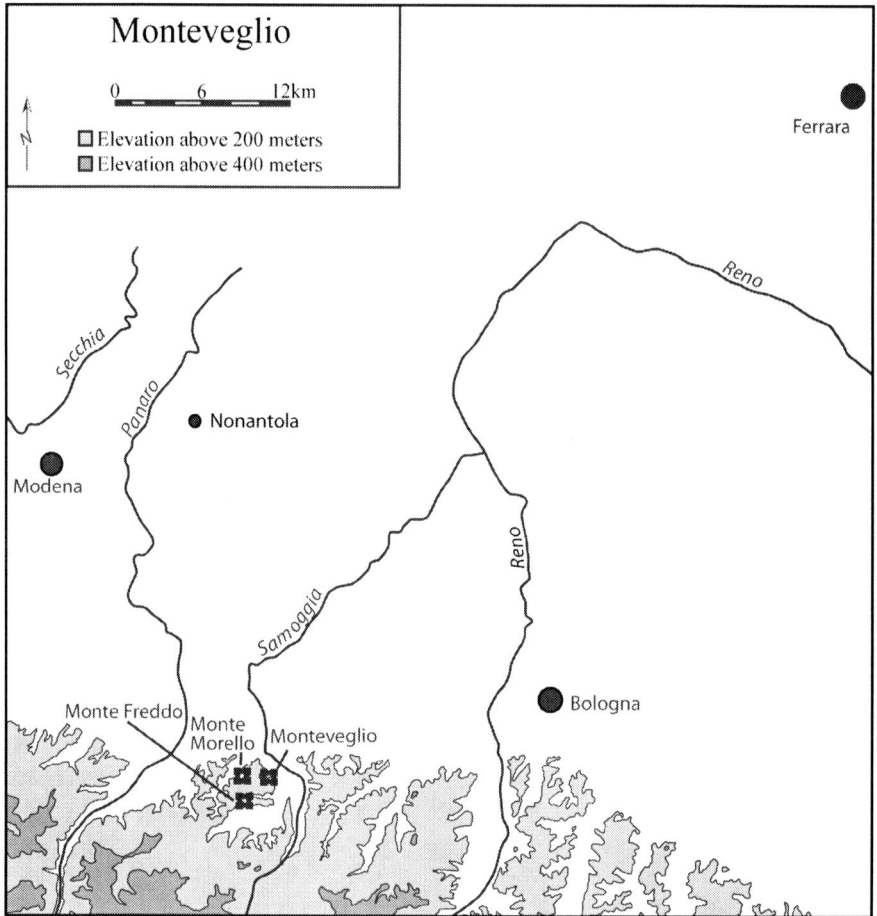

Enza and the Mincio.[90] Henry's successful operation at Mantua had disrupted this, and since Henry passed through Reggio in October, presumably neither this section of the Po nor the countryside of Reggio and Modena were still under Matilda's control. He then went southeast into the Modenese hills where *Mons Maurelli* surrendered without a fight. *Mons Alfredi* put up a stiff resistance (*certamine freni*), but at the price of the capture of Matilda's standard bearer, the eloquent Gerard.[91] Securing these two sites was preliminary to Henry's goal of

---

[90] Schumann, *Authority and the Commune*, p. 65.
[91] Donizone, *Vita Mathildis*, 2:7.600–10, pp. 75–76. *Certamine freni* is certainly not a cavalry action. Bethmann, *Donizonis vita Mathildis*, p. 391, suggests *effreni*; this is likely an example of Donizone's fondness for Grecisms, i.e., *phreni*; cp. the use of *falerati* at 2.3, 339, p. 67. Donizone also assumes that the adjective "eloquent" will be sufficient to distinguish the standard bearer from many others of the same name.

taking the fortress of *Montisbelli* (Monteveglio), but despite spending much of the summer in the effort, the siege failed. There had been no successful investment of Monteveglio; Donizone reports that Henry had been unable to prevent either entering or leaving the castle. Hopes that Matilda's supporters were about to desert her also came to nothing. A council held in Carpineti was unexpectedly swayed by the preaching of the monk John (*heremita Johannes*);[92] Henry's offers of peace, offers which demanded only that Matilda cease her opposition to Clement III, and which had, according to Donizone, greatly appealed to her following, were rejected.[93] At least one of his siege engines (*machina*) was burned. The castle successfully resisted the emperor who also lost one of his sons in the failed siege. The summer of 1092 had not been nearly as productive for him as the previous two years.

The site of the castle of Monteveglio is 20 kilometers west of Bologna, 25 kilometers southeast of Modena, near the left bank of the Samoggia River; it is built on a hill that rises very sharply to an elevation of 280 meters. Archeology shows that almost every group known to have inhabited northern Italy has left its traces at or near Monteveglio. It was part of the Byzantine defensive system until taken by the Lombards in the eighth century.[94] First described as a castle in 822 in a document of Louis the Pious, Monteveglio came into the possession of Matilda's family when her great-grandfather Adalberto-Azzo became count of Modena.[95] The castle is at the northern end of the routes through the Apennines from Bologna to Florence,[96] and marks the eastern extremity of the Apennine defensive system at Matilda's disposal. Having pushed Matilda back into the mountains, Henry was now moving to limit her mobility within them. Presumably, Monteveglio was one of the places that Matilda strengthened while Henry was elsewhere occupied. He was successful in capturing its outliers, *Mons Maurelli* and *Mons Alfredi*, but had to fight hard for the latter. There is

---

92   *Vita Mathildis*, 2.7, 630–62, pp. 76–77; the abbot of St. Apollonio in Donizone's time was named John; *Vita Mathildis*, ibid., notes to line 647; for a discussion of other possibilities, see Golinelli, *Vita di Matilde*, pp. 144–45, n. 105.

93   Matteo Schenetti, "La vittoria de Matilde di Canossa su Arrigo IV," *Studi Matildici III*, pp. 235–42; Lino Lionello Ghirardini, "Il convegno di Carpineti (1092) e il sua decisiva importanza nella lotta per le investiture," *Studi Matildici II*, pp. 97–136. The contrasting images of Matilda in these articles are interesting. Schenetti's Matilda seems to be waiting for the men to tell her what to do; Ghirardini's Matilda "clearly conducted herself as *princeps*." Donizone once again assumes that *heremita Iohannes* (ll. 647–56) needs no further identification.

94   Renato Passeri, *La seconda Canossa: Storia di Monteveglio e di Montebudello* (Bologna, 1978), pp. 28 ff.; Gina Fasoli, "Appunti per la storia di Monteveglio tra il VII e il XII secolo," *L'Archiginnasio* 38 (1943), 92–99; Paul the Deacon discusses the wars of Lombard king Liutprand c.725, *Historia langobardorum*, book 6, cap. 49, pp. 234–35; Foulke, *History of the Langobards*, pp. 289–93.

95   Tiraboschi, *Dizionario topografico storico degli stati Estensi*, 2 (Modena, 1825; repr. Bologna, 1963), pp. 58–62; Passeri, *La seconda Canossa*, p. 49.

96   Paolo Mucci and Ezio Trota, "La strada medievale fra Nonantola e la Toscana," *Viabilità antica e medievale nel territorio modenese e reggiano: Contributi di studi*, ed. Giordano Bertuzzi (Modena, 1983), pp. 35–89.

some question as to the specific locations of these castles. Renato Passeri places them at modern Monte Morello and Monte Freddo. Monte Morello is 1.25 kilometers west of Monteveglio at a height of 351 meters; Monte Freddo is 1.1 kilometers south of Monte Morello at a height of 352 meters.[97] Their function was to defend Monteveglio by disrupting attacks from the west, that is, coming through the Panaro valley. Both of these places have been rebuilt a number of times, and archeology is less successful with Matilda's castles than with Etruscan or even Neanderthal habitations. There is likewise nothing remaining of the castle of Monteveglio itself. The topography of the mountain is the only hint as to the extent and shape of the castle.[98]

The other toponym given by Donizone is *Cucherla* where one of Henry's siege engines was burnt. Donizone's description of the incomplete investment of Monteveglio and the harassment of the besiegers by the castle's defenders suggests that the destruction of the *machina* took place during a raid on Henry's siege camp, but this would leave the problem of maneuvering a fully assembled siege engine up the steep hillside. Simeoni's proposal that the *machina* was a wooden siege tower is similarly ill-suited to the terrain.[99] Donizone's description of Henry's "thundering" against Monteveglio suggests rather stone-throwing artillery which would have an effective range of about 150 meters.[100] Passeri's lively reconstruction of the action, based on Donizone and his own imagination, does not discuss such questions, but he envisions *Cucherla* as a citadel or keep located across a dip in the mountaintop, 150 meters from the central part of the castle, from which a desperate sortie emerged to destroy the *machina* that was threatening the walls. That it was burned from underneath (*succensa fit*) indicates such an attack rather than the use of incendiary missiles. Occupying this spot would put Henry's artillery well within effective range of the castle. Absent the archeology to support it, Passeri's hypothesis remains suggestive.[101]

Donizone, of course, has no interest in such details but reports that the anti-pope Clement III came to Monteveglio to confer with the emperor (2.7, lines 623 ff.). Things were not going well at Rome.

In October, Henry finally gave up on Monteveglio. The trumpets announcing his departure sounded repeatedly through the fields; the description gives the impression that the besieging army had been rather large and moved out unit

---

[97]   Passeri, *La seconda Canossa*, pp. 65–67. Other locations have been proposed: Golinelli, *Vita di Mathilde*, p. 144, n. 99; Tiraboschi, *Dizionario topografico*, 2:53, 77.

[98]   For a discussion of the use of GIS technology to virtually reconstruct castles, including detailed discussion of the topography of the Panaro valley see Alberto Monti, "I castelli lungo il confine tra Bologna e Modena: Dati storici ed elaborazione digitali," in *Rocche e castelli lungo il confine tra Bologna e Modena. Attil della Giornata di Studio (Vignola, 25 ottobre 2003)*, ed. Pierpaolo Bonacini and Domenicio Cerami (Vignola, 2005), pp. 15–31.

[99]   *Vita Mathildis*, 2.7, 663–64 with note, p. 77.

[100] Kelly DeVries, *Medieval Military Technology* (Peterborough, ON, 1992), pp. 131 ff.

[101] An excellent aerial photo can be found in Franca Manenti Valli, "Lo scacchiere castellano matildico," in *Rocche fortilizi castelli in Emilia Romagna Marche*, ed. Giuseppe Adani (Milan, 1988), p. 34.

by unit. Henry headed west rather than to his usual winter quarters at Verona. After a short stay in Reggio, the emperor continued on toward Parma. Donizone describes this as a feint since he changed his line of march, turned back to *Cavillianum* (San Polo d'Enza)[102] and approached Canossa. At this point Donizone inserts a gleefully vivid recollection of Henry's humiliation in 1077 and his desire for revenge. When Matilda heard of Henry's approach she moved out to *Bibianellum* (Bianello), one of four smaller outlying castles downhill from Canossa, with a part of the garrison.[103] Donizone describes first Matilda's faith in St. Apollonio and then a tight maneuver during which the opposing forces could hear one another as they passed through the hills. Some of Matilda's leaders (*proceres*) then returned to Canossa; along the way they ignored the challenges called out by Henry's troops and successfully regained the castle where they urged a vigorous repayment for Henry's incursion.[104] Donizone then goes on to describe the king's banner flying, trumpets reverberating, the abbot and the monks chanting psalms, and the fog settling in so thickly that the castle became invisible to the would-be attackers. This apparently worked to the advantage of the defenders as Donizone reports that in the exchange that ensued the attackers suffered disproportionate casualties while the only defender wounded had already accounted for a number of the enemy. This is a rather common boast.

> The abbot prayed, the people, as mentioned, fought.
> The king's army is assailed, wounded by weapons of iron;

---

[102] Guido Agosti, "San Polo et il suo territorio: aspetti geo-morphologici," in *Milleni Sampolesi: Atti del Convegno di Studi Storici (San Polo d'Enza 4–5–6 Maggio 1984)*, ed. Gino Badini (Reggio Emilia, 1985), pp. 1–17 [hereafter *Milleni Sampolesi*]; idem, "Val d'Enza e Canossa," in *Quattro Castella nella Storia di Canossa: Atti del Convegno di Studi Matildici, 28–29 Maggio 1977*, ed. Gino Badini (Rome, 1977), pp. 227–39 [hereafter *Quattro Castella*]. Both have numerous photographs of the terrain.

[103] Although Bianello is the only one of the Quattro Castelli to be specifically mentioned, the entire complex is a cohesive unit within the larger defensive system. Arnoldo Tincani, "Quattro Castella: zona limitanea di difesa," pp. 83–92; Odoardo Rombaldi, "Il potere e l'organizzazione del territorio di Quattro Castella," pp. 7–49; Franca Manenti Valli, "Il Bianello nella vicenda architettonica e nella strategia difensiva," pp. 173–99, all in *Quattro Castella*; Franca Manenti Valli, "I Quattro Castelli: Avancorpo fortificato dei Canossa," in *Architettura fortificata. Atti del 1° congresso internazionale. Piacenza-Bologna 18–21 Marzo 1976. Castella 18* (Bologna, 1978), pp. 447–69.

[104] Donizone seems to be once again emphasizing the resolve and steadfastness, the professionalism, of Matilda's troops who were not distracted from their mission by taunts. This does not seem to be an offer to resolve the dispute by single combat although cutting them off from Canossa would have been desirable. As *proceres* these men may have been known to the Parmans in Henry's following. Matthew Strickland, "Provoking or Avoiding Battle? Duel and Single Combat in Warfare of the High Middle Ages," in *Armies, Chivalry and Warfare in Medieval Britain and France. Proceedings of the 1995 Harlaxton Symposium*, ed. Matthew Strickland (Stamford, UK, 1998), pp. 317–43; idem, *War and Chivalry: The Conduct and Perception of War in England and Normandy, 1066–1217* (Cambridge, 1996), pp. 160–62.

Of the people of the land only one is wounded,
Who had struck many arms with [his] weapon. (2.7, 701–04)[105]

[Abbas orabat, pugnabat plebs memorata.
Vulneribus ferri iaculatur contio regis;
Ex populo terrae iaculatur non nisi certe
Unus, qui multas pilo pulsaverat ulnas.]

Then the emperor's standard bearer, the son of Oberto (*natus Oberti*),[106] was unhorsed and the royal standard was captured. At this point Henry decided to retreat – sincerely wishing he had never even heard of the road to Canossa much less taken it – first to *Baianum* (Bibbiano) and then across the Po. Matilda's troops followed afterward, regaining much of the lands she had lost and a good bit of loot besides. As Donizone reports, from the moment he lost his banner Henry's fortunes declined.[107]

Scholarly opinion of Donizone's testimony and of the significance of the engagement itself has been divided. The notion of a pincer maneuver as a key element is apparently an old one, found in the seventeenth-century work of Pietro Valestri, abbot of St. Prospero in Reggio. The unpublished manuscript, written in a number of different hands, is a collection of excerpts from sources including Bernold, Donizone, papal letters and earlier historians with the abbot's commentary; it contains more than one account of the events of 1092.[108] Valestri, like Donizone, was not writing a biography, but a panegyric, a work of praise for one whose role in life was to provide a model of heroic virtue for royal women.[109]

Despite this, historians writing about the battle have commented on Valestri's work as though it was intended as a description of the battle. The comments are based on a paraphrase published by Angelo Ferretti who interprets Donizone's account as a brisk encounter with the defenders rushing out before any assault could begin. For Ferretti, there is no question that immediate assault was Henry's intention. The fighting was bloody, and things went badly for the emperor's troops who quickly withdrew after the loss of the imperial banner. Ferretti then

---

[105] For various translations of these lines see Golinelli, *Vita di Matilde*, p. 90; similarly, Bellocchi and Marzi, *Matilde e Canossa*, pp. 221, 223; conversely, Hay, *Military Leadership*, pp. 139–40.

[106] Oberto is presumed to be the defeated commander at the battle of Sorbara (1084). In Donizone's version of that engagement the marquis ignominiously fled after striking a single effective blow. *Vita Mathildis* 2.3, lines 338 ff., pp. 67–68; n. 123, below.

[107] *Vita Mathildis* 2.7, 672–735, pp. 76–79.

[108] Pietro Valestri, *La gran contessa Matilda, paragone genealogico ... perfettamente verificata.* Gino Badini, "Documenti Canossani dell'Archivio di Stato di Reggio Emilia," in *Canossa prima di Matilde* (Milan, 1990), p. 282. I have so far examined only a copy printed from microfilm.

[109] As such, the work is discussed in studies of Matilda's *Nachleben*. Odoardo Rombaldi, "Guido dal Pozzo autore del volume 'Meraviglie Heroiche di Matilda la Gran Contessa d'Italia,' Verona 1678," pp. 106–7; Clementina Santi, "Matilde negli scrittori reggiani," p. 156, both in *Matilde di Canossa nelle culture europee del secondo millennio: Dal storia al mito*, ed. Paolo Golinelli (Bologna, 1999).

adds details from Valestri's work although, he writes, he does not know where the Benedictine abbot got his information. In this version, Matilda entrusted the defense of Canossa to Welf, and it was her young husband who led the vigorous sortie. She herself pressed the attackers from behind, leading 3,000 foot and 800 horse and keeping herself closer to Bianello. Valestri's account, writes Ferretti, does not differ substantially from that of Donizone with the exception of Welf's role, and, given Donizone's silence on the subject of Matilda's husbands, this is hardly surprising. The successful two-pronged attack is attested by the existence of the oratory called Madonna della Battaglia between Canossa and Bianello. Ferretti then continues with a discussion of the terrain, the two-hour walk from Canossa to Madonna della Battaglia and the possibility that Matilda engaged with Henry's rearguard or "a detachment."[110]

German scholars writing at about the same time rely on Donizone's account. Hildenhagen adds the observation that a castle with Canossa's reputation for impregnability could be defended by relatively few. Matilda quickly returned from Bianello with reinforcements and attacked Henry outside Canossa. She was supported by a sortie from the castle; the fog that Donizone reports was an important element in Henry's defeat. Volkmar paraphrases Donizone adding only the comment that Henry found the garrison of Canossa prepared.[111]

In a very different interpretation, Simeoni remarks that the missiles that Donizone refers to could have been fired or thrown over the walls, that is, there was no sortie and therefore no pincer.[112] In Simeoni's discussion of the historicity of Donizone's work he dismisses the action as a "modest attempt by Henry to surprise Canossa" which Donizone aggrandizes because Matilda was personally present and, possibly, because he himself was somewhat "anxious."[113] In general, Simeoni seems reluctant to discuss war.

In marked contrast, Lino Lionello Ghirardini considers the battle (or failed assault) not only decisive for the course of the Investiture Controversy, but "influential for the future course of military operations" even though Donizone "often narrates in a confused way ... passing over even important matters in silence" and "is inaccurate in details."[114] Ghirardini envisions a field battle that centered around Madonna della Battaglia, the chapel noted by Ferretti. He also accepts the presence and active role of Welf. In this interpretation, Henry's actions are explained by faulty intelligence; the emperor believes that most of Matilda's forces are still in the area of Monteveglio, and Canossa is thus only

---

[110] Ferretti, *Canossa: Studi e richerche*, 2nd ed. (Florence, 1884), pp. 108–12; the location of this description in Valestri's manuscript is not specified; Donizone's version is followed closely on ff. 102r–v.

[111] Hildenhagen, *Heinrich IV.*, pp. 28–30; Volkmar, *Der dritte Römerzug*, pp. 8–9.

[112] *Vita Mathildis*, notes to 2.7, lines 680 ff., p. 78.

[113] Simeoni, "La *Vita Mathildis*," p. 38; similarly, idem, "Il contributo della contessa Matilde al Papato nella lotta per le investiture," *Studi Gregoriani* 1 (1947), 353–372.

[114] Lino Lionello Ghirardini, "'Madonna della Battaglia': lo scontro decisivo della lotta per le investiture (ottobre 1092)," *Bolletino Storico Reggiano* 11 (April 1971), 36–56, quote p. 38.

lightly defended. Ghirardini's discussion emphasizes the importance of a careful study of the terrain and also calls on "local tradition."[115]

Published in the same year, John Beeler's survey of medieval warfare included some brief remarks on the countess Matilda and interpreted the action at Canossa as "a classic pincer."[116] Most recently, Hay, like Simeoni, prefers a strict reading in which there was no sortie, no pincer, and thus no need to coordinate the actions; the capture of the emperor's banner was an act of personal bravado, and the resounding trumpets signal only that Donizone knows his Virgil.[117]

While all of these hypotheses have their appeal, none is particularly convincing in answering the questions that, as usual, Donizone's description raises. Canossa was part of a multi-level network of castles and outposts that extended across the north face of the Apennines between the Secchia and Enza rivers, in effect making the entire region one large fortress.[118] Donizone mentions only what he considers important. His silence about the Apennine defensive system is a far more serious impediment to understanding his description of the action than his neglect of Welf.[119] Matilda and St. Apollonio are important; Canossa is important.[120] San Polo and Bianello must be mentioned because the main characters, Henry and Matilda, went to those castles. But Guardasone, directly across the Enza from San Polo, and Rossena with its outlier Rossanella, a bit over two kilometers west of Canossa and the only castle actually visible from Canossa, were also there, as were castles further into the mountains such as the already-mentioned Baiso and Carpineti to the southeast. Matilda's father had held San Polo as a fief of the church of Reggio, a bishopric now in the hands of Henry's

---

[115] Welf's role is supported by citations to Ferretti's paraphrase of Valestri and to Bernold of St. Blasien, *Chronicon*, s.a. 1092, p. 453. "Heinricus quoque, imperator ipsius, in Longobardia iam biennio morabatur, ibique circumquaque terram Welfonis Italici ducis praeda ferro et incendio devastare non cessavit, ut eundem ducem et prudentissimam eius uxorem a fidelitate sancti Petri discedere, sibique adherere compelleret; set frustra." Local tradition is further discussed in Arnaldo Tincani, "Matilde nelle leggende popolari dell'Appennino," in *Matilde ... del secondo millennio*, pp. 179–205; similarly, Simeoni, "La *Vita Mathildis*," passim.

[116] Beeler, *Warfare in Feudal Europe*, pp. 205–06. In a personal communication Beeler wrote that his discussion was based on Leone Tondelli, *Matilda di Canossa*, 2nd ed. (Reggio Emilia, 1926).

[117] *Military Leadership*, pp. 139–42.

[118] Rocco Morretta, "L'Apparato difensivo," n. 39 above; in addition to the relevant works on the Quattro Castelli, cited n. 103 above, see Lino Lionello Ghirardini, "S. Polo nella sistema strategico-difensivo dell'appennino canossiano," in *Milleni Sampolesi*, pp. 99–115, who expresses some reservations about Morretta's view of this system, p. 104, and unfortunately cites few sources for interesting and potentially useful observations; Franca Manenti Valli, "Lo scacchiere," n. 101 above, pp. 25–46; idem, *Architettura di castelli nell'Appennino Reggiano* (Milan, 1987), pp. 19–24, 125–26, 169–70, 207–13, 241–42; Antonio Cassi Ramelli, *Dalle caverne ai rifugio blindati; trenta secoli di architettura militare* (Milan, 1964), p. 85.

[119] Welf acted together with Matilda until April 1095. Goez, "Welf V.," pp. 372–73.

[120] Canossa has been the subject of archeological research since the nineteenth century. Tonino Aceto, "L'apparato difensivo de Canossa," in *Studi Matildici III*, pp. 369–93; Franca Manenti Valli, "Canossa. Rivisitazione dei ruderi," in *Canossa prima di Matilde*, pp. 35–68.

supporter Lodovico, who was appointed sometime in 1091–92. Bonifacio gave Rossena to the church of Reggio and received it back in fief, an arrangement undoubtedly to his benefit. There is no specific information given as to who had control of these sites in October 1092, but since Henry went to San Polo it was either in the new bishop's hands or it was quickly taken, and Donizone does not mention the action.[121] Henry was not only moving toward Canossa, but into a well-fortified area.

Like all castles, Matilda's numerous strongholds had been built "to effectively oppose armed aggression and, in the second place, to support an action of attack or counter attack by its occupants." Since these defensive structures have as their primary function increasing the chances of survival in war, a great deal of resources – time, energy and ingenuity – was expended on them.[122] The Canossa complex was the basis for the rise to power of Matilda's family and, as Donizone has been at some pains to make clear, it functioned effectively. If, as now seems generally accepted, the Canossan castles functioned in concert, the elements had to communicate. Two expedient methods would be sending messengers, who doubtless has shortcuts that were not generally known, and the use of known aural signals that would result in a prearranged response. Lacking such communication there would be no defensive system in place, but rather a number of small isolated fortifications each concerned only with its limited immediate area.

Donizone describes the initial movement toward Parma as a feint. For a feint to be successful, it must be believable, that is, there had to be a reason for Henry to go to Parma. Certainly he had strong support there. Clement III was originally from Parma, and the extended family of the Otbertines that had supported Henry during the 1081–84 expedition had large holdings in the region. At least one member of that family was with Henry at Canossa, serving as his standard bearer.[123] Donizone reports that in the summer, Henry had crossed the Po with

---

[121] Ghirardini, "San Polo," notes that it would have been very dangerous for Henry to leave San Polo unsecured as he moved on to Canossa, pp. 111–12; the situation of Guardasone and Rossena is unclear, Manenti Valli, "Lo scacchiere," p. 37; Gerhard Schwartz, *Die Besetzung der Bistümer Reichsitaliens unter den Sächsischen und Salien Kaisern mit den Listen der Bischöfe, 951–1122* (Leipzig, 1913; repr. Spoleto, 1993), p. 198; Groß, *Lothar III.*, pp. 248, 256–57; Overmann, *Gräfin Mathilde*, p. 6.

[122] Monti, "I castelli lungo," p. 16.

[123] Determining which members of the extended Otbertine family are with Henry at this point is a complex exercise; the family has four major branches. Ferdinando Gabotto, "I marchesi Obertenghi fino alla pace di Luni," *Giornale storico della Lunigiana* 9 (1918), 3–47, is dated, but gives a detailed genealogical chart, n.p., between pp. 46–47; Schumann, *Authority and the Commune*, discusses the origins of the family, its holdings and the rivalry with the Canossans who rose to power at about the same time, pp. 60–64, 145–46, and accepts Gabotto's identification of Marquis Oberto as Oberto IV (born c.1020) and *natus Oberti* as his son, Oberto V (born c.1050). The identification rests on the fact that their descendant Oberto VI Pelavicino (c.1080–1147) did not join the papal party after the defeat of Henry IV, and thus remained hostile to Matilda longer than other Otbertines, pp. 214, 319. Schumann streamlines Gabotto's genealogy leaving out a candidate from a different branch of the family. Henry's staunch

a large number of both Italians and Germans (*Stipatus transit Longobardis, Alemannis*). Given the location, the Italians most likely came from the Modenese. The brief stop at Reggio, where his *castra* was probably located outside the city, would have been a good point for Henry to join up with an escort coming out from Parma and to release the troops that had been at Monteveglio. Henry's operational timetable would have called for him to move into Matilda's southwestern quadrant. The failure of the siege of Monteveglio was not a disaster for Henry. Piadena in Matilda's northwest sector had evaded his control as had Nogara in the northeast, and now Monteveglio in the southeast held out. Why Donizone does not describe any actions at Piadena or Nogara in 1090–91 is a question that cannot be answered here,[124] but the failures, if failures they were, did not disrupt Henry's apparently careful planning. Similarly, the presence of unconquered, but probably damaged, Monteveglio, with its outliers held by Henry's supporters could not be considered an immediate threat to operations conducted 70 kilometers away in the Parmense. Henry moved, apparently on schedule, into the southwest quadrant of Matilda's territory. The size of his following is not known, but if the emperor set out from Reggio with anywhere near the "under 40,000" estimated by Ghirardini no one is likely to have been surprised that he made use of them.[125]

Yet Donizone writes that Henry feinted toward Parma and – the weather was clear – turned back to San Polo. Since Henry's departure from Reggio was not secretive, in this scenario he intended to be seen, there is no reason not to assume that he took the easiest and most obvious route, the Via Aemilia, and reached and possibly crossed the Enza, about 17 kilometers west of Reggio, as would be expected, but then turned back (*rediit retro Cavilianum*). It is an intriguing but unprovable thought that he joined up here with more troops sent from Parma before turning south to San Polo, a distance of about 16 kilometers. Donizone's feint may be no more than Henry setting out for San Polo along the easiest road, which was also the road to Parma. He has so many times described Henry as treacherous that anything the emperor did could be so interpreted. That Matilda had arrived at Canossa, where she was seldom to be found, indicates that she knew perfectly well what Henry would be attempting.

Although her ancestors had never been counts of Parma, Matilda had interests in the Parmense. It was in Parma that her great-great grandfather Sigifredo from the county of Lucca settled, and her great-grandfather Azzo and his brothers established themselves there. The family had considerable holdings

---

supporter Adalberto Rufo had a younger brother, also called Oberto IV (c.1040/50–c.1101), by Gabotto, and Oberto's son Ugo II (c.1070/80–c.1101/22); without firmer dating of Ugo's birth the question remains open, but junior members of this large family would have strong motivation to take advantage of such an opportunity. Eads, "Mighty", pp. 103–11, 188–90. Hay, *Military Leadership*, p. 140, n. 144; n. 106 above. Another major branch of the same family included the Este and thus Welf IV and Welf V.

124 He does describe Henry's failure to take Nogara in 1095, *Vita Mathildis* 2.9, pp. 81–82.
125 Ghirardini, "'Madonna della Battaglia,'" p. 47.

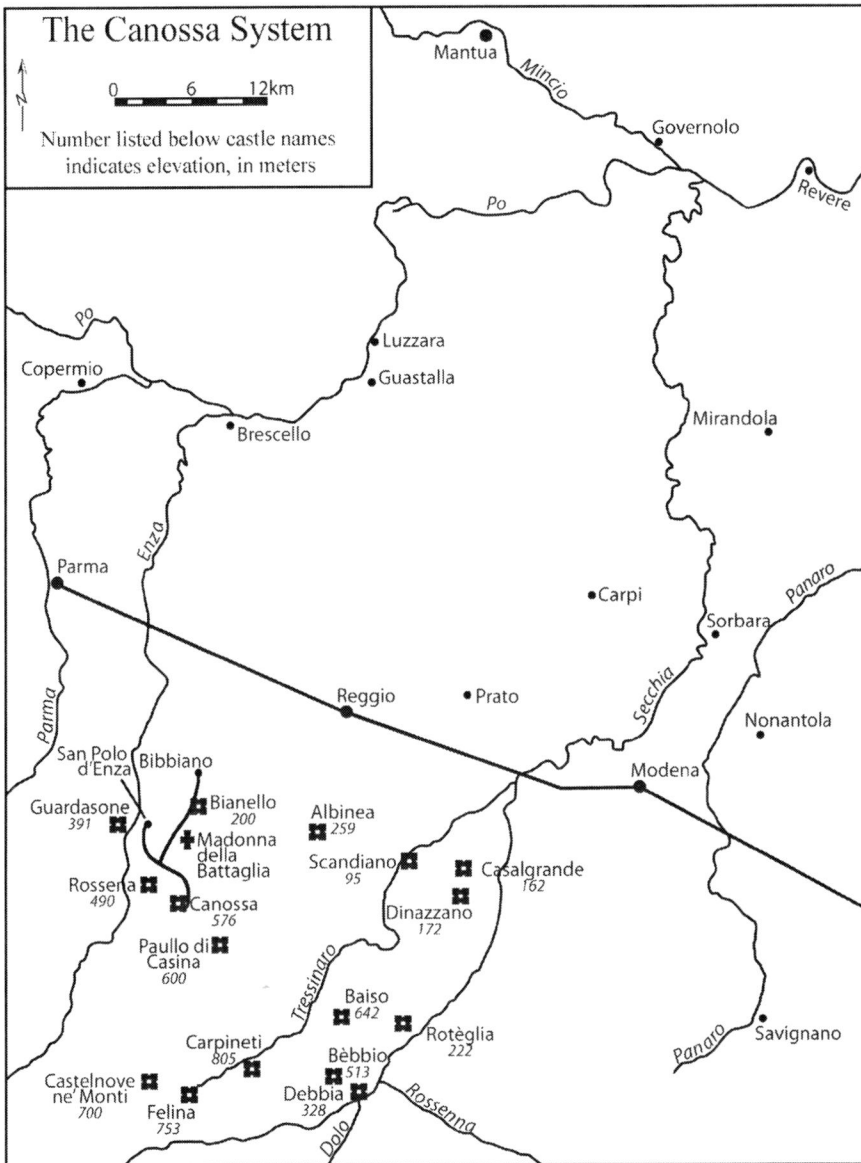

The Canossa System

Number listed below castle names
indicates elevation, in meters

0   6   12km

Mantua

Mincio

Governolo

Revere

Po

Po

Luzzara

Guastalla

Copermio

Mirandola

Brescello

Enza

Parma

Carpi

Panaro

Sorbara

Parma

Reggio

Prato

Secchia

Nonantola

San Polo
d'Enza

Bibbiano

Modena

Guardasone
391

Bianello
200

Albinea
259

Madonna
della
Battaglia

Scandiano
95

Casalgrande
162

Rossena
490

Canossa
576

Dinazzano
172

Paullo di
Casina
600

Tressinaro

Baiso
642

Rotèglia
222

Panaro

Savignano

Carpineti
805

Bèbbio
513

Castelnove
ne' Monti
700

Felina
753

Debbia
328

Dolo

Rossenna

in the region.[126] Among the locations associated with the Canossans were Brescello at the confluence of the Po and Enza rivers and the road from Brescello to the ferry at Copermio on the Parma River. Brescello, the *municipium* of Brixellum, had been an important transport and communication hub since the time of Augustus. The road that passed through Brescello and Copermio linked Parma to the north bank of the Po and the roads to Cremona, Mantua, Brescia and Verona and beyond.[127] In the other direction lay the routes toward Tuscany, the Cisa Pass and the Via Francigena. The support of Parma's noble families was vital during Henry's first Italian expedition of 1081–84. Matilda had been able to hinder his access to Rome to some degree even though Tuscany was in the hands of Henry's supporters. Without support from Parma, the war against Pope Gregory VII would have been all but impossible.[128]

Henry thus had reason to campaign in the Parmense. San Polo was well situated for actions around Brescello or Copermio, but he went to Canossa. Donizone narrates events one after another in a compact style giving the impression that Henry departed from Reggio, turned back to San Polo and moved on to Canossa in rapid succession, perhaps in a single day. This would require covering 39 kilometers including a steep stretch in the mountains rising from 170 meters at San Polo to 576 meters at Canossa. After this march a strongly fortified position was attacked leading to defeat and the retreat to Bibbiano, adding another 10 kilometers and requiring a descent through the hills from Canossa's height, perhaps while being harassed by the enemy and possibly in either fog or darkness. The straight-line distances are an understatement of the actual distances and effort that would be involved especially in the mountains where the roads switch back and forth between the numerous hills and rocky outcroppings (*calanchi*). It is more likely that Henry headed toward Parma and turned back to San Polo after a day or more, possibly with a larger force which would be more likely to be observed. Donizone's reference to clear weather may be intended either as a contrast to the fog that appears only a few lines later, or as an explanation of how the movement was observed. Once it was observed, Matilda quickly left Canossa for Bianello.

The description of the rapid journey to Bianello with the two groups passing within hearing of each other is another aspect of Donizone's story that gives the impression that everything happened at once, that Matilda had almost been caught in Canossa and barely escaped. There is more than one approach to Canossa from the area of San Polo. Had Henry marched further up the Enza

---

[126] Fabbi, "Le famiglie," n. 55 above; Schumann, *Authority and the Commune*, pp. 55 ff.; Fumagalli, *Le origine*, pp. 1–29; M. G. Bertolini, "Adalberto Atto di Canossa," *Dizionario biografico degli Italiani*, 1 (Rome, 1960), pp. 221–23.

[127] Schumann, *Authority and the Commune*, pp. 22, 27–28, 217; Matilda's control of the road to Copermio must have been especially annoying for the church of Parma which controlled the ferry itself, pp. 97, 213, 246; it is not clear how Brescello came into Azzo's hands, pp. 56–57.

[128] For a succinct discussion of Parma's role in Henry's long struggle with Matilda see Schumann, *Authority and the Commune*, pp. 160–62; for the role of the Via Francigena in the first Italian expedition see Eads, "Mighty", pp. 62–67; idem, "Geography of Power," pp. 368–73.

valley to Ciano d'Enza in order to approach Canossa from the south, the winding road through the hills would have lengthened the march and taken him directly past Rossena. There is no indication that he did so. If Henry had turned toward Canossa at the present-day Pieve San Polo, slightly north of San Polo d'Enza, he would have approached Canossa from the north, and Matilda would have been cut off from Bianello. There is no evidence that he took this route. The most likely approach from San Polo passes through the small villages of Le Vigne, Borsea and Grassano; it approaches Canossa from the north and passes it on the east side. Today the road passes almost directly under the remaining tower wall, but there have been landslides and in Matilda's time this would have been well within the walls. The suburb of the castle was on the east side. Just beyond Borsea a branch road turns north to the small village of Sedignano. This is the road that Matilda and her troops would have taken to Bianello, and it is most likely near this point that the two groups heard one another as they passed in opposite directions.[129] Beyond this point there is only one road south to Canossa, and it is at this point that Canossa first comes into view. While there were no doubt alternative routes used by the local residents, especially those on foot, Donizone writes only that when Matilda was at Mt. Giumegna, a large troop of the enemy was moving slowly over Mt. Lintergnano and, since the two hills are close together, each group was aware of and shrank from the presence of the other.

> [Dum fuit ad montem Iumingnae, densius hostes
> per Lintregnanum montem veniunt pede raro.
> Hi duo sunt montes vicini, sensit abhorrens
> Utraque pars strepitum,] (2.7, 686–69a)

Everyday sounds like a dog's barking echo in the hills, so it is not surprising that a troop of armed men, at least some of whom were mounted, would be heard. Since Matilda had already covered almost two-thirds of the distance from Canossa to Bianello the maneuver was not so close as Donizone's telling suggests, but no doubt closer than Matilda would have liked.

Henry's movements did not necessarily depend on Matilda's presence at Canossa. Whatever operations he intended to undertake in the Parmense, the Canossa system would have to be taken into account whether or not she was in the castle. The possibility that Henry hoped to find Canossa only lightly defended and thus to be easily taken does not seem sound. Donizone's earlier observations on the castle's immunity to siege engines, while possibly exaggerated, means that a long and costly siege was likely unless Henry had reason to expect the castle to be surrendered. The emperor was surely aware that the council at Carpineti had been leaning toward accepting his terms until John's sermon turned things around. It was not impossible that he could find another

---

[129] *Vita Mathildis*, notes to 2.7, lines 680 ff., p. 78; Golinelli, p. 145, n. 111; Ghirardini, "Madonna della Battaglia," pp. 38–39, 42–43; Istituto geografica militare, Carta d'Italia, topografica, Scala di 1:25,000, nos. 85.I.NE, 85.I.SE, 86.IV.NO, 86.IV.SO.

Hugo del Mansi. What is impossible, or at least highly improbable, is that Matilda would have been careless in providing for the castle's defenses. That Canossa was short of either food or arms is very unlikely.[130] Since Matilda could hardly be unaware of Henry's strategy, she would have organized what strength she still had at her disposal to defend the core of her power base.

The point that Matilda could not risk being pinned inside Canossa is a valid one. Trapping Matilda, and possibly Welf, in Canossa would likely end the war. But in order to do this Henry would not only have to appear very suddenly, but with sufficient force to invest the castle completely, something that he could not do at Monteveglio, where he had maintained the siege for some months. Donizone says that the defenders had been able to enter and leave the castle; he does not describe any attack in force on Henry's camp but rather harassing raids, perhaps ambushes of foraging parties.

> [Presidium monti confert huic contio fortis,
> Cuspide quae regem stimulare solebat inhertem.] (2.7, 620–21.)

He does not place Matilda within Monteveglio. If Matilda had considered relieving the castle, she found Henry's position too strong, especially since he held the western outliers near the Panaro valley. She had trusted to the defenses of Monteveglio, and Henry may have expected her to do the same thing at Canossa, and undoubtedly hoped that she would remain within its walls.

Donizone does not explain why Matilda went to Bianello, but if she feared the possibility of being trapped or betrayed in Canossa itself, surely smaller Bianello, which could more easily be completely surrounded, was no safer.[131] But, Bianello does not stand alone; east to west the hills of Montevetero, Bianello, Montelucio and Montezane rise within 850 meters. Franca Manenti Valli has raised the question of connecting passages between the Quattro Castelli and also between Rossena and Rossanella (300 meters apart). The proposed connections are not only between the four castles but also with the larger defensive perimeter that included Canossa, Rossena and Carpineti, and with the roads toward the Po.[132] Matilda did not go to Bianello for safety, but to be able to move as events unfolded. She was prepared to abandon Canossa because even if the castle could endure Henry's siege she could not. If the emperor's forces had her pinned inside Canossa, Matilda's ability to function effectively was ended. Henry could count on her party quickly disintegrating once he made it known

---

[130] Hay, *Military Leadership*, pp. 136–38, discusses possible effects of the war that had been going on for two years on Matilda's ability to supply her troops or to replace those lost. Had it come to a question of feeding her troops, there is little doubt that Matilda would have turned to the churchmen of the papal party as she had during the previous hostilities. Eads, *Mighty*, pp. 158–60.

[131] The question has been asked by Simeoni, *Vita Mathildis*, notes to lines 680 ff., p. 78; Ghirardini, "'Madonna della Battaglia,'" p. 42; Hay, *Military Leadership*, pp. 138–39.

[132] *Architettura di castelli*, p. 125; "I quattro castelli," pp. 456–57, maps the hypothetical reconstruction, p. 459.

that Matilda was trapped in Canossa. He would thus avoid the risks attendant on a prolonged siege.

Assuming that Matilda was concentrating her forces for the defense of her southwest quadrant, they had to be quartered. Canossa, however imposing, is not very large. Any sizable body of troops had to be parceled out among the castles of the system as Matilda traveled quickly through the hills from Monteveglio to Canossa. Donizone writes that it was some of her most important people (*proceres*) who returned to Canossa from Bianello to organize the defense. Bianello was also where her important guests were housed, not at Canossa itself. The exception was Pope Gregory VII who stayed in Canossa in 1077 because of the need to insure his safety; Henry IV stayed at Bianello and returned there each night after his daily penance. In 1110 and 1111 Henry V also came to Bianello. In 1092 it seems likely that Matilda went to Bianello both to avoid being pinned inside Canossa and so that she and the commanders from Canossa could confer with the other leaders who were quartered there with their troops. The first and most obvious decision was to hold Canossa and await events. It is likely that contingency plans were already in place since Henry would have had to come to Canossa at some time; the plans would be those that the entire system had been designed for – making use of the protection of the walls and watching until circumstances or a misstep by the enemy made an attack from the hills advantageous. This could conceivably involve nothing more than defending the walls and waiting until the enemy departed, with the worst-case scenario being that the enemy did not depart or make any mistakes in which case the castle would be lost.

Canossa, however, was not a single castle. Given that the various fortifications could not communicate by line of sight, there had to be signals arranged for such basic actions as attack and retreat or to give the enemy's location. Equally important in fog or darkness would be signals to tell friend from foe. Some of Matilda's commanders returned to Canossa both to encourage the garrison, as Donizone reports, and probably to efficiently assign the newcomers as well. The return trip to Canossa is one of the most difficult problems Donizone sets. Henry was moving slowly enough to not tire his troops during the steep ascent, but he was at least halfway to Canossa if the close encounter between his troops and Matilda's took place near Sedignano. This left little time for conference at Bianello before heading back to Canossa. Even taking into consideration the necessity for communications routes between the various elements of the system, there would be a difficult uphill ride and, as Donizone reports, a narrowly avoided encounter with Henry's troops.

For all the importance he attaches to Canossa, Donizone gives few details about the encounter at the castle itself and, as usual, the sequence seems improbable as written. This is no doubt why many details of his account have been questioned. The answer may lie in the fact that, although he was at Canossa during Henry's attempt, he was with the abbot and his fellow monks chanting psalms in the church of St. Apollonio and not among the defenders. Donizone reports only a generic encounter or exchange in which the defenders naturally came off well, but this occupies only two lines and comes after the sounding of the trumpets, the singing of the psalms and the descent of the fog.

That the monks combated the heretic emperor with their prayers is unquestioned. That there was a volley of arrows is likely enough, but surely Henry did not come into the mountains to send a few arrows over the outer walls of Canossa. Donizone's use of *jaculatur, pilo* and *ulnas* gives the impression of javelins in use although it is unclear at what point, and these words have general or metonymic uses that better suit Donizone's approach to battle descriptions. He mentions no siege engines, no ladders, no assault on the walls. Donizone is using the words that best fit his loosely defined hexameters and describing a hostile exchange that he in fact heard rather than saw. He heard the trumpets sound. Perhaps they did merely announce the presence of the enemy, but to whom? Obviously, those inside Canossa knew they were under attack. The inhabitants of the suburb had probably taken shelter within the walls by the time Matilda departed for Bianello. But Matilda and the troops at Bianello needed to know that the assault had begun so they could begin whatever action had been decided on. They obviously could not simply charge uphill from Bianello to Canossa, but could move out and await events. The garrisons of the castles further into the hills had to be put on alert, and doubtless messages had been sent as soon as Henry's move out of San Polo was known.

Henry was also awaiting events, watching as his troops tested the defenses of Canossa; he watched as the fog came in and he could no longer see the castle in front of him. This is one of Donizone's clearest statements, and it is literally true. He had lived with the autumn fog of the Apennines his entire life, but this fog had been sent when most needed in answer to the prayers of the monks of St. Apollonio of Canossa. There is, of course, no way to prove that just as Henry IV began an assault on Canossa a clear day turned to dense fog, but there is no reason to question the thick fog in Donizone's account.

*

The fog affected everyone, but not equally. Henry had spent several years in Italy; he surely knew about the weather conditions around Canossa although he may not have experienced them before. Certainly the Parmans or Reggians among his troops would have known of the possibility of fog, but they were now effectively blinded in the course of an attack on a well-defended castle. Those who lived with the fogs knew how to get around with minimal visibility, and it stretches credibility to think that only one of the defenders of Canossa took the opportunity to slip outside the wall and strike a blow at the disconcerted invaders. It seems that the capture of Henry's banner involved at least two people: one who aimed the blow that the standard bearer barely avoided and caused him to fall from his horse, and another who ran up and snatched the banner pole. Donizone does not clearly state that at a specific signal the entire garrison rushed out and fell upon the attackers because Canossa was designed with partial walls and switchbacks along the rising road to make an opposed entry as difficult as possible. This design would also make a sortie en masse

Top: view from within the southeast tower on a foggy day. Bottom: the tower photographed from below on a clear day.

impossible, but it would not prevent skirmishing, an activity in which the fog greatly favored the defenders. Although no doubt accompanied by a bodyguard, Henry was no more proof against attack than his standard bearer. When he realized that the defenders were quickly becoming the attackers, and word that the imperial standard had been lost may have quickly spread among his troops, he decided to withdraw, an action for which there was no doubt a signal.

Donizone has not been so thoughtful as to note at what time of day Henry began his retreat or when the fog began to lift. Neither does he say how far out from Bianello Matilda's troops had moved through the fog or that any troops from Canossa followed Henry on the steep downhill road. He does, however, say that Henry went not to San Polo but to Bibbiano (*Baianum*). This may be no more than the decision to get a bit further along the road back toward the Po, but it could also mean that the road from Canossa to San Polo was cut off. If San Polo was a secure base, then preventing Henry from regaining it was a reasonable objective for the troops from Bianello. Ghirardini's surmise that there was a significant battle at Madonna della Battaglia, less than two kilometers uphill from Bianello, may represent Henry's attempt to make a stand and avoid being herded toward Bibbiano which is about four kilometers north of the Bianello complex. This assumes that the emperor's troops, however many he may have started out with, retained any cohesion at this point. There is some level ground around the small church, but Donizone is no help here. Once Henry left Canossa for Bibbiano, something that Donizone could only have learned after the fact, the narrative returns to the ceremony at Canossa when Henry's banner was installed in St. Apollonio's chapel. Only then does he mention that these events took place in October, and that Matilda's troops followed as Henry withdrew across the Po where she regained what was lost. What is important to the monk is not tactics or logistics, but that the party of the pious had great gain in that year.

Many of the difficulties presented by Donizone's account have been attributed to his effort to imitate the meter, if not the graphic depictions of bloodshed, of epic poetry. That an event occurs in epic is not proof that it does not occur in fact. Despite the fogs that appear in the *Iliad*, dense fog is a feature of autumn weather in the Apennines; although trumpets sound in the *Aeneid*, the castles of Matilda's defensive system still had to communicate.[133] Donizone reports King Adalbert at Canossa and Henry IV at Monteveglio using horns and trumpets to signal movements. He also reports the use of trumpets at Canossa in 1092, and there seems no reason to question this point or assume the usage is unusual. It seems reasonable to assume that the army of Matilda of Tuscany operated no differently from any other army of the same time and place.

Donizone wrote his work for presentation to Matilda in order to persuade her to be buried at Canossa. He omitted not only things that she might not wish to be reminded of, such as her marriages or the defeat of her army at Volta

---

[133] Golinelli, *Vita di Matilde*, p. 145, n. 113; Hay, *Military Leadership*, pp. 140–41.

Mantovana, but also matters that did not seem important. As the end of her life approached Donizone doubtless thought that Matilda would prefer to contemplate her life as a testing by God, a trial that was rewarded with success in this world and for which greater reward awaited her in the next.[134] Such things as a precise sequence of events, clearly specified locations, ratios of horse and foot, the names of many participants in these events and how the Apennine defense system worked must be reconstructed from whatever hints Donizone inadvertently gives. He tells us, however, that Matilda paid attention to these things. She knew where Henry was and how great a force he had; she repaired and supplied her fortifications.[135] The one thing she could not prepare against was betrayal. The citizens of Mantua betrayed her; Hugo del Mansi betrayed her; Canossa did not. That is Donizone's point. In making it the monk has left a complex riddle to solve, but without his difficult and occasionally infuriating work there would be a large gap in the historical record of two important eleventh-century military careers.

Appendix

Henry IV's Military Actions

1063   September. Expedition to Hungary to restore Salomon, betrothed to Henry's sister, to the throne. The death of his opponent, Bela I, gives Henry a bloodless victory.

1065   29 March. Henry IV girded with a sword and declared of age to rule.
May. Planned expedition into Italy deferred due to wrangling among Henry's advisors.

1066   June. Marries Bertha of Savoy-Turin; the alliance is intended to strengthen Henry's position in Burgundy and to counter the combined house of Canossa-Lorraine in northern Italy.

1067   January. Calls muster at Augsburg for expedition to Italy; Godfrey II, Duke of Lower Lorraine and Marquis of Tuscany, departs before Henry arrives; expedition abandoned.

1069   Early. Expedition against the Liutizi; successive destructive invasions significantly weaken the Liutizi confederation.
Supports Archbishop Siegfried of Mainz in a dispute with Dedi I of

---

[134]   For example, *Vita Mathildis*, 2.7, 612–15, p. 76.
[135]   *Vita Mathildis*, 2.6, 564–68, p. 74.

Lower Lusatia; captures two of Dedi's castles in Thuringia; the rebels surrender.

1070   August. Lays waste to the estates of Otto of Northeim, Duke of Bavaria, recently condemned for treason and deposed; Otto raises an army and attacks the king's Thuringian estates.

2 September, Eschwege. Otto defeats the Thuringians while Henry IV defends Goslar.

1071   Early. Duke Otto, attempting to force a battle, occupies Hasungen; the Saxon princes defend Goslar while the king goes to Bavaria and confers the duchy on Welf IV.

12 June (Whitsun). Otto submits and is imprisoned along with his ally Magnus Billung.

1072   28 March. Seizes the Billung fortress of Lüneburg.

1073   Summer. Prepares an expedition against Duke Boleslav II of Poland who broke a truce.

29 June, Goslar. The Saxon princes demand the settlement of grievances before they will undertake the Polish expedition; the king withdraws to the Harzburg; when the princes camp outside to press their demands, Henry flees.

13 August, Hersfeld. Polish expedition aborted; Henry lacks sufficient strength to move against what is now a full-scale rebellion of the Saxons and Thuringians.

Summer. Lüneburg, not provisioned for a siege, is recaptured; to save his garrison, Henry frees Magnus Billung; Saxons and Thuringians led by Frederick II of Goseck destroy the castle of Heimburg; Hasenburg and the Harzburg remain under siege at the end of the year.

October. Henry is unable to mount an expedition against the rebels; a number of powerful south German magnates join the king's opponents.

1074   Early. Plan to launch a surprise attack in January fails due to insufficient forces; rebels burn and besiege Spatenberg and *Vokenroht*; but allow Queen Bertha, who is awaiting the birth of a child, to leave.

27 January. The two armies are encamped on opposite banks of the frozen Werra River; Henry's troops are unwilling to fight under unfavorable conditions so he must negotiate.

2 February, Gerstungen. Henry's representatives accept peace on the Saxons' terms, but the common people (*plebs, vulgus, rustici*), who suffer most from the presence of the royal castles, are not satisfied.

End of March. Saxon *vulgus* attack Hartzburg; destruction of the chapel and desecration of the royal graves violates treaty of Gerstungen; some south German princes return to Henry's side.

August, Hungary. Expedition to support Henry's brother-in-law, Salomon.

1075   8 June, Breitungen. Royal army musters.

9 June. Battle at Homburg on the Unstrut. Henry's rapid march from Breitungen catches the Saxons by surprise; numerous desertions give

Henry numerical superiority; the Saxon nobles flee while their infantry suffers heavy losses.

22 October, Gerstungen. Many south German princes ignore summons to muster for further campaigning in Saxony; Duke Godfrey III of Lower Lorraine supports the king.

26–27 October. Saxon princes surrender.

Christmas. Otto of Northeim, released and restored to royal favor, is commissioned to rebuild the Harzburg.

1076   February. Henry IV excommunicated at Lenten synod by Pope Gregory VII; those imprisoned or exiled in 1075 are released.

August. Expedition into Meissen with Duke Vratislav of Bohemia; withdraws when faced with strong opposition; Vratislav's garrisons are expelled; Otto of Northeim returns to the Saxon side.

16 October – 1 November, Tribur/Oppenheim. Meeting of lay and ecclesiastical magnates. Henry avoids deposition, awaiting the pope's arrival and judgment.

December. Henry flees into Italy.

1077   25–28 January, Canossa. Henry performs penance and is released from excommunication.

13 March, Forcheim. Rudolf of Rheinfelden elected as as anti-king.

April. Henry IV returns to Germany.

May–June. Raises an army in Regensburg; forces Rudolf to withdraw into Saxony.

Summer, Mainz. Prepares for Saxon expedition.

August, Würzburg. Rudolf besieges the city; Henry moves to intercept reinforcements sent by Welf IV and Berthold of Zähringen, but is outnumbered; he avoids battle and withdraws to Worms; Rudolf abandons the siege and attempts to force a battle, but Henry's camp between the Rhine and the Neckar is secure, and he refuses to accept either battle or single combat. Without the king's approval, the princes agree to a meeting in November with Welf and Berthold.

Late summer, Swabia. Henry is reinforced; undertakes punitive expedition against Rudolf's supporters.

November. Henry's army prevents the planned meeting of the princes from both sides.

November to March 1078, Bavaria. Succesful expedition against Rudolf's supporter, Ekbert of Formbach.

1078   May, Metz. Royal army takes the city.

Summer, Swabia and Franconia. Rudolf's south German allies attack Henry's supporters; Rudolf moves out of Saxony for a joint attack on Henry.

7 August, Battle of Mellrichstadt. Henry stations 12,000 Franconian foot on the Neckar; succeeds in keeping the two parts of Rudolf's forces separate, but cannot defeat either; Rudolf, although victorious, flees the field; both sides suffer serious losses for no gain.

Autumn. Rudolf gathers a large army to defend Saxony.

November, Swabia. Expedition against Rudolf's allies.

1079   Early. Rudolf's army forces tribute from Westphalia; burns monastery attempting to take control of Fritzlar.

March. Henry distributes Rudolf's Swabian lands to his own supporters. Frederick of Büren is appointed duke and betrothed to Henry's daughter, Agnes.

24 March – 12 May (Easter to Whitsun). Successful expedition against Marquis Leopold II of Austria; Welf IV drives Frederick of Büren from Ulm.

August. Henry mobilizes against the Saxons, but a truce is brokered; Henry is able to encourage some defections from Rudolf.

Winter. Henry gathers troops in Burgundy, Franconia, Swabia, Bavaria and Bohemia.

1080   Mid-January. Departs from Mainz heading into Saxony; Rudolf moves into Thuringia to meet him.

27 January, Battle of Flarchheim. Rudolf of Rheinfelden holds the field, but lacked the capacity to follow up the victory.

7 March. Henry IV excommunicated for the second time.

Summer. Henry's supporters Duke Vratislav of Bohemia and Count Wiprecht of Groitzsch campaign in Saxony; both Henry and Rudolf gather forces.

15 October, Battle on the Elster. Rudolf of Rheinfelden is victorious but dies of his wounds.

"A few days later," Volta Mantovana. Henry's Italian supporters defeat the troops of Pope Gregory VII's ally, Matilda of Tuscany.

December. Henry undertakes winter campaign in Saxony; the Saxons bar his way to Goslar and force negotiations.

1081   February, forest of Kaufungen. The Saxons grant a truce of only four months.

March. Henry departs for Italy; most of his loyal supporters must stay behind.

June. Truce expires; Saxons and Swabians invade Franconia; meet at Bamberg.

Summer. Henry, lacking siege equipment, withdraws from Rome.

Summer and autumn. Makes dispositions for the longer campaign to come; Count Ugiccio of Lucca places troops at Henry's disposal; harries Countess Matilda's forces in Tuscany then moves north of the Apennines.

August, Ochsenfurt. Hermann of Salm elected anti-king.

1082   9 March – 23 April, Rome. Henry continues siege of Leonine City; on 17 April the south wall is breached, but the attack is repulsed.

17 March, Farfa. Henry expels Rusticius Crescentii, Gregory VII's supporter and kinsman.

12 May, Mailberg. Henry's ally, Vratislav II of Bohemia, soundly defeats Leopold II of Austria, a papal ally.

Summer, Rome. Siege is maintained by Archbishop Wibert of Ravenna; punitive expedition against Matilda of Tuscany, who sends much-needed funds to the pope during Henry's absence; Emperor Alexius Comnenus funds Henry's expedition against Robert Guiscard, the pope's ally and Alexius's enemy.

Autumn, northern Italy. Henry attacks lands of Guido of Sezze.

End of the year. Unfounded rumors that Hermann of Salm is moving toward Italy; Henry returns to Rome with reinforcements from Milan.

1083   11 January. Death of Otto of Northeim ends any threat from Germany.

Lent. Henry's renewed attack on the Leonine City disrupts Lenten synod.

3 June. Leonine City falls; Henry sets up his headquarters in the imperial palace and fortifies the Palatiolus to the east of St. Peter's basilica.

29 June. Henry dismisses his Italian troops.

Late summer and autumn. Henry goes first to Tuscany with his German troops; he then sets siege to Carpi, near Modena. Romans capture and raze the Palatiolus.

1084   January. Wibert of Ravenna returns and assumes command of operations at Rome; Welf IV captures Augsburg.

1 February to mid-March. Henry moves south against Robert Guiscard; both appear to be avoiding an encounter.

21 March. Rome surrenders; Wibert of Ravenna consecrated Pope Clement III; crowns Henry IV emperor on Easter.

April to early May. Unsuccessful siege of Castel Sant'Angelo still held by Gregory VII; systematically moves against a number of remaining fortified holdouts in North Rome, Tivoli, Porto; the Septizonium successfully resists.

21 May. Henry leaves Rome as Robert Guiscard approaches.

28 May, Rome. Robert Guiscard rescues Gregory VII, but because of the destruction caused by the Norman's army, the pope cannot remain in the city.

17 June. Henry departs Italy; his heir, Conrad, remains.

2 July, Sorbara. Matilda of Tuscany's troops defeat an army of Henry's Italian supporters with a surprise attack on their encampment.

7 August, Augsburg. After fourteen-day siege Henry retakes city from Welf IV.

1085   May/June. Confiscates Matilda of Tuscany's lands in the Lorraine; castle of Briey successfully resists.

Early summer, Saxony. Anti-king Hermann of Salm and the rebel bishops flee; Henry concedes principal Saxon demands, but is forced out of Saxony within two months.

1086   27 January. Moves toward Saxony with a large army; the rebels retreat.

14 February. Withdraws from Saxony; a conspiracy within his army is blamed for the failure to force a settlement.

April, Regensburg. Welf IV unsuccessfully besieges Henry.

Early July, Würzburg. Saxons and Swabians begin a siege to restore their communications lines; they go out to meet Henry as he comes to lift the siege.

11 August, Battle of Pleichfeld. Henry is badly defeated by Welf IV; Würzburg surrenders, but as soon as the Saxons and South Germans leave, Henry returns and retakes it.

24 December. Welf IV and Berthold of Rheinfelden compel Henry to abandon the siege of an unnamed castle in Bavaria.

1087   2 July, Henry's ally, Vratislav of Bohemia, defeats Ekbert II of Brunswick.

August. A general peace conference in Speyer fails; Ladislaus of Hungary sides with the rebels.

October. Planned expedition delayed by Henry's illness; the Saxons offer terms that include the rehabilitation of Ekbert II; Henry's acceptance angers important allies, and as soon as he dismisses his army Ekbert repudiates the agreement.

1088   January. Ekbert II tries and fails to be chosen king; he turns against his previous associates and backs Henry; Hermann of Salm must abandon Saxony.

April, Regensburg. Welf IV retakes and devastates the city.

14 August. Ekbert II rebels again; Henry besieges his castle at Gleichen; Ekbert counters by attacking Quedlinburg; Henry despatches a part of his force to defend Quedlinburg.

28 September. Death of Hermann of Salm.

24 December. Ekbert stages a surprise attack and defeats Henry's depleted army at Gleichen; Henry must withdraw.

1089   Ekbert continues successful campaign in Saxony.

Autumn, Henry moves against Ekbert, his fifteenth and last expedition to Saxony; no engagement. In Italy, Matilda of Tuscany marries Welf V, son of Welf IV.

1090   March, Henry departs for Italy leaving many loose ends in Germany.

21 April. Siege of Mantua begins.

Before 26 June. Ripalta, upriver from Mantua, surrenders.

3 July. Ekbert II betrayed and killed in Germany.

Before the end of the year. Gubernolo, downriver from Mantua, surrenders.

1091   10 April. Mantua surrenders.

Summer. Castle of Minervia falls.

Winter, Tricontai. Matilda of Tuscany's troops betrayed and defeated.

End of the year. Henry holds the region north of the Po except Piadena and Nogara.

1092   Early in the year Henry sends his son Conrad to secure the March of Turin after the death of Countess Adelheid.

June. Henry moves south of the Po; Monte Morello surrenders; Monte Alfredo is taken.

Summer. Siege of Monteveglio.

September. Matilda of Tuscany convenes a council at Carpineti; Henry's offer of terms is rejected; soon after, Henry abandons the siege of Monteveglio.

October. Henry moves against Canossa and is quickly forced to withdraw.

Before the end of the year. Matilda of Tuscany regains Gubernolo and Ripalta.

Some of the emperor's supporters and their troops must return to Germany; Welf IV and the Gregorian bishops are trying to revive the rebellion.

1093   Mid-March to late July. Henry's son Conrad, with his troops, defects. Henry is effectively cut off in Italy.

May. The league of Lombard cities (Milan, Lodi, Cremona and Piacenza) forces Henry to withdraw from Pavia where he had wintered.

1094   Early. Henry's second wife, Praxedis, separates from him; Matilda of Tuscany rescues her from Verona.

Late (or early 1095), Nogara. Failed siege; Matilda of Tuscany relieves the city.

1096   Early. Henry IV seeks aid from Coloman of Hungary against Welf IV. Reconciles with Welf IV; returns the duchy of Bavaria.

1097   Spring. Returns to Germany after seven years in Italy. Numerous reconciliations follow.

1098   Worms. Henry IV and Welf IV settle the inheritance of Bavaria and Welf's possessions in Swabia on his sons Welf V and Henry the Black.

May, Mainz. Henry V, twelve years old, elected king.

Mainz. Henry demolishes the city's walls.

1099   29 June, Bamberg. Henry declares Peace of God; his protection of the churches conflicts with the long-established custom of supporting troops on church benefices.

1101   Spring, Cambrai. Henry IV sends troops to Bishop Walcher, under siege by the returned crusader Count Robert II of Flanders, who is acting on the initiative of Pope Pascal II.

21 April, Liège. Henry V girded with a sword and declared of age.

16 May. Captures and destroys fortresses held by Henry of Limburg.

1102   March. Pope Pascal II renews excommunication of Henry IV.

October, Cambrai. Lifts the siege and pursues Robert of Flanders, who refuses battle; Henry leaves with a promise to return if Robert does; Robert then carries out a night attack, and the citizens of Cambrai agree to surrender if Henry does not return in the spring.

1103   29 June. Robert and Henry reconcile.

1104   Late November. Mounts a punitive expedition against Theodoric III of Katlenburg who had imprisoned Herman and Hartwig of Magdeburg.

12 December, Fritzlar. Henry V secretly departs from the camp; Henry IV abandons the expedition.

1105   Early. Kin of murdered Sigehard of Burghausen join Henry V.

Mid-summer, Mainz. Henry V attempts to restore Bishop Ruothard; Henry IV pays all boat owners not to ferry Henry V's army across the Rhine.

Nuremberg. Henry V besieges city.

August, Würzburg. Henry IV restores Bishop Erlung; tries to raise troops to relieve Nuremberg.

September, Nuremberg surrenders to Henry V.

End of September, Regensburg. Henry IV surprises his son who has dismissed his army and returned to Regensburg; Henry V escapes, but Henry IV has regained control of the city.

Regensburg. Leopold III of Austria and Borivoi of Bohemia reinforce Henry IV; Henry V returns with an army recruited in Bavaria and Swabia. The two armies face off across the River Regen for three days but only single combats are undertaken. The princes on both sides hold peace talks among themselves; Leopold and Borivoi go over to Henry V, and Henry IV flees during the night.

31 October. Henry V, who had been expected to attack Mainz, crosses the Rhine to Speyer and gains the city and its treasury; fearing betrayal, Henry IV leaves Mainz for Hammerstein.

21 December, Koblenz. Henry IV and Henry V meet; after an apparent agreement, Henry IV dismisses most of his troops and starts toward Mainz; the next day, Henry V's following increases greatly.

23–31 December, Böckelheim, Ingelheim. Henry IV is imprisoned, abdicates.

1106   Early February. Henry IV flees Ingelheim for Lower Lorraine; receives support in Cologne, Aachen and Liège; Henry of Limburg and Robert of Flanders, his former opponents, support him.

22 March, Liège. Destroys all the bridges on the River Maas except Visé. Henry V's force of three hundred suffers heavy losses in a failed effort to take the bridge.

July, Cologne. Henry V's siege fails; he withdraws to Aachen after three or four weeks due to heat, supply problems and high casualties.

End of July – early August. Negotiations for a truce and plans for another meeting.

7 August, Liège. Death of Henry IV.

3

Jaime I of Aragon: Child and Master of the Spanish Reconquest[1]

Donald J. Kagay

If "Africa begins at the Pyrenees" (a shaky truism that far too many medievalists still adhere to),[2] the discussion of a Spanish ruler's reconquest career as a prime example of military leadership during the European Middle Ages may seem at worst pointless and at best ill-conceived. Since such geo-cultural divisions themselves would surely have seemed beyond the pale in the thirteenth century, however, this paper will proceed to assess the accomplishments of one of southern Europe's greatest generals of the high Middle Ages, Jaime (Jaume) I "the Conqueror" (r.1214–76).

Early Life

The stellar military record of this long-lived Aragonese sovereign was clearly the result of a fiery determination that transcended and redefined both royal and martial traditions of the day. Coming to the thrones of upland Aragon and maritime Catalonia as a six-year-old orphan who had lost his father, Pedro II (r.1196–1213), at the battle of Muret (12 September 1213),[3] he quickly under-

---

[1] I would like to extend my sincere thanks to Dr. Clifford Rogers for his careful reading of this article and for his insightful suggestions, many of which I have followed.

[2] For the discussion of Spain's supposed separation from the other "civilized" parts of Europe, see William Atkinson, "Spain: The Country, its Peoples and Languages," in *Spain: A Companion to Spanish Studies* (London, 1929), p. 2; John A. Crow, *Spain: The Root and Flower: A History of the Civilization of Spain and of the Spanish People* (New York, 1963), p. 6; Helen Wattley-Ames, *Spain is Different* (Yarmouth, Maine, 1999), pp. 7–8.

[3] For Jaime's early life and stormy accession to the Aragonese throne, see *The Book of Deeds of James I of Aragon: A Translation of the Medieval Catalan* Llibre dels Feyts [hereafter *BD*], trans. Damian Smith and Helena Buffery (Aldershot, Hampshire, 2003), pp. 15–24 (chaps. 1–10); Martín Alvira Cabrer, *12 de Septiembre de 1213: El Jueves de Muret* (Barcelona, 2002); Ferran Soldevila, *Els primers temps de Jaume I* (Barcelona, 1968), pp. 15–77; Salvador Sanpere y Miguel, "Minoría de Jaime I," in *Congreso de Historia de la Corona de Aragó* [1 CHCA], 2 vols. (Barcelona, 1909–13), 2:581–608; F. Darwin Swift, *The Life and Times of James the First the Conqueror, King of Aragon, Valencia, and Majorca, Count of Barcelona and Urgel Lord of Montpellier* (Oxford, 1894), pp. 11–16. The other translation of the *Llibre dels Feyts* used in this paper is *The Chronicle of James I, King of Aragon, Surnamed the Conqueror*, trans. John

stood and took as his own the prevalent royal cant that made the ruler in eastern Spain into the principal protector of the "homeland" (*patria*) and its "common-wealth" (*cosa publica*).[4] Despite the possibilities inherent in the royal office, the young king, surrounded by over-mighty relatives who hoped to claim the Aragonese throne for themselves, spent the next decade in defending his royal rights while attempting to direct the energies of his querulous barons toward more profitable activities that he could control.[5] When still a teenager in 1225, Jaime hit upon a plan well known for some centuries to other rulers of Christian Iberia – the weakening of domestic unrest by diverting baronial energies against the *taifas*, the mini-states of Muslim Hispania. From his upbringing with the Templars at Monzón, the Aragonese king would quickly assimilate in theoretical and practical terms the pressure that drove sovereigns to military leadership. He would have thoroughly learned from direct experience all of the martial lessons discussed by his son-in-law, Alfonso X of Castile (r.1252–84) – not an untalented soldier himself – in the *Siete Partidas*, one of the greatest legal mirrors of contemporary medieval society.[6] In the great memoir summarizing his life and work, the *Liber dels Feyts*, Jaime would repeatedly demonstrate his intimate familiarity with the aspects of behavior and knowledge that Alfonso pointed to when discussing how a king was transformed into a successful military leader. These qualities included: (1) clear communication with his troops (2) balance between excessive prudence and boldness of action (3) strategic and tactical skill in the deployment of troops to gain numerical and positional superiority and (4) the full reconnaissance of an enemy's position and intentions before engaging him in combat.[7]

Taking into account Jaime's psychological background (fashioned by the loss of his parents while still a child and his transition to adolescence surrounded by few adults he could trust), the emergence of the Aragonese king as a great military leader seems surprising until one considers how thoroughly he was

Forster (London, 1883). Electronic version: *Library of Iberian Sources Online* (http://libro.uca. edu/title.htm). The principal Catalan editions used are: (1) *Llibre dels Fets del rei En Jaume*, ed. Jordi Bruguera, 2 vols. (Barcelona, 1991) and (2) *Libre dels feits del rei En Jaume* in *Les quatre grans Cròniques*, ed. Ferran Soldevila (Barcelona, 2007).

4 Donald J. Kagay, "Rule and Mis-Rule in Medieval Iberia," in *War, Government, and Society in the Medieval Crown of Aragon* (Aldershot, Hampshire, 2007), study IV, p. 50.

5 Donald J. Kagay, "Royal Power in an Urban Setting: James I and the Towns of the Crown of Aragon," *Mediaevistik* 8 (1995), 127–36; idem, "Structures of Baronial Dissent and Revolt under James I (1213–76)," in idem, *War*, study VII, p. 62; Soldevila, *Primers temps*, pp. 169–201; Swift, *James*, pp. 21–26.

6 Robert I. Burns, S.J., "Castle of Intellect, Castle of Force: The Worlds of Alfonso the Learned and James the Conqueror," in *The Worlds of Alfonso the Learned and James the Conqueror: Intellect and Force in the Middle Ages* (Princeton, 1985), pp. 12–13. For *Siete Partidas*, see Robert A. MacDonald, "Law and Politics: Alfonso's Program of Political Reform," in Burns, ed., *Worlds*, pp. 180–82; Joseph F. O'Callaghan, *The Learned King: The Reign of Alfonso X of Castile* (Philadelphia, 1993), pp. 274–76.

7 *Las Siete Partidas*, trans. Samuel Parsons Scott, ed. Robert I. Burns, S. J., 5 vols. (Philadelphia, 2001), 2:441–43 (Part. II, tit. xxiii, laws iv–vi)

involved with war from a relatively early age. Thus, through what Alfonso el Sabio calls "practice and skill,"[8] the young Aragonese sovereign understood the norms of warfare he had inherited and then proceeded to expand their horizons.

Christian and Muslim Warfare in the Peninsula

Except for the internecine conflict which marred the realms of Christian Iberia from their beginnings,[9] the principal military arena that occupied Spanish armies from the eighth century onward was the seven-century-long struggle known as the "reconquest" (*reconquista*).[10] In this asymmetrical conflict, periods of armed peace were interspersed with relatively rare outbursts of bitter fighting that attempted to advance the frontiers and consequently the victor's power. Such episodes of conflict were largely prevented, however, by the establishment of "artificial border wastes" that maintained virtual no-man's lands between Christian and Muslim polities. Such a zone was known in Christian realms as a *marca* and in the *taifas* as a māfasa or thagār.[11]

When combat did take place, it was fought by Christian and Muslim units that grew increasingly similar in fighting style and equipment. Christian armies were composed of heavily armored knights and lightly protected infantry. In Aragon, the footsoldiers were bolstered by hardy auxiliaries, the *almogaveres*. These frontiersmen lived off the land and carried few weapons besides a "long knife" (*coltell*), a short spear, and several darts.[12] While cavalry and infantry were often assembled in separate divisions, pitched battles normally devolved

---

8 *Siete Partidas*, ed. Burns, 2:444 (Part. II, tit. xxiii, law viii).

9 For the violent interchanges common between Aragonese kings and their subjects, see *BD*, pp. 29–33 (chaps. 15–16); Donald J. Kagay, "Violence Management in the Twelfth-Century Crown of Aragon," in *Marginated Groups in Spanish and Portuguese History*, ed. William D. Phillips, Jr., and Carla Rahn Phillips (Minneapolis, 1990), pp. 11–21; idem, "Structures," pp. 64–65.

10 The most important modern works on this phenomenon are: Charles Julian Bishko, "The Spanish and Portuguese Reconquest, 1095–1492," *The Fourteenth and Fifteenth Centuries*, ed. Harry W. Hazard, vol. 3 of *A History of the Crusades*, ed. Kenneth H. Setton, 6 vols. (Madison, WI, 1975–85), pp. 396–456; Derek W. Lomax, *The Reconquest of Spain* (London, 1978); Joseph F. O'Callaghan, *Reconquest and Crusade in Medieval Spain* (Philadelphia, 2003); *La reconquista española y la repoblación del país*, ed. José María Lacarra (Zaragoza, 1951).

11 Julian V. Minghi, "Boundary Studies in Political Geography," *Annals of the Association of American Geographers* 53 (1963), p. 407; Thomas F. Glick, *Islamic and Christian Spain in the Early Middle Ages: Comparative on Social and Cultural Formations* (Princeton, 1979), pp. 59–62; Mikél de Epalza, "Islamic Social Structures in Muslim and Christian Valencia," in *Iberia and the Mediterranean World of the Middle Ages*, ed. Paul E. Chevedden, Donald J. Kagay, Paul G. Padilla, and Larry J. Simon, 2 vols. (Leiden, 1984), 2:188.

12 *Chronicle of Muntaner*, 1:22, 139 (chaps. 10 (n. 12), 62); Bernat Desclot, *Chronicle of the Reign of King Pedro III of Aragon*, trans. Frank L. Critchlow, 2 vols. (Princeton, 1928–34), 1:4; Paul Douglas Humphries, "'Of Arms and Men': Siege and Battle Tactics in the Catalan Grand Chronicles (1208–1387)," *Military Affairs* 49 (1985), 174; María Teresa Ferrer i Mallol, "La organización militar en Cataluña en la Edad Media," *Revista de Historia Militar*, separate volume (2002), pp. 181–86.

into a melée of horsemen and footmen fighting individual adversaries or groups of enemy soldiers.[13] Despite the importance of pitched battles such as Zallaqah (Sagrajas) (1086), Alarcos (1195), and Las Navas de Tolosa (1212) to the course of the Reconquest,[14] most Christian military operations against Spanish Islam centered on siege operations. The secret to defeating heavily fortified urban sites and castles was skillful patience in stopping the flow of food and water into the besieged site. With the influence of the crusades, heavy counterweight artillery had slowly begun to feature in siege warfare by Jaime's day. Though more expensive than pitched battles, siege operations involved far less risk and were more often rewarded by the gain of new territory.[15]

Muslim armies of the reconquest retained the tripartite division of Umayyad and Abbasid forces, maintaining separate commanders, and cavalry and infantry corps for each wing. Like their Christian counterparts, raiding across lightly defended frontiers was the principal form of military endeavor that Muslim troops engaged in across the Peninsula since such *razzias* involved minimal risk and could be extremely profitable. When Muslim armies took to the battlefield, they emulated their Christian adversaries by relying on the terrorizing effect of charging cavalry against infantry arrays. Despite their similarities, Muslim armies of the Peninsula greatly differed in several aspects from their Christian rivals. Quickly rejecting the use of local militia recruited from across Andalusia, Cordovan caliphs increasingly relied on Berber and black African troops who served as mercenaries or slaves. These units were supplemented by *jihad* or "holy war" volunteers. Foreign infantrymen thus anchored the Muslim army while light-armored cavalry units were used to mount flanking attacks on enemy formations or to utilize the time-honored tactic of "simulated flight" (*kerr-wa-furr*) in order to draw the front ranks of Christian horsemen and infantry into ill-considered pursuit.[16] With the emergence of the great general, al-Mansur, in the late tenth century, the caliphal army became a truly professional force that proceeded to crush every Christian army it encountered.[1717] Within a very short time after the great general's death in 1002, however, the Caliphate of Cordova itself collapsed, shattering into *taifas*, small principalities centered on Andalusia's important cities that now fought to hold out against the ascendant Christian

---

[13] Humphries, "Arms and Men," pp. 174–75.

[14] Ambrosio Huici Miranda, *Las grandes batallas de la Reconquista durante las invasiones africanas* (Madrid, 1956), pp. 48–82, 135–69; 241–327.

[15] Humphries, "Arms and Men," pp. 176–77.

[16] Philippe Contamine, *War in the Middle Ages*, trans. Michael Jones (Oxford, 1990), p. 58; Richard Fletcher, *Moorish Spain* (Berkeley, 1992), pp. 60–61; Hugh Kennedy, *The Armies of the Caliphs: Military and Society in the Early Islamic State* (London, 2001), pp. 10–11, 21–25, 99–106, 113, 183; Alberto Montaner Frutos and Alfonso Boix Jovani, *Guerra en Šarq Al'Andalus: Las batallas cidianas de Morella (1084) y Cuarte (1094)* (Zaragoza, 2005), pp. 133–35.

[17] David Wasserstein, *The Rise and Fall of the Party-Kings: Politics and Society in Islamic Spain 1002–1086* (Princeton, 1985), pp. 31–32, 41–42; Lomax, *Reconquest*, pp. 46–50.

states of the Peninsula.[18] In the era of this political and military sea-change, Jaime I came to power.

Jaime I's Wars

While "the Conqueror" was virtually orphaned by war, he was just as inexorably apprenticed to the battlefield and eventually became a master of combat through years of martial experience. If there are seven ages of man, as medieval thinkers believed,[19] then each of Jaime's were filled to overflowing with war. As a teenager, he was thrown into war unprepared by the interlinked revolts of Aragon's nobility and by his unsupported expedition against the Muslim fortress of Peñiscola (1225).[20] With the peace of Alcalá in 1227,[21] the king gained breathing room which he ultimately used to great advantage to conquer the *taifas* of the Balearics (1229–33),[22] Valencia (1234–38),[23] Jativa

---

[18] Wasserstein, *Rise*, pp. 55–81; idem, *The Caliphate in the West: An Islamic Political Institution in the Iberian Peninsula* (Oxford, 1993), pp. 146–61.

[19] J. A. Burrow, *The Ages of Man in Medieval Writing and Thought* (Oxford, 1986); Nicholas Orme, *Medieval Children* (New Haven, 2003), p. 6; Beryl Rowland, "Classical and Medieval Ideas on the 'Ages of Man' and the Middle English Poem 'The Parliament of the Thre Ages'," *Poetica* 3 (1975), 17–29.

[20] *BD*, pp. 42–42 (chap. 25); Luis González Antón, "La revuelta de la nobleza aragonesa contra Jaime I en 1224–7," *Homenaje a Don José María Lacarra de Miguel en su jubilación del profesorado*, 2 vols. (Zaragoza, 1977), 2:143–63; F. Olivan Baile, "¿Fue traidor al rey de Aragón el señor de Albarracín, Don Pedro Fernandez de Azagra?" *Teruel* 24 (1960), 210–19.

[21] *BD*, pp. 52–54 (chap. 33); *Documentos de Jaime I de Aragón* [hereafter *DJI*], ed. Ambrosio Huici Miranda and Maria Desamperados Cabanes Pecourt, 5 vols. to date (Zaragoza, 1975–86), 1:180–82 (doc. 91); *El libro de la cadena de Jaca: Documentos reales, episcopales y municipales de los siglos X, XI, XII, XIII y XIV*, ed. Dámaso Sangorrín y Diest-Garcés (Zaragoza, 1920), p. 321; González Antón, "Revuelta," pp. 142–46.

[22] *BD*, pp. 69–135 (chaps. 47–126); Miquel Barceló, "Expedicions militars i projectes d'atac contra les Illes orientals d'Al-Andalus (al-Jaza'ir al Sharqiyya al-Andalus) abans de la conquesta (1229)," *Estudi General* 1 (1981), 291–321; Pablo Cateura Bennàsser, "Sobre la aportación aragonesa a la conquista de Mallorca (1229–1232)," in *X Congreso de historia de la corona de Aragón* [hereafter *X CHCA.*] 3 vols. (Zaragoza, 1979), Comunicaciones, 1–2:17–40; Micaela Danús, "Conquista y repoblación de Mallorca: Notas sobre Nicoláu Bovet," in *X CHCA*, 1–2:41–64; Alvaro Santamaria, "La expansion político-militar de la corona de Aragó bajo la dirección de Jaime I: Baleares," in *X CHCA*, Ponencias, 93–146; Jose Maria Quadrado, *Historia de la conquista de Mallorca*, 2 vols. (Palma de Mallorca, 1958).

[23] *BD*, pp. 137–233 (chaps. 127–289); Robert I. Burns, S.J., "The Many Crusades of Valencia's Conquest: An Historiographical Labyrinth," in *On the Social Origins of Medieval Institutions: Essays in Honor of Joseph F. O'Callaghan*, ed. Donald J. Kagay and Theresa M. Vann (Leiden, 1998), pp. 167–77; Miguel Gual Camarena, "Reconquista de la zona castellonense," *Boletín de la sociedad castellonense de cultura* 24 (1949), 417–41; Pedro López Elum, *La conquista y repoblación valenciana durante el reinado de Jaime I* (Valencia, 1995); José Martínez Ortiz, "Turolenses en la conquista e integración de Valencia y su reino," in *X CHCA*, 1–2:101–18; Antonio Ubieto Arteta, "La reconquista de Valencia y Murcia," in *X CHCA*, Ponencias, pp. 149–64.

and Biar (1244–45),[24] and Murcia (1265–66).[25] While establishing governments for these vast new territories, Jaime, now famed as a warrior, had to put down a massive rebellion led by the Mudéjar prince of southern Valencia, Al-Azrak.[26] He also was forced to deal with insurrections mounted by Aragonese and Catalan nobles[27] as well as by such members of the royal family as Prince Alfonso and Ferran Sanchez de Castro.[28] Though he attempted to cap his crusading career by leading an expedition to the Holy Land in 1269–70, this venture proved unsuccessful[29] and the Conqueror spent the last months of his life in beginning to put down another uprising of his Valencian Mudéjars (Muslims under Christian rule).[30]

With this rich background pastiche of military episodes large and small, Jaime attained the skills of a warrior in much the same way he established administrations for the lands he had conquered so suddenly – by trial and error. His military success was a true institutional development that altered over time to establish a custom of war, which the king repeatedly drew on to

---

[24] *BD*, pp. 235–82 (chaps. 290–377); Isabel A. O'Connor, *A Forgotten Community: The Mudejar Aljama of Xàtiva, 1240–1327* (Leiden, 2003); Josep Torro Abad, *El naixement d'una colònia: Dominació I resistència a la frontera valencia (1238–1276)* (Valencia, 1997); Robert I. Burns, S.J., and Paul E. Chevedden, "'The Finest Castle in the World'," *History Today* 49 (11) (November, 1999), 10–17.

[25] *BD*, pp. 283–327 (chaps. 378–465); Josep-David Garrido i Valls, *Jaume I i el regne de Múrcia* (Barcelona, 1997); Miguel Gual Camarena, "La Corona de Aragó en la repoblación murciana," in VII *Congreso de Historia de la corona de Aragón*, 3 vols. (Barcelona, 1963–64), Comunicaciones, 2:303–10; Juan Torres Fontes, *La reconquista de Murcia en 1266 per Jaime I de Aragón* (Murcia, 1999).

[26] Robert I. Burns, S.J., *Muslims, Christians, and Jews in the Crusader Kingdom of Valencia: Societies in Symbiosis* (Cambridge, 1984), pp. 1–51; idem, "The Crusade against Al-Azraq: A Thirteenth-Century Mudejar Revolt in International Perspective," *The American Historical Review* 93 (1988), 80–106; idem, "La guerra de Al-Azraq de 1249," *Sharq Al-Andalus* 4 (1987), pp. 253–56; idem, "A Lost Crusade: Unpublished Bulls of Innocent IV on al-Azraq's Revolt in Thirteenth-Century Spain," *The Catholic Historical Review* 74 (1988), 440–49; idem, "Príncipe almohade y converso mudéjar: Nueva documentación sobre Abu Zayd," *Sharq Al-Andalus* 4 (1987), 109–22; Robert I. Burns, S.J., and Paul E. Chevedden, *Negotiating Cultures: Bilingual Treaties in Muslim-Crusader Spain under James the Conqueror* (Leiden, 1999), pp. 3–11.

[27] V. Coma Soley, *Los vizcondes de Cabrera* (Barcelona, 1968), pp. 27–29; Joan Serra Vilaró, *La historia de Cardona*, 2 vols. (Tarragona, 1966), 1:199–204.

[28] Fernando Fondevilla, "La nobleza catalano-aragonesa por Ferran Sanchez de Castro," I *CHCA*, 2:1061–1176; Fernando de Sagarra, "Noticias y documentos inéditos referentes al infante D. Alfonso, primogénito de D. Jaime I y Da. Leonora de Castilla," *Boletín de la Real Academia de Buenas Letras de Barcelona* 9 (1917–20), 288–89.

[29] *BD*, pp. 337–44 (chaps. 482–93); Engracia Alsina Prats, "Jaime el Conquistador y sus relaciones con los Santos Lugares. Actuación de los sucesores en el trono de Aragón, destacado a Isabel de Castilla, reina de Sicilia por su matrimonio con Fernando de Aragón," in X *CHCA*, Comunicaciones, 1–2:7–16; Francesch Carreras y Candi, "La creuada a Terra Santa," in I *CHCA*, 1:106–38; Santiago Hernández Izal, "La maltempsada de la Mare de Déu de Setembre de 1269," *Acta historica et archaeologica medievalia* 10 (1989), 489–516.

[30] *BD*, pp. 375–78 (chaps. 555–60); Robert I. Burns, S.J., "Rehearsal for the Sicilian War: Pere el Gran and the Mudejar Countercrusade in the Kingdom of Valencia, 1276–1278," in XI *Congresso di Storia della Corona d'Aragona*, 3 vols. (Palermo, 1983), 2:259–87.

attain success. At the end of his life when Jaime attempted to export this tried-and-true way of war to the larger arena of eastern crusading, he found that his experience was irrelevant to the international war on Islam that by now had become moribund. In 1274, when called by Pope Gregory X (r.1271–76) to a council at Lyons, the Aragonese sovereign proposed a well-developed plan for the mounting of an expedition against Islamic rulers of the Holy Land that would operate in conjunction with Mongol forces striking from the east. When he found his martial experience denigrated as the barking of "a small dog at a big one who pays him no heed,"[31] Jaime lost no confidence in himself, but rather in the contemporary state of crusading. His way of war went on unchecked until his death two years later, and brought with it nothing but success. Despite the ungracious reception on the larger stage of holy war, Jaime died in 1276 with his warring reputation very much intact, the subject of both awe and envy among his immediate successors. To understand Jaime I's military accomplishments, it will be necessary to review his attainments as martial organizer, financier, quartermaster, strategist, and finally battlefield commander. To accomplish this complex task, all of the Conqueror's military actions will be compressed into one treatment of his many *feyts*.

Jaime I's Military Manpower

As with his parliaments, the very existence of his armies rested solely with the king himself. When deciding on war for whatever reason, Jaime set into motion processes that had become commonplace long before his birth. To inform the troops that made up his army of his intention of going to war, the king issued written summonses drawn up by his notaries and then delivered by his corps of messengers and post-riders (*cursores, trotarii*).[32] Like parliamentary summons, these documents indicated in general terms the reason the host was being assembled, its scale, the mustering place and time, and the promise of specific pay rates if the campaign exceeded customary terms of service.[33]

---

[31] *BD*, pp. 359–65 (chaps. 524–35); Norman Housley, *The Later Crusades: From Lyons to Alcazar 1274–1580* (Oxford, 1992), pp. 11–13; *Documents on the Later Crusades, 1274–1580*, ed. Norman Houseley (London, 1996), pp. 16–20 (doc. 1).

[32] Donald J. Kagay, "Army Mobilization, Royal Administration and the Realm in the Thirteenth-Century Crown of Aragon," in Paul E. Chevedden et al., eds., *Iberia and the Mediterranean World*, 2:99; José Martínez Aloy, "Los correos de la curia regia," *Analecta sacra tarraconensia* 18 (1944), 92–114.

[33] Archivo de la corona de Aragón [hereafter ACA], Cancillería real, Pergaminos de Jaime I, no. 1440; Registro [hereafter R.] 17, fols. 7, 12; R. 18, fols. 14v, 62, 65, 82v; R. 22, fol. 13; R. 23, fol. 24; *BD*, pp. 59, 155, 202 (chaps. 37, 153, 230); Joaquim Miret i Sans, *Itinerari de Jaume I el Conqueridor* (1918; repr. Barcelona, 2007), pp. 243, 499, 516; Fondevilla, "Nobleza," 2:1097–99, 1117–20, 1129–30, 1132–33, 1150–53; Humphries, "War," p. 174; Kagay, "Army Mobilization," p. 99; Swift, *James*, p. 291 (doc. 4). For parliamentary summonses, see Luis González Antón, *Las cortes de Aragón* (Zaragoza, 1978), p. 146; Donald J. Kagay, "The Devel-

To assure the summoned parties of his seriousness at having the military appointment kept, the king occasionally included a threat. "Do your duty or we will inflict on you "such harm and damage ... [that though] it will displease us after the fact ... it will displease you even more."[34] Despite these stark threats, the fulfillment of the military obligations stated in the summons often depended on the current relationship the king had with the summoned parties. When the king was a teenager and in a distinctly weakened position, his call for military service could very well be answered, but often in a haphazard way that made effective campaign planning impossible.[35] In his later years when his central-izing policies sparked the broad-based baronial insurrection of the *Unión* in Aragon and Valencia, Jaime's military summonses were intentionally ignored by men who would not follow the king to war before he settled their grievances.[36] Because of the varying results that such summonses could produce, Jaime often relied on full assemblies of his parliaments, such as those of Barcelona (1228) and Monzón (1236), to arrange all the particulars of a campaign months before troops took the field.[37]

Depending on the duration and nature of the campaign he planned, Jaime could draw from several sources of manpower to accomplish his aims. The prin-cipal source of his soldiery lay with the members of his feudal array. These vassals, who had sworn "homage and fealty" to their royal overlord in exchange for the lands and fortresses they held from him,[38] were bound to serve in the

opment of the *Cortes* in the Crown of Aragon, 1064–1327" (Ph.D. diss., Fordham University, 1981), pp. 361–66, 402–6; E. S. Procter, "The Development of the Catalan *Corts* in the Thir-teenth Century," *Estudis universitaris catalans* 22 (1936), 531; Esteban Sarasa Sánchez, *Las cortes de Aragón en la Edad Media* (Zaragoza, 1979), pp. 72–73.

[34] Carmen Battle Gallart, "Una conjura del Tarragonins contra l'autoritat," *Boletín Arqueológico* 133–40 [Època IV] (1976–77), 203–7; Kagay, "Structures," p. 46.

[35] *BD*, pp. 42–43 (chap. 25). In the Peñiscola campaign of 1225, Jaime waited at Teruel for three weeks until he decided to call off the planned *chevauchée* as the result of an agreement with Zeit Abuzeit, the Valencian ruler at the time. At that point, the Aragonese noble, Pedro Ahones, with a company of horse appeared, and ready for war, even though almost a month late. When he refused to comply with the royal ban on further campaigning, he paid for his arrogance with his life.

[36] *BD*, pp. 300–01 (chap. 406). Shortly after the first explosion of unionist dissatisfaction at Exea in April of 1265, Jaime called for 2,000 Aragonese knights to serve in the Murcian campaign and only received the support of 600 horsemen. For the Aragonese and Valencian *Unión*, see Luis González Antón, *Las uniones aragonesas y las cortes del reino (1283–1301)*, 2 vols. (Zaragoza, 1975), 1:22–24; Donald J. Kagay, "Rebellion on Trial: The Aragonese *Unión* and its Uneasy Connection to Royal Law, 1265–1301," in *War*, study VI, pp. 30–32; Joseph F. O'Callaghan, "Kings and Lords in Conflict in Late Thirteenth-Century Castile and Aragon," in Paul E. Chevedden et al., eds., *Iberia and the Mediterranean World*, 2:125–26.

[37] *BD*, pp. 73–78, 209 (chaps. 50–55, 241); *DJI*, 1:385–88 (doc. 238); Kagay, "Development," pp. 95–104, 110–13; Procter, "Development," pp. 532–33.

[38] *The Usatges of Barcelona: The Fundamental Law of Catalonia*, trans. Donald J. Kagay (Phila-delphia, 1994), pp. 39–44; Thomas N. Bisson, "The Problem of Feudal Monarchy: Aragon, Catalonia, and France," in *Medieval France and her Pyrenean Neighbors: Studies in Early Institutional History* (London, 1989), pp. 240–47.

royal "host" (*hueste, host*) with "arms, bread, and equipment" for up to three months at their own expense.[39] This also applied to their own vassalic retainers if the king could show he was in crucial need of such military aid.[40]

Besides the regular members of his host, Jaime increasingly came to rely on the important ancillary troops provided by his towns. These militias, made up of men whose military service was a clearly specified function of their urban citizenship, normally supported the host with garrison, picket, and transport duty. They served with valor as infantry and crossbowmen in a number of the Balearic and Valencian campaigns. Since their feudal relationship to the king was similar to that of Jaime's troops of noble extraction, they were expected to support themselves in the field from three days to three months. For longer periods, such forces could expect a daily wage paid in Barcelona or Jaca *sous*.[41]

In addition to their regular components, royal armies were occasionally complemented by mercenary troops whose relationship to the Aragonese king was entirely based on money. Like earlier counts of Barcelona, Jaime generally used such troops in amphibious operations against the Balearic Islands. In these complicated expeditions, Jaime had little choice but to buy the service of Genoese and Pisan ship masters in order to augment his own merchant marine and serve as transports between the Catalan coast and the Balearic ports.[42]

The only source of manpower the Conqueror did not utilize in his many campaigns was that guaranteed him by national law. In both Aragon and Catalan custom, a sovereign whose land was threatened by foreign invasion could call out an emergency force of "all men who are old and strong enough to fight" to defend the realm.[43] Since Jaime seldom engaged in defensive warfare, he had little use for this source of free soldiery, and, in fact, an Aragonese sovereign did not call out this type of *arrière ban* until 1285 when Catalonia was invaded

---

[39] Antonio Palomeque Torres, "Contribución al estudio del ejercito en los estados de la reconquista," *Anuario de Historia del Derecho Español* 15 (1944), p. 234; Kagay, "Army Mobilization," p. 99.

[40] *The Customs of Catalonia between Lords and Vassals by the Barcelona Canon, Pere Albert: A Practical Guide to Castle Feudalism in Medieval Spain*, trans. Donald J. Kagay (Tempe, 2002), pp. 38–39 (art. 38); Donald J. Kagay, "The King's Right Must be Preferred to the Lord's: Sovereignty and Suzerainty in the Treatise of Pere Albert," in *Law*, study V, pp. 693–703.

[41] Elena Lourie, "A Society Organized for War: Medieval Spain," *Past and Present* 35 (1966), 54–76; Carmen Pescador, "La caballería popular en León y Castilla," *Cuadernos de Historia de España* 33–34 (1961), 101–238; 35–36 (1962), 56–201; 37–38 (1963), 88–198; James F. Powers, *A Society Organized for War: The Iberian Municipal Militias in the Central Middle Ages, 1000–1284* (Berkeley, 1988), pp. 112–61; idem, "Two Warrior-Kings and their Municipal Militias: The Townsman-Soldier in Law and Life," in *Worlds*, pp. 95–128; Kagay, "Army Mobilization," p. 105.

[42] *BD*, pp. 123, 126 (chaps. 108, 111); David Abulafia, *The Western Mediterranean Kingdoms 1200–1500: The Struggle for Dominion* (London, 1997), pp. 50–51.

[43] *Usatges*, trans. Kagay, p. 80 (art. 64); Donald J. Kagay, "The National Defense Clause and the Emergence of the Catalan State: *Princeps namque* Revisited," in *War*, pp. 57–97.

by a French crusading force under Philip III (1270–85).[44] Though such national defense forces were utilized on many occasions during the fourteenth century, Jaime's successors soon found them to be almost useless in military terms and assuredly not without a maintenance expense.[45]

Jaime I's Military Financing

As his wars lengthened, Jaime found himself in a deepening financial bind that could pull defeat from imminent victory. Because his realms were "strong money" states that would not allow the devaluation of coinage to meet military payrolls,[46] Jaime had to work hard on several levels to keep his armies funded. Without access to the "household tax" (*fogatge, fogaje*), an impost crucial for military funding during the reign of his great-great-grandson, Pedro IV (Pere III) "the Ceremonious" (1336–87),[47] the Conqueror and his officials had to rely on individual taxes tied directly to war: the *redemptio exercitus*, a fee paid in lieu of military service,[48] and the *defectus servitii* or the *fallimentum*, a fine for not answering a military summons or for unsanctioned departure from the king's army.[49]

Though these exactions provided a tidy sum, it was rapidly consumed by the ravenous maw that military operations too often became. To keep his troops in the field, Jaime had no option but to appeal to ever-widening circles of funding. On rare occasions, as in his first Valencian campaign in 1225, he was fortunate to come across a good citizen of Teruel, Pascual Muñoz, who supplied the king's

---

[44] Joseph F. Strayer, *Medieval Statecraft and the Perspectives of History; Essays by Joseph R. Strayer* (Princeton, 1971), pp. 107–22.

[45] Manuel Sánchez Martínez, "The Invocation of *Princeps namque* in 1368 and its Repercussions for the City of Barcelona," in *The Hundred Years War: A Wider Focus*, ed. L. J. Andrew Villalon and Donald J. Kagay (Leiden, 2005), pp. 151–78.

[46] Octavio Gil Farres, *Historia de la moneda española* (Madrid, 1959), pp. 210–13; Peter Spufford, *Money and its Use in Medieval Europe* (Cambridge, 1988), pp. 314–15.

[47] María Teresa Ainaga Andrés, "El fogaje aragonés de 1362: Aportación a la demografía de Zaragoza en el siglo XIV," *Aragón en la Edad Media* 8 (1989), 33–59; Luis García de Valdeavellano y Arcimus, *Curso de historia de los instituciones españoles de los orgines al final de edad media* (Madrid, 1968), pp. 305–06; J. M. Pons Guri, "Un fogatjament desconegut de l'any 1358," 30 (1963–64), 322–498. For a similar French impost, the *fouage*, see John Bell Hennemann, *Royal Taxation in Fourteenth Century France: The Devlopment of War Financing 1322–1356* (Princeton, 1971), pp. 4–5, 211–15, 255–59, 281–83.

[48] ACA, Cancillería real, Cartas Reales (Jaime I) (extra series), no. 64 (3); R. 15, fol. 12v; R. 23, fols. 8v–9; Robert I. Burns, S.J., "The Crusade against Murcia: Provisioning the Armies of James the Conqueror, 1264–1267," in *Jews, Muslims, and Christians in and Around the Crown of Aragon: Essays in Honour of Professor Elena Louris*, ed. Harvey J. Hames (Leiden, 2004), p. 62; Kagay, "Army Mobilization," p. 102.

[49] ACA, Cancillería real, Pergaminos de Jaime I, no. 1916; R. 23, fol. 70v; Kagay, "Army Mobilization," p. 102. Such payments are discussed in *Usatges*, trans. Kagay, 73 (arts. 30–31). The *fallimentum* in this context is defined as seeing one's lord in danger and not helping him.

army for three weeks free of charge.[50] Even though these sources could provide the king with a great deal of capital, they seldom came without conditions and restrictions. The easiest money the king could lay his hands on was provided from the "arbitrary exaction" (*questia*). Though such grants were supposedly voluntary, it was clear to the Jewish and Muslim communities (*aljamas*) from which they were normally extorted that giving money on these terms might free them from such contributions for a while.[51] For the king, these populations constituted a "royal treasure" that could be drawn on by the Crown whenever needed.[52] Despite this institutional blank check, he was careful not to overtax this resource and occasionally either returned a portion of grants pledged by his Muslim and Jewish subjects or waived these "donations" altogether.[53]

While these extorted funds could be drawn on throughout a campaign, the Aragonese king found that true loans from his Christian subjects were best attained within the first phases of the conflict before battlefield losses deadened financial enthusiasm. Even without royal pressure, individuals and groups might loan money to the Crown to assure the protection of the king's armed forces from the "madness" of a neighboring noble who had risen in rebellion or, more importantly, to curb "the perfidy of the pagans [Muslims]."[54] Some of these advances made to the royal host and its leader were in the form of supplies or transport given "out of sheer generosity." While these granters were hopeful that they might be rewarded in other ways if the king gained victory, they were adamant that their present generosity should not lapse into some future fiscal precedent.[55] Individuals who loaned Jaime or his sons money to help with the mobilizing of forces or moving them to the front had their monetary advances recognized and were then granted a repayment schedule that was tied to the diversion of royal revenues of various sorts until the loan was fully repaid.[56] The possibility of repayment in such arrangements was generally considered a good one even when the loan was quite a large one.[57] To the creditor, however, this

---

50 *BD*, p. 42 (chap. 25); Martínez Ortiz, "Turolenses," pp. 110–11.

51 ACA, Cancillería real, Cartas reales, Jaime I (extra series), no. 61 (2); R. 18, fol. 105; Yitzak Baer, *A History of Jews in Spain*, trans. Louis Schoffman, 2 vols. (Philadelphia, 1961), 1:84–86; Francisco de Bofarull y Sans, "Los judios en el territorio de Barcelona (siglos X a XIII). Reinado de Jaime I (1213–1276)," in I *CHCA*, 2:924–25, 934–35 (docs. 131, 150).

52 J. Lee Shneidman, *The Rise of the Aragonese-Catalan Empire, 1200–1350*, 2 vols. (New York, 1970), 2:462–64.

53 ACA, Cancillería real, R. 17, fol. 66v; Burns, "Crusade," p. 65.

54 ACA, Cancillería real, R. 23, fols. 223v–225; Kagay, "Army Mobilization," p. 102.

55 ACA, Cancillería real, Pergaminos de Jaime, no. 363; *DJI*, 1:205–06, 229–30, 263–64 (docs. 110, 123, 146); Kagay, "Army Mobilization," p. 102.

56 ACA, Cancillería real, R. 17, fols. 33v, 77; *Transition in Crusader Valencia: Years of Triumph, Year of War, 1264–1270*, vol. 3 of *Diplomatarium of the Crusader Kingdom of Valencia: The Registered Charters of its Conqueror Jaume I, 1257–1276*, ed. and trans. Robert I. Burns, S.J. (Princeton, NJ, 2001), pp. 135, 147, 168–69 (docs. 605, 613ª, 631ª).

57 ACA, Cancillería real, R. 13, fol. 283; *Diplomatarium*, 3:181–82 (doc. 640). When the Catalan "first men" (*prohoms*) living in Valencia put up 100,000 s. to underwrite Jaime's attack on Murcia, the donation was to be paid back from the all the major Catalan dioceses.

process could also appear a virtual bait-and-switch, especially when the king specified the same revenues to pay off more than one of his debts, effectively forcing the creditor to stand in line to get repaid.[58]

With the added expenses that war brought in its wake, both Jaime and his sons negotiated a plethora of loans with municipal financial agents, both Jewish and Christian. These new fiscal bonds were forged for reasons ranging from the purchase of supplies to the acquisition of a new horse.[59] As these debts added up, Jaime's fiscal officers would consolidate the list of minor advances into one grand total and then issue to the creditor, a pay voucher or IOU (*albaranum, albarà*) that would contain the king's recognition of the full amount owed, but seldom specified when it would be repaid.[60] Jaime had learned this type of fiscal hopscotching early and would continue it for his entire life. He was always careful to pay off his IOUs, but often took quite a long time in doing so.[61] If the loan amount was large enough, the king often simplified the process of reimbursement by converting the creditor into a tax farmer who could collect profitable imposts or "annuities" (*violaris*) for up to two years. In this way, the creditor could make back his original outlay with a good deal to spare.[62]

As campaigns lengthened, the Conqueror needed money in greater increments than that guaranteed him by individual loans. Seeking much greater outlays, he turned to both persons and groups who acted as moneylenders for both profit and influence. In 1231, he negotiated a sizeable loan of 100,000 s. with the Navarrese king, Sancho VI "the Strong" (r.1194–1234), capping this deal with a diplomatic pact that attempted to use Aragonese power as a counterpoise to growing Castilian aggression.[63] Within his own realms, Jaime could turn to another set of international lenders, the Knights Templar or the Hospital of St. John, to deposit funds and to find ready financing terms when needed.[64] When particularly strapped for cash, the king might use these organizations as receivers for general loans to support expeditions against "the enemies of the Christian faith." In such ventures, the Aragonese king, often acting without direct papal authorization, assured his subjects, both Christian and Jewish, that

[58] ACA, Cancillería real, R. 17, fol. 36; *Diplomatarium*, 3:162–63 (doc. 624).

[59] ACA, Cancillería real, R. 17, fols. 32, 33, 35v; *Diplomatarium*, 3:156–58, 160–61 (docs. 619ª, 621ª, 622). Such loans could involve more than one party, as did a transaction in 1265 in which Prince Pedro borrowed money from one man to buy a warhorse from another, which he clearly planned to give to another person.

[60] ACA, Cancillería real, R. 17, fol. 32; *Diplomatarium*, 3:156–58 (doc. 619ª).

[61] Thomas N. Bisson, "Las finanzas del joven Jaime I (1213–1228)," in X *CHCA, Comunicaciones 1–2*, 161–208; Kagay "Army Mobilization," p. 98.

[62] ACA, Cancillería real, R. 13, fols. 282–83; *Diplomatarium*, 3:176–81 (doc. 639ª).

[63] ACA, Cancillería real, Pergaminos de Jaime I, no. 445; *DJI*, 1:264–66 (doc. 147); *BD*, p. 152 (chap. 149); Angel J. Martín Duque and Luis J. Fortún Pérez de Cirriza, "Relaciones financieras entre Sancho el Fuerte de Navarra y los monarcas de la Corona de Aragón," in X *CHCA, Comunicaciones 3, 4 y 5*, 171–82; Miret i Sans, *Itinerari*, p. 92; Swift, *James*, pp. 288–90 (doc. 2).

[64] Alan J. Forey, *The Military Orders from the Twelfth to the Early Fourteenth Century* (Toronto, 1992), pp. 117–18; idem, *The Templars in the Corona de Aragon* (London, 1964), p. 350.

"they could legally lend their money" to ecclesiastical agents who could be trusted to transfer these funds to the war effort.[65]

When the sources of impromptu funding began to dry up, the Conqueror was then forced to make his fiscal case before more formal arenas. The first of these, the institutional mechanisms associated with the papal crusade, was one Jaime was perfectly adapted to from his troubled upbringing as well as his "childlike reverence for the Papacy."[66] As a "servant of God and the Church of Rome,"[67] he utilized the well-developed institutions of crusading in all of his major campaigns against Spanish Islam. After attaining a papal bull that defined the limits of the enterprise and the indulgence granted for such campaigning,[68] the Aragonese king could then begin the process of diverting certain clerical revenues to his military coffers for up to three years.[69] As we have seen, much of this clerical money was diverted to other creditors for repayment. This fiscal pragmatism as well as the high-handed use of clerical revenues in his new lands dimmed the Conqueror's luster as a crusade figure in papal circles and, on at least one occasion, earned for him the shameful characterization as "an indecent and shameful despoiler of a Papal subsidy."[70] When Jaime had his confessor's tongue hacked off in 1246 for revealing the details of the latest royal peccadillo, he became known in papal circles as a "despoiler of his own clergy."[71] Despite their hesitation in entrusting Jaime with crusading funds, popes continued to issue crusading bulls for Jaime's assaults on Muslim outposts such as Jativa and Murcia or to put down insurrections among his own Muslim subjects.

The second large-scale organization Jaime relied on to raise money was the parliament, known in Aragon as the Cortes and in Catalonia as the Corts. Like similar bodies throughout Europe, over the course of the thirteenth century these outgrowths of the royal courts underwent a glacial transformation from occurrences to free-standing institutions.[72] Even with its uncertain status, however, Jaime grudgingly agreed that "in matters as important as ... [war], it was neces-

---

65 ACA, Cancillería real, R. 13, fol. 196; Burns, "Crusade," p. 53.
66 Robert I. Burns, S.J., "The Spiritual Life of James the Conqueror King of Arago-Catalonia, 1208–1276: Portrait and Self-Portrait," *The Catholic Historical Review* 62 (1976), 14.
67 Ibid., p. 15; *BD*, p. 366 (chap. 537).
68 José Goñi Gaztambide, *Historia de la bula de la cruzada en España* (Vitoria, 1958), pp. 59–62; *The Crusades: Idea and Reality*, ed. Louise and Jonathan Riley-Smith (London, 1981), pp. 73–74 (doc. 12); Richard A. Fletcher, "Reconquest and Crusade in Spain," in *The Crusades: The Essential Readings*, ed. Thomas Madden (Oxford, 2002), pp. 62–67; O'Callaghan, *Reconquest and Crusade*, pp. 21–22.
69 Martin Fernández de Navarrette, "Disertación crítica sobre la parte que tuvieron los españoles en las guerras de ultramar o de la cruzadas," *Memorias de la Real Academia de Historia* 5 (1817), 168–70; Kagay, "Army Mobilization," p. 103.
70 Maureen Purcell, *Papal Crusading Policy, 1244–1291*, vol. 11 of *The History of Christian Thought*, ed. Heiko Oberman, 14 vols. (Leiden, 1975), p. 145; Kagay, "Army Mobilization," p. 103.
71 *DJI*, 2:228–20 (docs. 432–33).
72 Robert Howard Lord, "The Parliaments of the Middle Ages and the Early Modern Period," *The Catholic Historical Review* 16 (1930), pp. 127–29; Antonio Marongiu, *Medieval Parliaments:*

sary to celebrate the Corts."[73] His hesitance about use of the parliament to attain
support for reconquest operations sprang from his knowledge (informed by long
experience) that parliamentary "members are generally divided in opinion and
... [can] never be made to agree."[74] Despite these concerns, these assemblies
provided a "complete council"[75] in which the sovereign could lay out his case
for war before the most important clerics, nobles, and townsmen of his realms.
By doing so, he could guarantee the vast majority of manpower for an upcoming
army volunteered in one session, as in the assembly of 1228.[76] Even if he failed
in attaining such immediate military support, he might gain a sizeable amount
of funding from the vote of a subsidy collected across an entire kingdom. These
subventions could be of an extraordinary nature designed to provide funding
to deal with a specific emergency or customary grants such as the *bovatge* or
monedaje.[77] Besides these fiscal advantages, parliamentary support lent Jaime's
military ventures a "national" tone with generally accepted decisions on such
crucial matters as the division of booty. Even with these advantages, however,
the Aragonese sovereign grew to dislike coming before the increasingly tight-
fisted members of the Cortes who attempted to apply ever-greater limitations
to his war-making even when he promised to reimburse their grants many times
over.[78]

No matter how money was pledged to Jaime's war effort, the collection and
disbursement of such funds was seldom carried out at an expedited pace, despite
the king's constant assurances that he would "work signally" to have these loans
repaid rapidly.[79] Instead, royal officials and commanders grew used to payment
by promise as both had to rely on the issuance of IOUs, "letters of credit"
(*cartas de creença*), and "muster lists" (*mostras*).[80] With the Aragonese king
and his officials constantly on the move from one military theater to another,

A Comparative Study, trans. S. J. Woolf (London, 1968), pp. 45–46; H. G. Richardson and G.
O. Sayles, Parliaments and Great Councils in Medieval England (London, 1961), p. 9.
73 BD, p. 286 (chap. 381); Kagay, "Army Mobilization," p. 103.
74 BD, p. 287 (chap. 382).
75 Ibid., p. 286 (chap. 381).
76 BD, pp. 74–77 (chaps. 51–54); Marongiu, Medieval Parliaments, p. 67; Procter, "Development," p. 542.
77 Ferran Soldevila, "A propòsit del servei del bovatge," Anuario de Estudios Medievales 1 (1954),
753–87; Thomas N. Bisson, Conservation of Coinage: Monetary Exploitation and its Restraint
in France, Catalonia and Aragon c1000–1225 AD (Oxford, 1979), pp. 59, 61, 75, 78, 90–95;
Kagay, "Development," p. 386.
78 BD, p. 291 (chap. 390); Kagay, "Army Mobilization," p. 103. In the Cortes of Zaragoza in 1264,
Jaime tried to sell the pledging of military subsidies as a sound investment that would return
60% profit in very short order.
79 ACA, Cancillería real, R. 13, fol. 196.
80 For a similar system in place under Pere III (1336–87) during the War of the Two Pedros
(1356–66), see ACA, Cancillería real, R. 1381, fol. 192; Donald J. Kagay, "A Government
Besieged by Conflict: The Parliament of Monzón (1362–1363) as Military Financier," in The
Hundred Years War: A Wider Focus, ed. L. J. Andrew Villalon and Donald J. Kagay (Leiden,
2005), pp. 138–39.

this system of transferring and recording money seemed to take on a life of its own with the issuance of blank sheets "on which nothing was written" that royal agents could fill in later as they received and disbursed funds.[81] Though this tenuous paper trail gave ample opportunity for malfeasance of many types,[82] the greatest evil this "system" imposed on Jaime's soldiers was the woefully irregular delivery of pay packets.

As with his raising of military monies, Jaime was extremely creative in the way he distributed these funds. He designated trusted barons and knights to serve as frontier commanders and castellans, specifying how many troops they were to muster, how long they were to serve, and what their daily pay rate would be. These orders also indicated the number of "beasts" (*bèstias*) – horses and mules – the commander had to take to the front. To see that this entire force would be properly supported, the king assigned a global total (*porcio*) to the credit of the commander who would then have to act as both quartermaster and paymaster with the disbursal of these funds. The commanders thus spent royal money to pay the daily salaries of soldiers and to purchase rations for their men and fodder for their "horses armored and unarmored" (*equos armatos et disarmatos*).[83] These funds were also used to repay commanders and soldiers who suffered financial losses on the battlefield (including horses) and who had provided money from their own pockets to supplement the *porcio*.[84] The obvious weak link in this fiscal chain was the slowness of the royal government in delivering these funds. The frustration of many a frontier commander who had to support his men and their mounts from his own resources grew as the only thing he had to show from Jaime's officials was one scrap of paper after another that contained royal debt recognitions for tours of duty long past.[85]

In all of these inter-connected means of raising and disbursing funds, Jaime adroitly utilized loans and subsidies of all kinds to gather and maintain armies, while manipulating the contracted service of these troops to keep them in the field for long periods without directly paying them. Despite the economic dangers of such "crisis financing," Jaime became a master at living from loan to grant and back again.

---

[81] ACA, Cancillería real, R. 13, fol. 271v; R. 17, fol. 32; Burns, "Crusade," p. 61.

[82] For a discussion of this type of malfeasance in a later reign, that of Joan I (1387–96), see Donald J. Kagay, "Poetry in the Dock: The Court Culture of Joan I on Trial (1396–1398)," in *War*, study XI, pp. 48–99.

[83] ACA, Cancillería real, R. 10, fol. 65; R. 14, fols. 58, 60; R. 15, fol. 10; R. 19, fol. 189; R. 20, fol. 345; Miret i Sans, *Itinerari*, pp. 275, 371–72, 405–06, 508, 533. For a complete run of such campaign expenses, see ACA, Cancillería real, R. 17, fols. 117–44; Carreras y Candi, "Creuada," pp. 123–38.

[84] ACA, Cancillería real, R. 17, fols. 66r–v, 68v.

[85] ACA, Cancillería real, Pergaminos de Jaime I, no. 1899; Miret i Sans, *Itinerari*, p. 399.

Provisioning of Jaime I's Armies

Another phase of army management that Jaime I learned through hard experience was that of provisioning troops operating far from home bases. He understood first in theory and then in practice lessons that writers before and after his time would harp on: "the principal point of war is to secure plenty of provisions and to weaken or destroy the enemy by famine" (Vegetius);[86] "food is something without which men cannot live; it is necessary that they have it continually" (Alfonso X);[87] "invade with a large force and you are destroyed by hunger; invade with a small one and you are overwhelmed by a hostile population" (Henry IV of France [1593–1610]);[88] and "war is an insatiable consumer of supplies" (John Millett).[89]

Without an official commissariat, however, the Aragonese king supplied his armies much as he did his household – by continual purchases made in local markets by royal agents who were reimbursed later from the king's treasury. As with the provisioners for his court and those of his wife and sons, the men ordered to fill an immediate supply need were expected to do so as quickly and cheaply as possible. This normally meant that these agents would purchase the commodities from sites as near as possible to the king's military operations.[90] To make the court truly mobile, Jaime was frequently forced to instruct his stewards to provide sufficient "straw, fodder, and stabling" for the many horses and pack animals necessary for campaigns.[91] In all of these purchases, Jaime's men were to use their own money or that available to them from their offices to obtain these crucial supplies and then had to be content with the king's IOU "by reasons of expenses … incurred" in lieu of immediate repayment.[92] The only immediate advantage they attained from this duty was the king's solemn promise that they would be free from every impost and toll in purchasing and delivering the provisions.[93]

From the debt recognitions Jaime issued for the purchase of comestibles, we can glean some idea of what his armies ate in the field. The basic commodities mentioned time and again in the records are "wheat, barley, and wine."[94] The

---

[86] *Vegetius: Epitome of Military Science*, trans. N. P. Milner (Liverpool, 1993), p. 67 (book III, chap. 3).

[87] *Siete Partidas*, ed. Burns, 2:386 (Part. II, tit. xviii, law 10).

[88] Colonel C. E. Callwell, *Small Wars: Their Principle and Practice* (1906, repr. Lincoln, Neb., 1996), p. 60.

[89] John D. Millett, "Logistics and Modern War," *Military Affairs* 9 (1945), 206.

[90] ACA, Cancillería real, R. 10, fol. 52; R. 14, fols. 89, 99; R. 20, fol. 277; Lope Pascual Martínez, "Los oficios en la corte de Jaime I," X *CHCA, Comunicaciones 1–2*, pp. 509–13; Miret i Sans, *Itinerari*, pp. 273, 427, 522.

[91] Miret i Sans, *Itinerari*, p. 407.

[92] ACA, Cancillería real, R. 14, fol. 99; R. 15, fol. 63; Miret i Sans, *Itinerari*, pp. 400, 427.

[93] ACA, Cancillería real, R. 23, fol. 54; Miret i Sans, *Itinerari*, p. 534.

[94] *BD*, pp. 183, 191–92 (chaps. 201, 214–15); ACA, Cancillería real, R. 14, fol. 67.

bread made from the rough-ground flour obtained from the whole grains was eaten as round loaves baked above campfires (*pa cuyt*), biscuits, and porridge.[95] This simple fare was augmented with condiments such as salt, mustard, and vinegar, vegetables such as cabbage and peas, and meat (either salted or fresh) such as lamb, mutton, beef, chicken, wild fowl, and fresh water fish.[96] Besides these varied food stocks and water, Jaime's agents also bought firewood and food-preparation utensils, as well as straw and oats for the army's mounts.[97] Bands of cowboys/butchers drove herds of cows and sheep from Jaime's frontier depots down to the war zone.[98] The royal shopping list was normally fairly basic in its content if not in its size. It could, however, include very specific requests tailored to the king's taste and that of his sons that included various grades of wine, conger eels, "sheep of Armengot," and "oil of Benifalet."[99] Royal purchasing agents, however, did not always spend their time buying in bulk; they occasionally turned their efforts to procuring for their royal master luxury items such as "green, Persian cloth" for a tunic, silk to make a war banner, fowls for the king's falcons, and extremely expensive mules reserved as gifts to recognize the extraordinary service of his soldiers.[100]

Though the amounts of these commodities were expressed in archaic measures (*cafiz*, quarter of Aragon and Valencia, almud),[101] the customary daily rations for both Aragonese armies remained constant for the next half-century: "thirty ounces of baked bread" or one kilo of flour and a half-liter of wine per person per day. War horses and pack animals would receive a daily rate of approximately twelve kilos of oats.[102] These compare favorably with the daily statistics for Castilian armies and horses of the same period (35 liters of water, 5 kilos of hay, 5 of oats) as well as with the logistical estimates one modern historian made for Alexander the Great's army and mounts (one kilo of grain and one liter of water per man; 13 kilos of fodder and 30 liters of water per horse).[103]

95 José Balari Jovany, *Origenes históricos de Cataluña*, 2 vols. (1899; repr. Abadia de San Cugat de Valles, 1964), 2:628; Manuel Gómez de Valenzuela, *La vida cotidiana en Aragón durante la alta edad media* (Zaragoza, 1980), pp. 180–81.

96 ACA, Cancillería real, R. 10, fol. 52; R. 14, fol. 119; Miret i Sans, *Itinerari*, pp. 273, 450.

97 Clifford J. Rogers, *Soldiers' Lives through History: The Middle Ages* (Westport, Conn., 2007), p. 75; Miret i Sans, *Itinerari*, p. 407.

98 Ferrer i Mallol, "Organización," p. 210.

99 ACA, Cancillería real, R. 17, fol. 33; Gómez de Valenzuela, *La vida cotidiana*, p. 181. Alfonso X suggests that a castle should be supplied with food as well as "hand-mills, charcoal, wood, and all those other articles called utensils": *Siete Partidas*, 2:387 (Part. II, tit. xviii, law x).

100 ACA, Cancillería real, R. 17, fols. 34r–v; Miret i Sans, *Itinerari*, p. 407.

101 ACA, Cancillería real, R. 17, fol. 34; Gómez de Valenzuela, *La vida cotidiana*, pp. 115–16.

102 "Ordenacions fetes per lo molt als senyor En Pere terç Rey d'Aragó sobra lo regiment de tots los officials de la sua cort," in *Colección de documentos inéditos del archivo general deo la corona de Aragón* [hereafter abbreviated *CDACA*], ed. Próspero de Bofarull y Moscaró, et al., 41 vols. (Barcelona, 1847–1910), 5:171–72; Ferrer i Mallol, "Organización," p. 210.

103 Donald W. Engels, *Alexander the Great and the Logistics of the Macedonian Army* (Berkeley, 1978), pp. 123–28; Francisco García Fitz, *Castilla y León frente al Islam: Estrategias de expansión tácitas militares (siglos xi–xiii)* (Seville, 1998), p. 93.

While the king could depend on his noble and urban units to provide their own supplies for a limited time,[104] or might have the good fortune to receive foodstuffs as presents from Muslim defectors or provisions captured with enemy fortresses,[105] the ultimate responsibility for transporting stores and equipment of all types to the battle zone fell on him. Taking into account the long coastline and maritime orientation of Catalonia and his major conquests, the most economical and rapid means open to Jaime for conveying supplies and equipment to the battle zone was by ship. Since the Aragonese possessed no professional navy of any kind until the era of Pedro III (r.1276–85),[106] the Conqueror depended on the vessels of his merchant marine of Barcelona and Tortosa fitted out for battle to help support his lengthy expeditions against the Balearics and Valencia.[107] The various types of "galleys" (*galeae*), barques (*llenys*), and transports (*uxers, tauridas*) were well adapted to Mediterranean waters and could serve equally well in transporting men, provisions, and horses to distant campaigns as they had for countless crusaders.[108]

The king himself could negotiate terms with individual captains for the royal use of their vessels for up to a year in exchange for a lump sum or a share of the plunder garnered by the expedition or won by individual vessels. As with individual soldiers moving to the front, such ships were not to pay either royal imposts or local tolls.[109] In his largest campaigns, Jaime enjoyed for many months the volunteered service of a large "fleet" (*estoleum, armada*) of merchant ships especially "armed" for combat.[110] At times, the king cut out the middleman by having hulls of the mercantile type built in the shipyards of his largest ports and then rigged for war service.[111]

With this naval advantage, Jaime could freely move between the war zone

---

[104]   ACA, Cancillería real, R. 17, fol. 12; R. 18, fols. 14v, 62, 65, 82v; R. 22, fol. 13; R. 23, fol. 45; Cartas reales (Jaime I) (extra series, no. 33 (1)); Fernando Fondevila, "La nobleza catalano-aragonesa por Ferran Sanchez de Castro de 1274," I *CHCA*, 2:1097–99, 1117–20, 1129–30, 1132–33, 1150–53; Humphries, "Arms," p. 174; Kagay, "Structures," p. 64.

[105]   *BD*, 132, 139, 173 (chaps. 121, 128, 184); Kagay, "Army Administration," p. 107, n. 57.

[106]   For the emergence of the Catalan-Sicilian fleet during the Ward of the Sicilian Vespers (1282–1304), see Lawrence V. Mott, *Sea Power in the Medieval Mediterranean: The Catalan-Aragonese Fleet in the War of the Sicilian Vespers* (Gainesville, 2003), pp. 52–185.

[107]   ACA, Cancillería real, Pergaminos de Jaime I, no. 1975; *BD*, pp. 77–78, 139, 338 (chaps. 54–55, 130, 484); *Consulate of the Sea and Related Documents*, trans. Stanley S. Jados (University, Alabama, 1975), p. 233 (chap. 298).

[108]   John E. Dotson, "Ship Types and Fleet Composition at Genoa and Venice in the Early Thirteenth Century," in *Logistics of Warfare in the Age of Crusades: Proceedings of a Workshop held at the Centre for Medieval Studies, University of Sydney, 30 September to 4 October 2002*, ed. John H. Pryor (Aldershot, 2006), pp. 63–75; Mott, *Sea Power*, pp. 186–204; Archibald Lewis and Timothy J. Runyan, *European Naval and Maritime History, 300–1500* (Bloomington, 1985), pp. 70–75.

[109]   ACA, Cancillería real, R. 20, fol. 296; *BD*, 78, 120 (chaps. 55, 104); Santamaria, "Expansion," p. 124.

[110]   ACA, Cancillería real, R. 12, fol. 141; R. 13, fols. 55, 171; Burns, "Crusade," p. 51; Miret i Sans, *Itinerari*, pp. 311, 340, 347–48.

[111]   ACA, Cancillería real, R. 14, fol. 55; Miret i Sans, *Itinerari*, p. 355; Burns, "Crusade," p. 51.

and his other territories while transporting men, food stores, armor, horses, disassembled artillery, stone shot and other equipment to the vicinity of the battlefield.[112] Despite its many advantages, naval transport could prove an extremely fragile lifeline between the king's home ports and the landing areas for his troops. As a matter of fact, on more than one occasion, Jaime found his logistical plans shattered "by the force of the weather" since the Mediterranean "becomes hostile in the winter ... [bringing] shipping to a standstill."[113]

Though eastern Spain was hardly "the society without wheels" that Richard Bulliet characterized the Middle East as being during the Middle Ages,[114] it was an area in which the fine road system of Roman Hispania had been badly treated by the Visigothic and Muslim conquests.[115]

As Jaime's armies veered away from the remnants of the *Via Augusta* that traversed all of the Mediterranean littoral of the Peninsula down to Cadiz, these forces increasingly came to depend on mules and other pack animals (*bestias, atzemblas*) to maintain supply lines. With a daily range of 25 miles a day fully loaded with up to 200 pounds, mules were essential for transport across the mountainous, Iberian landscape.[116] While Jaime was so certain of the importance of this form of transport that early in his reign he put "muleteers" (*arrieros*) and their pack trains under his "special protection," the pressures of keeping his troops fed and supplied often led the king to confiscate the services of the muleteers and their animals to transport matériel to the front without any guarantee that they could find consignments on the return trip.[117] With lengthy sieges, Jaime had little time for such concerns and, in fact, utilized ever larger pack trains that could mount up to 2,000 animals bearing loads of as much as 400,000 kilos.[118]

Over his long years of campaign and camp life, Jaime had learned by trial and error "my way of conquering lands."[119] He anchored this methodology

---

[112] ACA, Cancillería real, R. 14, fols. 110, 119; R. 20, fol. 296; *BD*, 123 (chap. 107); Miret i Sans, *Itinerari*, pp. 446, 450, 524.

[113] *BD*, pp. 120, 339–40 (chaps. 104, 485–88); Fernand Braudel, *The Mediterranean and the Mediterranean World in the Age of Philip II*, trans. Siân Reynolds, 2 vols. (New York, 1972), 1:248–53; Norbert Ohler, *The Medieval Traveller* (Woodbridge, Suffolk, 1989), p. 11.

[114] Richard W. Bulliet, *The Camel and the Wheels* (New York, 1990), pp. 216–36.

[115] Marjorie Nice Boyer, "A Day's Journey in Medieval France," *Speculum* 26 (1951), 604–06; Raymond D. Chevallier, *Roman Roads*, trans. N. H. Field (London, 1976), p. 157; S. J. Keay, *Roman Spain* (Berkeley, 1988), p. 61.

[116] Richard Ford, *A Hand-Book for Travelers in Spain and Readers at Home*, 3 vols. (1945; repr. Carbondale, IL, 1966), 1:70–73; Braudel, *Mediterranean*, 1:189, 284–85; Albert C. Leighton, "The Mule as Cultural Invention," *Technology and Culture* 8 (1967), 51; Thomas Savery, "The Mule," *Scientific American* 223 (1979), 104–5.

[117] ACA, Cancillería real, R. 21, fol. 148; *DJI*, 1:53 (doc. 18); Miret i Sans, *Itinerari*, p. 482.

[118] *BD*, p. 194 (chap. 219). For the load capacity of mules in pre-modern armies, see John Haldon, "Roads and Communications in the Byzantine Empire: Wagons, Horses, and Supplies," in *Logistics*, ed. Pryor, pp. 150–57; John H. Pryor, "Introduction: Modelling Bohemond's march to Thessaloniki," in *Logistics*, p. 19; Engels, *Alexander*, pp. 20–21.

[119] *BD*, p. 323 (chap. 455).

on matters he could control – the raising of funds, accumulation of matériel, and transport of supplies and equipment to the front. By close escapes caused through the lack of such provisions or poor planning in moving them to the war zone, the Aragonese king became an expert in both collecting stores and equipment, loading them on mule trains, and having them escorted to troops who would surely go down to defeat without them.[120] Like modern commanders, Jaime often grew frustrated that his army often functioned "as a mere escort for its food"[121] or that he spent much of his time as "a collector of supplies. ... [rather than] a leader of men."[122] The importance of his logistical role dawned on the Conqueror slowly, however, and only after he had neglected it, flirting with disaster in the process.

In his earliest campaigns, the Aragonese king depended on his feudal retainers to bring their own provender and underestimated his function as military provider. This was surely due to the fiscal pressure he was under due to his mounting debts. As one of Jaime's disgruntled retainers said of his early Valencian campaigns:

> you have made a great outlay in vain ... [you have] no treasury, no great revenue, no bread ... [and] are financially embarrassed in going about the land.[123]

This fear of civilian bankruptcy caused by ever-advancing military spending often put the king's troops in "great distress."[124] The lack of food for the royal army led many of his great ecclesiastical and baronial retainers to chide their young sovereign about poor planning in provisioning his troops, who were at the point of desertion from sheer hunger. "There are no supplies with the army," warned Prince Ferran, "and without them the troops cannot endure the labor of besieging a castle."[125] Other royal commanders warned that unless this problem was solved, many of the townsmen would take the lack of food as a signal for the end of military action and would go home "to get their crops in."[126]

In the face of crises of such disastrous proportions, Jaime put aside all of his nagging fiscal concerns and turned to provisioning his troops with both skill and energy. He did so by squeezing supplies from every reasonable source his realms could provide, even some that were completely unexpected. In addition to using found, donated, or diverted stores to make up dangerous supply

---

120 Ibid. When during the Murcian campaign certain of his nobles wished to raid Alicante, the king told them in great detail how to load shields and armor on mules and then to lash provisions on top. He surely remembered the pack trains in the Majorcan campaign that were so well-loaded that grapes loaded on the top were "neither broken nor bad." Ibid., p. 96 (chap. 71). For mule loading and driving, see Ford, *Hand-Book*, 1:71; Savery, "Mule," p. 104.
121 Callwell, *Small Wars*, p. 59.
122 Millett, "Logistics," p. 195.
123 *BD*, pp. 171, 204 (chaps. 180, 233).
124 Ibid., p. 191 (chap. 214).
125 Ibid., pp. 181–82 (chap. 199).
126 Ibid., p. 163 (chap. 166).

shortfalls,[127] Jaime also even utilized his hunting skills to bag "boars, cranes, and partridges" to put fresh meat in the army's larder.[128] None of these actions did much more than temporarily stave off hunger in the royal camp. Even in the midst of a full-scale siege operation, Jaime repeatedly took it on himself to leave the front lines and take a small party back to the nearest town and then to confiscate mules to bring supplies back to his men, even if this meant crossing enemy territory.[129] During such periods of logistical crisis, he would scour for supplies all of his realms that bordered the war zone, even diverting to the use of one campaign provisions destined for another military theater or for the royal court itself.[130] He also gathered substantial herds of cattle or sheep and had them pastured near his camp as a ready source of fresh meat.[131]

While these daring reactions saved several of the northern Valencian towns during his earlier campaigns, Jaime would be the first to admit that the crises he had to deal with were the result of poor planning. When he decided to establish a camp in 1237 outside of Valencia at Puig de Cebolla, he scolded its commander for "playing the mean trick" of not bringing adequate supplies for the garrison.[132] By going through such emergencies, the king grew convinced that he had to take all such logistical concerns on himself to be sure that his army was properly fed and equipped for long periods. To do so, he established simple supply depots – as at Puig – where stockpiled matériel was guarded for future use.[133] With the destination for these provisions assured, the Conqueror than turned to his naval supply lines by forming convoys of transports and "armed ships" that traveled "all in a body."[134] As a result of these actions, Jaime's military camp, often the scene of near-starvation, could become a natural entrepôt where "one could sell or buy everything as in a great city."[135] Such plenty, however, was not without problems of its own. With the spawning of so much commercial activity within the war zones in service of Jaime's army and extended court, prices often escalated due to profiteering and the rapid disappearance of such goods, making re-supply much more difficult. To see that provisions were adequately supplied to his men, Jaime instructed his stewards and bailiffs to allocate stores according to the "list of rations" provided by the army's commanders.[136] To assure that

---

127 Ibid., pp. 132, 174 (chaps. 121, 184); ACA, Cancillería real, R. 14, fol. 119; Miret i Sans, *Itinerari*, p. 450.
128 *BD*, p. 175 (chap. 186); Burns, "Crusade," p. 40.
129 Ibid.; *BD*, pp. 180–81 (chap. 197).
130 Ibid., p. 192 (chap. 216); ACA, Cancillería real, R. 15, fol. 63; R. 20, fol. 206; Miret i Sans, *Itinerari*, pp. 400, 512.
131 *BD*, p. 157 (chap. 156); Ferrer i Mallol, "Organización," p. 210.
132 *BD*, p. 191 (chap. 214). The commander was Bernat Guillem d'Entença and Jaime assured him that if he had not been closely related to him, he would have taken immediate vengeance on him for this criminal oversight. In Jaime's mind because of this botched logistical assignment, "Valencia is lost now and perhaps forever after."
133 Ibid., p. 189 (chap. 209).
134 Ibid., p. 220 (chap. 265).
135 Ibid., p. 221 (chap. 265).
136 Ibid., p. 183 (chap. 201).

prices of commodities destined for the front were maintained at a reasonable rate and delivered in suitable quantity during his Murcian campaign (1265–66), he appointed a special military quartermaster (*admudazaf* [Aragonese]; *almud-afás* [Catalan]) who acted to gather provisions, maintain reasonable prices, and oversee equitable supply distribution.[137]

From sheer necessity, then, Jaime had become a logistician of some merit. He understood how the market system of his realms could be utilized to maintain the flow of supplies to his fighting men. The demands of commerce, however, were never placed above the needs of his armies; when his forces faced starvation, he engaged in a "crisis provisioning" by which he bent every effort to adequately re-supply his troops. Like his old enemy, Al-Azrak, Jaime had come to realize over his long career that he owed his soldiers "a good deal of [his own] substance."[138]

Jaime I as Commander and Strategist

Jaime I's record as a battlefield and siege commander can perhaps best be approached through his Herculean efforts in mastering the art and business of war, through his never-ending enterprise in bending the will of his men to that of his own martial aims, and, finally, through his drive to overcome his own inadequacies to live up to his duty as a faithful vassal of the Almighty.

Of all these interconnected concerns, that of the management of military operations was surely the most enjoyable for the Aragonese king since his mastery of the art of waging war represented an increasing control over situations that could be exceedingly fluid. Like an apprentice in the contemporary guild system, experience endowed Jaime with confidence in responding to rapidly changing situations. In essence, for much of his early life, the Conqueror was a student both of and in war. Unlike Alfonso X, whose knowledge of the world of war was augmented by an academic patina from the works of Isidore of Seville and Vegetius,[139] the Aragonese ruler acquired a hard-won military mastery by learning from actual warfare itself a number of useful, even life-saving lessons.

As with his role as logistician, Jaime began to learn military precepts at an early age and saw that the core of such useful knowledge was organization and careful planning. He attributed his father's disastrous defeat at Muret to the disorder of a force in which "each noble fought for himself and broke with

---

[137] ACA, Cancillería real, R. 13, fol. 287v; Burns, "Crusade," pp. 71–73; Miret i Sans, *Itinerari*, p. 382.

[138] *BD*, p. 280 (chap. 374).

[139] Nancy Joe Dyer, "Alfonsine Historiography: The Literary Narrative," in *Emperor of Culture: Alfonso X the Learned of Castile and his Thirteenth-Century Renaissance*, ed. Robert I. Burns, S.J. (Philadelphia, 1990), pp. 145–46.

the rules of arms."[140] Though seldom having the opportunity to test his own practical organizational skills in great battles, the Aragonese king lent a careful hand to his army's transport and encampment. When moving through enemy territory, Jaime divided his forces between a vanguard, main body, rearguard and outriders. If attacked, the king, who normally rode in the rear, had trumpets sounded to signal his men whether to take up defensive positions or move to the attack.[141] He attempted to maintain some semblance of this order even when crossing swollen rivers such as the flooded Jucar above Cullera.[142] To keep track of smaller units engaged in reconnoitering, Aragonese armies also used bonfires placed on neighboring hills to indicate a safe line of march for the main force.[143] When engaged in amphibious landings as in Majorca (1229), Jaime often exchanged caution for speed by transporting small units from landing craft to defensible positions that would protect the general disembarkation.[144]

Since the majority of Jaime's military activity was directed toward the sieges of Muslim fortresses, the movement of his army to the front directly served this aim. His prime objective in the opening phases of such siege operations was to weaken and terrorize the garrisons of targeted castles by destroying standing crops, cutting down fruit and olive trees, and damming up water supplies to threaten enemy populations.[145] In this way, they would suffer "great weakness ... and need through hunger."[146] Jaime viewed this kind of time-consuming and difficult activity as an essential part of softening up a besieged fortress. Indeed, he compared it to the rewards gained by "the ripening of a fruit that one wishes to eat."[147] He used the self-interest of his merchant marine, operating singly or grouped in fleets under a royal admiral, to stop the maritime flow of goods to enemy territory by designating captains as privateers who would profit from all foreign shipping they captured.[148]

Since such attempts at devastation entailed a degree of danger that was often as great to the king's forces as to his Muslim enemies, Jaime routinely relied on a deception that was a hallmark of his military success. As a survivor of a dangerous adolescence surrounded by powerful enemies, he internalized quite deeply the valuable axiom: "guile is worth more than force."[149] Nowhere was this

---

[140] *BD*, p. 24 (chap. 9).

[141] Ibid., p. 309 (chap. 424).

[142] Ibid., p. 247 (chap. 312).

[143] Ibid., p. 175 (187). For similar signal fires during the French crusade against Catalonia (1285), see Bernat Desclot, *Chronicle, of the Reign of King Pedro III of Aragon*, trans. F. L. Critchlow, 2 vols. (Princeton, 1934), 2:235 (chap. 67).

[144] *BD*, pp. 82–83 (chap. 59).

[145] *BD*, pp. 156, 251–52 (chaps. 155, 321). For attempts of such military crop devastation in the ancient world, see Victor Davis Hanson, *Warfare and Agriculture in Classical Greece* (Berkeley, 1998).

[146] *BD*, p. 140 (chap. 131).

[147] Ibid., p. 187 (chap. 206).

[148] ACA, Cancillería real, R. 12, fol. 142; *DJI*, 5:82, 85 (docs. 1381, 1385).

[149] *BD*, p. 64 (chap. 43).

truth more valuable than in seeing his own troops across Muslim territory while simultaneously sowing disinformation among his enemy. A master of appearances across the wide treeless vistas of the Iberian landscape he was so familiar with, the Conqueror was known to make a small foraging party look much more fearsome at a distance by having its members – the knights – dismount and walk next to their horses. By having them make extra battle banners from their horse blankets and position shields and lances, and armor over their saddles while they continued to wear their helmets, the king was able to give an illusion of a much larger force of cavalry and infantry than the small squad of horsemen he actually commanded.[150] His greatest act of deception occurred in 1231 when, with an imposing force of six knights, five squires, four horses, and a shield, the Aragonese king intimidated a major Muslim garrison of Menorca to surrender by projecting the presence of a massive Christian army through the setting of 300 fires in and around the royal camp.[151]

In Jaime's mind, the most significant state in the opening phase of any siege operation was the proper placement of the camp both to protect his own men and menace the enemy. Laying out thirty such encampments by 1238,[152] the king gained valuable experience in choosing, setting up, and fortifying such positions – sometimes under strong enemy attack. Potential camps required certain very obvious qualities. They had be quickly defensible by being located within an existing fortress (as at Puig de Cebolla in 1237[153]) or on a hill endowed with natural defenses (as at Jativa in 1244[154]). The prime requirement, however, was a reliable water source for both the army and its animals.[155] In the Valencian and Murcian campaigns, this was often provided by the complex irrigation network that crisscrossed the southern Iberian *huerta*.[156] The king also used such land-forms to divide his camp between Aragonese and Catalan soldiers who often displayed deep-seated enmity even though fighting under the same banner.[157] Their royal master took great care in the selection of his camps to tighten the noose around the besieged enemy garrisons and to prevent the necessity of having to move his encampment later. Its placement – at Valencia halfway between the city and the dockyard suburb (*grao*) – could transform the camp

---

[150] Ibid., p. 196 (chap. 221).
[151] Ibid., p. 131 (chap. 120). When the French attacked across the Pyrenees in 1285, Pedro III's small force lit 200 fires so "It might seem as though all the armies of Spain were gathered there." Desclot, *Chronicle*, p. 235 (chap. 67).
[152] *BD*, p. 233 (chap. 270).
[153] Ibid., pp. 187–88 (chap. 206).
[154] Ibid., p. 260 (chap. 339).
[155] Ibid., p. 95 (chap. 70).
[156] Ibid., p. 92 (chap. 67). For the irrigation system in eastern Andalusia, see Thomas F. Glick, *Irrigation and Society in Medieval Valencia* (Cambridge, Mass., 1970); idem, *Islamic and Christian Spain in the Early Middle Ages: Comparative Perspectives on Social and Cultural Formation* (Princeton, N.J., 1979), pp. 68–76.
[157] *BD*, p. 92 (chap. 67).

into an entrepôt of sorts.[158] Because it was so convenient to the shipping of many supplies, Jaime's camp outside of Valencia provided both the sick and well with most urban commodities "as if they were in Barcelona or Lerida."[159] Several of his camps, such as Puig de Santa Maria, did not disappear after the siege concluded but became part of the new Christian cites' subsequent urbanization.

Having exercised great care in bivouacking his soldiers, Jaime showed equal care in carrying out the details of siege warfare that generally led to a successful conclusion. From his first initiation into military life in his early teens, the Aragonese king saw new martial technology as a way of quickly turning the tables against the Christian and Muslim castle holders he would contend with for the rest of his life. As Burns has observed, Jaime absolutely "delighted in artillery"[160] and was surely introduced to such engines of war as a boy of five during his father's siege of Muret in 1213.[161]

In fact the Conqueror's life had serendipitously intersected with the development and transmission of counterweight artillery from the Holy Land to Italy, the Midi, and Andalusia in the twelfth century.[162] The various forms of traction and counterweight artillery pieces Jaime mentions in the *Liber dels Feyts* – the *almangenech*, *fenevol*, *brigola*, *manganel*, and *trabuquet* – were all used to demolish fortress defenses and terrorize besieged populations.[163] The scale of fire with these machines – up to 1,000 stones a day – could quickly demoralize a garrison forced to suffer through such a bombardment.[164] The Conqueror demonstrated a very rapid learning curve concerning the use of these weapons and the advantage they gave him. He also quickly became somewhat of an expert in the rapid transport of artillery into war zones.[165] In some sense, though, his connection to artillery was not wholly utilitarian. Besides aiding in the rapid and efficient defeat of his enemies, these machines represented for the young king a phase of military accomplishment he could master even when peace reigned. From his earliest campaigns, he showed his skill at having artillery transported and set up for optimum effect against enemy garrison and the artillery they

---

[158] Ibid., p. 216 (chap. 256).
[159] Ibid., p. 223 (chap. 270).
[160] Burns, "Spiritual Life," p. 33.
[161] Jim Bradbury, *The Medieval Siege* (Woodbridge, Suffolk, 1992), p. 136; Jonathan Sumption, *The Albigensian Crusade* (London, 1978), pp. 150–51.
[162] Paul E. Chevedden, "Artillery in Late Antiquity: Prelude to the Middle Ages," in *The Medieval City under Siege*, ed. Ivy A. Corfis and Michael Wolfe (Woodbridge, Suffolk, 1995), pp. 131–76; idem, "The Invention of the Counterweight Trebuchet: A Study in Cultural Diffusion," *Dumbarton Oaks Papers* 54 (2000), 102–06; Paul E. Chevedden, Les Eigenbrod, Vernard Foley, and Werner Soedel, "The Trebuchet," *Scientific American* (July, 1995), 58–63; Paul E. Chevedden, Donald J. Kagay, Zvi Shiller, and Samuel Gilbert, "The Traction Trebuchet: A Triumph of Four Civilizations," *Viator* 31 (2000), 433–86.
[163] Paul E. Chevedden, "The Artillery of James I the Conqueror," in Paul E. Chevedden et al., eds., *Iberia and the Mediterranean World*, 2:68–76; Joseph Goday y Casals, "Medis d'atach y de defensa en la Crònica del Rey D. Jaume," I *CHCA*, 2:803–805.
[164] *BD*, p. 30 (chap. 15).
[165] Ibid., pp. 177–78 (chap. 192).

possessed.[166] By associating with engineers who built and helped service his artillery, the king gained a technical expertise that few men in his armies could match. If professional engineers, such as the well-paid Italian Nicoloso who served at Valencia, were not available, he could and did rely on sea captains and sailors who constructed trebuchets from ship masts and timbers.[167]

Jaime's fascination with artillery is apparent when during the Murcian campaign he helped aim an engine that immediately put out of commission an enemy artillery piece.[168] He thus looked on artillery as essential to the success of every siege he commenced. He protected his machines by surrounding them with light screens (*cledas*) and small squads of soldiers who kept watch day and night. When an enemy raiding party set on fire one of his artillery pieces during the siege of Albarracín in 1220, the king began customarily posting sizeable units of knights around the machines for up to five days at a stretch and even occasionally served such guard duty himself.[169] When artillery malfunctioned – normally from the tangling of the firing rope around the throwing arm – he had the crippled machine moved out of the range of enemy fire and replaced with other engines despite subjecting his troops to heavy casualties in the process.[170]

Besides the technical advantage afforded, the Conqueror soon learned that, though machines could tip the military balance in any siege, the ultimate success in any such operation relied on getting over or pulling down enemy defenses. Unlike Geraldo the Fearless, a twelfth-century marcher lord on the Leonese-Portuguese frontier who captured castles using stealth attacks,[171] Jaime forbade assaults launched at night to stop his troops "from behaving badly under arms" and to prevent a shift of momentum to a besieged enemy who might more easily beat back an attack made under the cover of darkness.[172] He instead relied on directly attacking the walls or burrowing under them. In the first case, he turned to the same engineers who had made his artillery to fashion multi-floored, wooden towers or belfires that could be propelled toward an enemy fortress with the use of wheels or log rollers. Protected on the outside by animal skins, this intimidating contraption could be drawn up to a fortress wall which could then be attacked when a plank was lowered, allowing Jaime's troops to scamper over on to the enemy battlements. The basic problem in this mechanism was that it had to be advanced by ropes and this exposed the pullers to terrible casualties. At Valencia, Jaime had to abandon his expensive belfry to incessant Muslim artillery fire that at first demolished it and then set it on fire.[173]

---

[166] Ibid., pp. 177–78 (chaps. 192–93).
[167] Ibid., pp. 93, 158 (chaps. 69, 157); Burns, "Spiritual Life," p. 33.
[168] *BD*, p. 326 (chap. 462); Burns, "Spiritual Life," p. 33.
[169] *BD*, pp. 30, 167–68 (chaps. 15, 174); Goday y Casals, "Medis," pp. 802–3.
[170] *BD*, p. 326 (chap. 461).
[171] Lomax, *Reconquest*, pp. 113–15.
[172] *BD*, p. 106 (chap. 83).
[173] *BD*, pp. 158–61 (chaps. 158–63); Bradbury, *Medieval Siege*, pp. 242–45; Nicolle, *Medieval Warfare Source Book*, 1:151.

While "going over the top" gave Jaime's armies limited success, wall mining was the king's preferred method of opening breaches in enemy walls. In both the Balearic and Valencian campaigns such excavations took place behind mantlets, moveable wooden screens constructed of timber frames, covered with planking and animal hides that served as flame retardants.[174] To protect sappers attempting to open large excavations under long sections of curtain wall, Jaime had several mantlets set up on the precipice of the moat that surrounded the besieged position. Shielded from enemy fire, mining operations could safely proceed down through the moat and under wall and tower foundations where setting fire to the props emplaced during the mining could effectively bring down large sections of a town's or castle's outer defenses.[175] Since the enemy often knew what his mining engineers were up to, they might start a counter-mine to thwart their efforts or send out raiding parties in an attempt to set the mantlets on fire. As with his artillery, Jaime stationed large parties of knights around the mantlets for days on end to protect the sappers.[176]

After several weeks spent in weakening enemy defenses, Jaime carried out the siege's end-game. Coordinating his final attack with the collapse of a curtain wall or tower brought down with the successful undermining, he ordered his men to attack the resulting breach with both speed and fury. He often maintained troops in the tunnels hacked below the walls and into the besieged fortresses. When the king's trumpeters gave the signal for the final attack, the king's subterranean troops, many of them sappers, rushed to attack the enemy while the rest of the army rushed through the breach.[177] To allow his men to get at the walls, the king's mining engineers filled stretches of moat with rubble so it could be crossed.[178] To open up breaches or demolish gates, some of the besiegers constructed battering rams, complete with iron heads and "rings through which ropes could be attached."[179] Once the frontal attack commenced, Jaime ordered his men to maintain the momentum through the breach unless they received "a mortal wound."[180] Only after this bloodiest phase of the operation was completed and the enemy garrison had surrendered did the Aragonese king declare victory. This was not always immediately accomplished because of the king's liberal surrender terms which gave Muslim garrisons up to five days to vacate the conquered fortress with everything they could carry.[181]

When the modern investigator attempts to assess Jaime I as a strategist, he is often stymied by the king's own narrative of military events in the *Liber dels Feyts*. Like many another aged campaigner over the centuries, the Aragonese

---

[174] Goday y Casals, "Medis," pp. 802–03; Bradbury, *Medieval Siege*, pp. 242–45.
[175] *BD*, pp. 93, 166 (chaps. 69, 177).
[176] Ibid., pp. 93, 166, 219 (chaps. 69, 172, 262); Goday y Casals, "Medis," p. 801.
[177] *BD*, pp. 168–69 (chap. 175).
[178] Ibid., p. 219 (chap. 262).
[179] Ibid., p. 238 (chap. 296).
[180] Ibid., pp. 104–05 (chap. 81).
[181] Ibid., p. 169 (chap. 177).

ruler was occasionally guilty (perhaps even unconsciously) of a chronological foreshortening that attributed the successful completion of a campaign solely to his perceptive pre-planning. Since many passages of his memoirs were written long after the events they commemorate, the king occasionally attributed to his own brilliance or courage military successes that might have come about from other causes. When standing between the reader and the events of his military life, the warrior-king reads history from back to front, projecting his own influence over matters that may have been caused by the actions of his enemies, of frontier commanders or even by chance.[182]

At the opening of the Valencian campaign in 1234, for instance, he seems to foresee in global terms how this conflict would unfold – first by the winning of Burriana and its satellite fortresses and then by the conquest of the critical hill fortress of Puig de Cebolla that led to the eventual fall of Valencia and Jativa.[183] Since these events took place in the exact sequence Jaime had predicted so long before, one is left to ponder whether the Aragonese king was a military seer or whether he, like his fellow humans, was equipped with a human memory that occasionally distorted the circumstances of the life that it was set to record.

Despite his occasional melding of past and present military memories, Jaime was clearly capable of drawing up general military plans. In 1274, for example, when at the Council of Lyons, he engaged in theoretical planning for a new assault on the Holy Land. By this extempore instrument, he suggested that a crusading army could attain success by sending a small party to garrison Acre and prepare the way for a much larger invasion some two years later.[184] Though never acted on, this operational directive reflects the Aragonese king's cautious yet effective "way of conquering lands."[185] Like all other medieval generals, Jaime's practice of strategy "cannot be understood outside the context of siege warfare and the castle's military role."[186]

Behind the many aphorisms scattered through his autobiography are the military life lessons of a successful commander: "it is better to figure things out before hand than just to find them out;"[187] "it is better that damage happens to another rather than to us;"[188] "since times change, one should be prepared in advance;"[189] "the sooner one seeks advice on damage received, the better it

---

[182] Donald J. Kagay, "The Line between Memoir and History: James I of Aragon and the *Llibre del Feyts*," in *War*, study XII, p. 174.

[183] *BD*, pp. 138, 145–65, 188–89 (chaps. 129–31, 206). For the relationship of memory and historical consciousness, see Mary Carruthers, *The Book of Memory: A Study of Memory in Medieval Culture* (Cambridge, 1994), p. 193; *The Medieval Craft of Memory: An Anthology of Texts and Pictures*, ed. Mary Carruthers and Jan M. Ziolkowski (Philadelphia, 2002), p. 39.

[184] *BD*, pp. 363–64 (chaps. 531–32).

[185] *BD*, p. 323 (chap. 455).

[186] Sean McGlynn, "The Myths of Medieval Warfare," *History Today* 44(1) (January, 1994), 32.

[187] *BD*, p. 178 (chap. 193); Burns, "Spiritual Life," p. 23.

[188] *BD*, p. 290 (chap. 388); Burns, "Spiritual Life," pp. 23–24.

[189] *BD*, p. 275 (chap. 366); Burns, "Spiritual Life," p. 24.

is."[190] With these and many other precepts learned from hard experience, Jaime became a master of an Iberian style of fighting that preferred steady siege operations advanced by repeated pillaging raids to the winner-take-all dynamic of the pitched battle.[191]

Reconnaissance of lands to be attacked became a watchword for the Aragonese ruler who commenced none of his major campaigns before consulting with individuals who had knowledge of the enemy territories he prepared to invade.[192] The realities of travel and provisioning shortened yearly attacks, forcing the king to prioritize attacks on the strongest fortresses in a given district while sowing as much terror as possible among the surrounding Muslim population.[193] In this way, Aragonese armies won military and supply bases that often suggested the direction of the next year's campaigning. A string of such sites might also come into the Conqueror's hands without direct combat due to a combination of Muslim fear and the king's well-known reputation for granting ostensibly liberal surrender terms.[194]

In sum, Jaime I stands as more of expert in tactical practicality than strategic theory. His armies (unknowingly following the counsel of Sun Tzu proffered centuries before) adapted to their Muslim enemies "as water does to the ground over which it flows."[195] The Aragonese king would surely have agreed with twentieth-century staff officers such as Helmuth von Moltke who counseled military adaptability rather than persistent and often-fatal adherence to a plan established before a campaign commenced.[196] Jaime clearly had military objectives when he led his army into the field, but as the expedition unfolded, his list of prioritized targets might alter as a result of unexpected enemy reactions or from his own desire to maintain administrative control over shifting situations.[197] His quick mind coupled with vast military experience allowed the

---

190 *BD*, p. 272 (chap. 361); Burns, "Spiritual Life," p. 24.

191 Philippe Contamine, *War in the Middle Ages*, trans. Michael Jones (Oxford, 1996), p. 219.

192 *BD*, pp. 69–70, 137–38 (chaps. 47, 128). Before the Balearics campaign, Jaime consulted with Pere Martell, a Catalan merchant who had traded throughout the archipelago. Before his attack on Valencia, he sought advice from his troublesome noble, Blasco de Alagon, who had traveled through the southern region when exiled from Jaime's lands.

193 Jaime's actions in this regard often seem to suggest the advice of the great military theorist of the nineteenth century, Carl von Clausewitz. Carl von Clausewitz, *On War*, ed. and trans. Michael Howard and Peter Paret (Princeton, 1989), pp. 456–59 (chap. 23); Michael Howard, *Clausewitz: A Very Short Introduction* (Oxford, 2002), p. 15.

194 After the siege of Burriana, for example, Peñiscola, Chivert, Polpis, and Almazora surrendered within a few days (*BD*, pp. 172–77 (chaps. 182–91)). For the mechanism of Jaime's peace treaties with Valencian Muslims, see Robert I. Burns, S.J., and Paul E. Chevedden, "Al-Azraq's Surrender Treaty with Jaume I and Prince Alfonso in 1245: Arabic Text and Valencian Context," *Der Islam* 66 (1989), 1–37; idem, *Negotiating Cultures: Bilingual Surrender Treaties in Muslim-Crusader Spain* (Leiden, 1999).

195 B. H. Liddell Hart, *Strategy* (New York, 1955), p. 13.

196 Howard, *Clausewitz*, pp. 64–65.

197 Like England's great crusading king, Richard I (1189–99), Jaime most often looked on the successful waging of war as "a matter of effective administration." John Gillingham, "Richard

Conqueror to assess in extremely logical terms the varied siege circumstances that confronted him on every expedition. He then transformed this "snap-shot" vision into a tactical certainty that manifested itself in clear orders.[198] This capability of well-conceived military thinking proved invaluable in both communicating plans to his captains and in holding to courses of action he believed in even when all of his subordinates opposed them.

Jaime I's Relations with his Armies

As with every medieval ruler, Jaime I spent much of his time in maintaining control over his people, many of whom sprang from origins almost as elevated as his own. The quandary of attaining the support of the king's over-mighty subjects and then directing it into channels he chose was nowhere more apparent than in the dynamics of the royal army. As a commander whose very life rested on maintaining discipline over his troops, Jaime often acted as a military instructor who issued and repeatedly explained instructions concerning group assembly and attack.[199] He constantly counseled the cautious approach toward Muslim positions, not so much for fear of the enemy, but because disordered attacks on small, Muslim contingents or fortified posts might lead to the loss of a great number of horses, and in the type of warfare he had spent his whole life waging "one horse … [was] worth more than twenty Saracens."[200]

While often harping on the benefits of indirect attacks that involved less danger to man or beast, the king surely knew but seldom admitted that his control over large segments of his army was superficial at best. In the first phases of the Balearic campaign when he had sent small units to reconnoiter Majorca's defenses, the king must have been shocked to hear that those very scouting parties had launched unbridled attacks against part of the city's garrison who had sallied out from the walls.[201] At Valencia, he categorically rejected a suggestion by one of his captains concerning mounting the final assault on the city under the cover of darkness since he knew too well that at night "men are not ashamed of behaving badly under arms."[202] Even while admitting that the control over his troops might be decreased in the heat of battle, he was quick to utilize and even depend on the frenzy of his attacking soldiers. In the final assault on Majorca, for instance, he instructed his men to maintain their attack (no matter how wild and disordered) until the city was taken.[203]

I and the Science of War in the Middle Ages," reprinted in *Medieval Warfare, 1000–1300*, ed. John France (Aldershot, 2006), p. 311.

[198]   *BD*, pp. 179, 218–19 (chaps. 194, 261).
[199]   *BD*, p. 304 (chap. 415).
[200]   Ibid., p. 84 (chap. 60).
[201]   Ibid., pp. 84–85 (chap. 60).
[202]   Ibid., p. 106 (chap. 83).
[203]   Ibid., pp. 104–05 (chap. 81).

With little realistic possibility of establishing complete power over the greatest members of his host, Jaime occasionally utilized psychological means to attain this end. At critical points in campaigns, he delivered stirring orations that bound his soldiers to the honorable and chivalric mission he had chosen for himself.[204] The inspirational effect the Aragonese king had on his troops was undeniable. A number of the king's greatest retainers made out wills before joining the army, convinced that they might not return from their military service.[205] When these premonitions came to pass – as with Guillem and Ramon de Montcada in the early Balearic expedition – Jaime, though sorely tempted to give in to grief, used such casualties as a way of firmly tying his men to the campaign's fundamental objective.[206] This is not to suggest that the Aragonese king displayed no affection for the men he served with. He risked his life to recover the bodies of the dead and attend to the wounds of the living.[207] The morale of his troops was a constant concern for a commander who maintained very little separation between himself and his men. He mingled with the common soldiers in the camp and on the front lines, always encouraging them to carry out "a good stroke of war."[208]

Jaime's expectations of his soldiers were at times even loftier than his affection for them, and, when disappointed, could bring a cruel and immediate response. When front-line troops, even those who had been wounded, dared to leave their comrades on the field to seek medical treatment, Jaime had only one name for them: traitor.[209] He applied this high standard to his own battlefield demeanor. When wounded in operations outside Valencia, he broke off the crossbow quarrel which had pierced through his helmet into his skull and "went away laughing so the army would not take alarm."[210] Despite the harsh standard the king often set for his men, their affection for him could at times not be contained. No example of this was more striking than his farewell speech in 1231 to a Balearic army he had spent over a year with. After tendering his heartfelt thanks for their loyal service neither he nor they managed any further words and remained silent "out of grief."[211]

Like his court and parliament, Jaime's army was a temporary organization that was completely dependent on his will for its very existence.[212] It mirrored both the bonds of loyalty and dissent that tied the Aragonese ruler to his subjects. As a young man engaging in his first martial action, Jaime, though the acclaimed sovereign of Aragon and Catalonia, was treated as a military novice by the army's principal commanders. His older vassals roughly instructed their

---

204 Ibid., pp. 104–05, 304 (chaps. 81, 415).
205 Miret i Sans, *Itinerari*, p. 108.
206 *BD*, pp. 90–93 (chaps. 66–68).
207 Ibid., pp. 91, 167 (chaps. 67, 173).
208 Ibid., pp. 96–97, 105, 129 (chaps. 72–73 82, 117).
209 Ibid., pp. 89, 201–02 (chaps. 64, 229).
210 Ibid., p. 221 (chap. 266).
211 Ibid., pp. 120–21 (chap. 105).
212 Luis Felipe Arregui Lucea, "La curia y las cortes en Aragón," *Argensola* 4 (1953), 2–3.

liege lord in the cautious way of fighting that would become a hallmark of his later generalship. Disregarding the dominance of the royal office, old hands in the Balearic campaign, such as the Montcada brothers and Nuño Sanchez, boxed their young charge's ears, while sarcastically referring to him as "a lion of combat."[213] When the young king's tactical exuberance and desire for glory got the better of him, resulting in his command of small parties of knights against much larger Muslim units, one of his senior captains talked to him as to a child: "your impetuousness on this day will be the cause of our death."[214] Remembering the lethal price his father had paid for disregarding battlefield caution, the king showed himself an extremely quick study who seldom neglected the advice of his senior subalterns.

Thanks to this rapid military learning curve, Jaime quickly realized how fraught with jealousy and dissension his armies could become. Though the baronial anarchy of his youth had been quieted by his tremendous success in Majorca and Valencia, Jaime was always aware how close it was to the surface in the operations of his host. In the Murcian campaign, after long experience as a military leader, Jaime had to lecture his troops concerning the noxious effect of private quarrels on an army's effectiveness. Unless the members of the army kept such disputes in check, he warned that "our army will be thrown into confusion and we will have to give up the campaign."[215] Many of these differences, however, had nothing to do with longstanding feuds, but rather centered on differing visions of the army's principal objectives. At several critical junctures of the Valencian war, his barons, convinced that the region could not be conquered in its entirety and that the king would lose his entire army if he maintained military operations, counseled their royal master to consolidate his gains and renew hostilities against the truncated Muslim state at some time in the future when his finances were repaired.[216] The Conqueror, incensed at what he perceived as traitorous attacks, swore he would not leave the battle zone until he had gained final victory.[217] Unfortunately, royal frustration often followed in the train of such righteous anger, since the king could not always afford to dispense with the service of the principal troublemakers, as their units often comprised the majority of his troops on hand. He was thus left to ruminate concerning the "disloyal and false people" who surrounded him,[218] ultimately concluding that "in the world there are no people as arrogant as knights are."[219] Such concerns were also aired by his constant supporters "who did not desert [the king] until death."[220] They grew furious at their lord who, in acting to keep

213 *BD*, p. 90 (chap. 65).
214 Ibid., p. 90 (chap. 64).
215 Ibid., p. 304 (chap. 415).
216 Ibid., pp. 204–6 (chaps. 233–34, 237).
217 Ibid., p. 99 (chap. 75).
218 Ibid., p. 165 (chap. 169).
219 Ibid., p. 206 (chap. 237).
220 Ibid., p. 165 (chap. 169).

the army together, forgave his "great vassals, [thus] emboldening them to do evil against him."[221]

Some of the disputes that wracked his armies had less to do with the king's rocky relationship with his barons and more with national and class fissures within his realms. When the source of these feuds sprang from ancient hatreds between the various nationalities he ruled, the king attempted to defuse such geopolitical differences by separating, Catalan, Aragonese, and southern French troops both in the siege camp and in the formations of the field army.[222]

This simple expedient could scarcely be applied to all matters that divided the army across class lines. Though after a set term of service all members of the royal host could expect to receive from the king a customary daily wage and to be reimbursed for any losses they might suffer on campaign,[223] the army often badly divided between the wealthier and poorer as well as the privileged and unprivileged soldiers. Despite Jaime's earnest attempts to quash them, these rifts widened exponentially when the question of plunder won from Muslim *Hispania* came up. In all of his major campaigns, the Aragonese king attempted to settle the fractious issue by imposing the legal and administrative principle of "booty-division" (*repartamiento*). After winning large swaths of Muslim territories, Jaime appointed commissions of royal officials known as "dividers" (*divisores, partidores*) whose principal duties were to remove Muslim populations from the largest urban sites of a conquered district and replace them with Christian settlers. The divisions allotted to the new settlers were by no means equal, with the Church, the nobility and the larger town councils gaining the lion's share of the captured property.[224] The written records of this process, the registers known as the *libros de repartamiento*, were issued after the final conquest and are essential for the understanding of how Christian polities with all their own class divisions were grafted on to societies that had been Muslim for six centuries.[225] Though from the long distance of historical investigation this

---

221 Ibid., p. 325 (chap. 459).

222 Ibid., pp. 37–38 (chap. 21). Though attempting to show no open preference between his various realms, Jaime, when especially angry with the Aragonese as in 1264 when they failed to aid the Murcian campaign, let slip his preference for Catalonia "as the most honorable land in Spain." When his southern French subjects failed to freely give him financial aid in the midst of his Holy Land crusade, Jaime accused them of being self-seeking and stingy vassals. Ibid., pp. 293, 244 (chaps. 392, 493).

223 For military salaries in the last half of Jaime's reign, see ACA, Cancillería real, R. 20, fols. 324, 345; Miret i Sans, *Itinerari*, pp. 442, 532–33; Carreras i Candi, "Creuada," pp. 124–30; Kagay, "Army Mobilization," p. 105. For reimbursement policies, see ACA, R. 20, fol. 350v; *BD*, p. 92 (chap. 68); Miret i Sans, *Itinerari*, p. 142; Donald J. Kagay, "The Town in Service of War in the Medieval Crown of Aragon," *De re militari* website, http://www.deremilitari.org (accessed 23 June 2008).

224 Robert I. Burns, S.J., *The Crusader Kingdom of Valencia: Reconstruction on a Thirteenth-Century Frontier* (Cambridge, Mass., 1967), pp. 104–5, 243–45.

225 "Repartamiento de Mallorca," in *CDACA*, 13:1–141; "Repartaminento de Valencia," in *CDACA*, 11:143–656; Miret i Sans, *Itinerari*, pp. 75–76.

process seems fairly logical, while not thoroughly fair to all parties, in the midst of a campaign it could be positively explosive.

With the conquest of Majorca, for instance, Jaime had to prevent his army from dissolving into a leaderless horde through its thirst for booty by first attempting to have everything won during the campaign divided among the feudal lords in the army who would then take over the process of distributing plunder to their own retainers. The wealthier members of his host, however, rejected this egalitarian solution and demanded that all plunder be divided into lots and sold at auction to the highest bidder. The king opposed this solution as a "cheating transaction," disadvantageous to the poorer members of his army, but gave in to pressure from the "best people" and allowed the sale to go forward. This sparked a riot among "the knights and the common people" and only after they had vented their anger against their richer colleagues for several days was the royal commander able to restore peace by promising an equitable division of unsold plunder to the poorer members of his host.[226] This course of events, so profoundly shocking to Jaime, served to remind him in graphic terms that his army was a microcosm of his realms, complete with class hatreds and fears.[227]

When war lapsed into the fragile peace that followed each of Jaime's major campaigns, the king's army dissolved yet again into its component parts. The men who served in combat, however, never escaped the shadow of their military experience. They remained bound to the king by the duty of military service they owed him both as sovereign and feudal lord as well as by ties of appreciation for favors he had bestowed on them after successful tours of duty. Because of the "labors and immense expenses" many of his town councils had incurred during expeditions taking place in their vicinity, the king attempted to compensate these bodies for all the fiscal hardships they had undergone by exempting them from all royal taxation for up to five years.[228] To further show his gratitude, the king repeatedly cajoled his officials to expedite the repayment of loans made by these corporate bodies in support of military operations.[229] He could not forget, however, that his lands were surrounded by dangerous frontiers and war could commence again without warning. For this reason, soldiers cashiered out of military service were never far from the battlefield. Garrison duty along the Aragonese and Valencian border thus continued for vassals who held fortresses and fiefs in these dangerous regions.[230] What is more, the danger inherent along

---

[226] ACA, Cancillería real, Pergaminos de Jaime I, nos. 365, 384; *BD*, pp. 110–12 (chaps. 89–91); *DJI*, 1:213–15 (docs. 113, 124). The poorer soldiers said they had engaged in rioting because they were "dying of hunger" after the long siege.

[227] For a similar phenomenon in crusading armies, see Christopher Tyerman, "'Princeps et Populus': Civil Society and the First Crusade," in *Cross, Crescent and Conversion: Studies on Medieval Spain and Christendom in Memory of Richard Fletcher*, ed. Simon Barton and Peter Linehan (Leiden, 2008), pp. 127–51.

[228] ACA, Cancillería real, R. 13, fol. 285; R. 15, fol. 87v; Burns, *Diplomatarium*, 3:191–93, 319 (docs. 652ª, 764ª); *DJI*, 1:263–64 (doc. 146); 4:101 (doc. 1007); Miret i Sans, *Itinerari*, p. 108.

[229] ACA, Cancillería real, R. 14, fol. 114; R. 21, fol. 34; Miret i Sans, *Itinerari*, pp. 447, 464.

[230] ACA, Cancillería real, R. 15, fol. 32; Burns, *Diplomatarium*, 3:248 (doc. 764ª).

these frontiers could even override exemptions to royal military service and induce the king to call cashiered units back to active duty.[231] By and large, men in his earliest campaigns viewed military service with Jaime as a profitable venture which they did not oppose engaging in more than once. In the last decades of the Conqueror's life, however, few Muslim lands remained to be conquered and men increasingly hid behind national custom to avoid risking their lives in economically useless wars.

Jaime I's Psychological Relationship to War

Because of his sad youth and the glorious accomplishments of his young adulthood, Jaime I might have looked on himself as a self-made man who could attribute his amazing military successes to both talent and determination. For the Conqueror, however, human war was fought "in partnership with God."[232] Even if defeat loomed, the Aragonese king felt protected by Jesus and Mary, who were the ultimate intercessors before God for military triumph.[233] He looked on himself and his men as the vassals of the Almighty who engaged in battle with the infidels to either convert or destroy them.[234] This certainly gave rise to a comfortable circular argument for both the king and his subjects; that is, Jaime's "power and advancement" were "works of God" and his feats of military prowess brought about "the honor of God and of all the heavenly court."[235] With this kind of rock-hard attitude in place when he stepped on the battlefield, Jaime and many of his great men essentially saw human conflict in cosmic terms. As his relative and right-hand man, Nuño Sanchez, said, the war against Islam was a "good and meritorious work" as well as a "work of God."[236] Since, for the Aragonese king, human death is part of God's plan,[237] the king had no fear of it and counseled his men to feel the same. Though he grieved when his comrades fell in battle, he was never inconsolable since he was certain they "died in God's service" and this assured their glorious entry into heaven.[238] To hedge his bets in this regard, the king frequently attended Mass and confessed his sins, often encouraging his troops to do so on the eve of battle.[239]

---

231 *DJI*, 2:299 (doc. 489).
232 Burns, "Spiritual Life," p. 10.
233 Ibid., p. 16.
234 *BD*, p. 86 (chap. 61).
235 *BD*, p. 75 (chap. 52).
236 Ibid., p. 74 (chap. 51).
237 The equality of death for the rich and poor, young and old, is a topos in many of Jaime's battle orations. Ibid., pp. 151, 188, 205–06 (chaps. 147, 207, 236); Burns, "Spiritual Life," p. 17.
238 *BD*, p. 188 (chap. 207).
239 Ibid., pp. 34, 50, 86, 133, 157, 172, 179, 193, 198, 202–03, 205, 241, 248, 251, 271, 273, 285, 319, 321, 378 (chaps. 19, 31, 61, 122, 156, 183, 194, 217, 224, 230, 232, 236, 303, 314, 321, 361, 364, 380, 445, 451, 562); Burns, "Spiritual Life," p. 15,

Even though Jaime's "good deeds" (*bons feyts*, *bones obres*) were ultimately attributable to God who used the Aragonese king as a military pawn of sorts, he was also certain that Almighty directed him "to leave a good reputation through the good works we do."[240] His drive to bequest a "good name" to posterity was also connected to the royal office he possessed. Kingship thus forced on Jaime a demeanor that was complementary to his role as a warrior. He held in his hands justice and protection for all his subjects, especially the weaker ones. In effect, God chose him as both ruler and soldier "to do right."[241] This tie between successful king and triumphant soldier embodied in Jaime was obvious during the final assault on Murcia in 1266 when he urged his sons, Pedro and Jaime, to fight honorably so "everyone will recognize who you are and from where you came." If they failed to comport themselves well in light of the lofty offices they held, he threatened to disinherit them.[242]

Perhaps because of the upheavals of his early childhood that was marked by fear of family disintegration, Jaime was determined to display his courage, especially when he commanded an army. This bravado, as we have seen, was quickly knocked out of him by more experienced military commanders. Though they taught him a more cautious way of war, Jaime never devalued courage as a way of inspiring the troops and even recognized bravery in his enemies.[243] When wounded, he continued to fight and only tended to his wounds after the battle was decided. He treated as cowards or worse those of his men who did not maintain this high standard. When one of his soldiers, a famous tournament champion, left the field heavily bleeding with a cut on his upper lip, Jaime sarcastically informed him that a "good knight" did not desert his post for such a minor wound.[244]

Even with his determination to display his courage before the troops, Jaime actions sometimes concealed the feelings of inadequacy he carried with him to the battlefield. He brought along on every major campaign "a good sword from Monzón," nicknamed La Tizóna after one of the Cid's mighty weapons. Though carrying it on to the battlefield, the king never wielded it, using it, instead, to produce good luck for his military enterprises.[245] Despite such paranormal guarantees of ultimate success, Jaime seemed plagued with deep doubts and an almost paranoid fear of admitting that he was afraid of breaking off military engagements since this might communicate weakness to his troops. If the choice was presented him, he preferred either injury or death to the lamentable fate of being publically branded a coward.[246]

---

240 *BD*, pp. 16, 71, 151, 236 (chaps. 1, 48, 147, 292); Burns, "Spiritual Life," pp. 8–9.
241 *BD*, pp. 51–52, 55, 57 (chaps. 32, 34, 36). For theories of good and bad rulership in medieval Iberia, see Donald J. Kagay, "Rule and Mis-Rule in Medieval Iberia," in *War*, study IV, pp. 48–66.
242 *BD*, p. 311 (chap. 427).
243 Ibid., pp. 32, 84 (chaps. 16, 60); Burns, "Spiritual Life," p. 18.
244 *BD*, p. 89 (chap. 64).
245 Ibid., p. 168 (chap. 174).
246 Ibid., pp. 165, 208 (chaps. 169, 239).

When this kind of primal insecurity loomed, however, the king fell back on his feudal relationship with God and this invariably renewed his confidence and buoyed his certainty that "the light of good works dispels darkness."[247]

Conclusion

Jaime I never resigned from the profession of soldering. In this sixty-eighth year, he responded rapidly to an uprising of his Muslim subjects in southern Valencia as he had for the past five decades: after scouting the territory around the rebels' fortresses, he ordered the devastation of all crop land that could help sustain a besieged garrison. He then issued a general military summons, but before it could be properly acted on by his vassals, the great warrior fell ill and started giving orders through his son, Pedro.[248] Before his malady worsened, the Conqueror addressed the crown prince and his greatest nobles. Summarizing his life's work, he thanked God for his sixty-two-year reign ("longer than any king in the memory of man") as well as for "the love and affection of his people."[249] When he died on 27 July 1276, the great king's body was taken across Valencia and Catalonia to the burial site of Aragonese kings, the Cistercian monastery of Poblet. Following the bier was a cortege swollen by mourners of all ages and classes. At the end of this doleful procession came ten horses whose tails had been bobbed in Turkish fashion in honor of the deceased sovereign.[250] One of the clearest assessments of the character Jaime projected to the outside world came from a chivalric poet of contemporary Galicia:

> The King of Aragon is a king of good sense
> a king of merit, a king of all good
> a true king of Aragon.[251]

Though Jaime had enjoined his son to live up to his glorious record[252] and Pedro himself burned "to follow the praiseworthy footsteps of his predecessors,[253] there was very little left to do when he finally suppressed the Muslim revolt in 1277.[254] With the Murcian war of 1265–66, the Aragonese reconquest had effectively

---

247 Ibid., p. 71 (chap. 48).
248 *BD*, pp. 375–78 (chaps. 555–60); Robert I. Burns, S.J., "Muslim-Christian Conflict and Contact in Medieval Spain: Context and Methodology," *Thought* 54 (1979), 248; idem, "Los mudejares de Valencia: Temas y metodologia," in *Actas del I simposio internacional de mude-jarismo* (Madrid, 1981), pp. 468–69.
249 *BD*, p. 378 (chap. 562).
250 Ramon Muntaner, *Chronicle*, trans. Lady Goodenough (Cambridge, Ont., 2000), p. 58 (chap. 28).
251 Quoted in O'Callaghan, *Reconquest*, p. 105.
252 Muntaner, *Chronicle*, p. 58 (chap. 28).
253 *The Chronicle of San Juan de la Peña: A Fourteenth-Century Official History of the Crown of Aragon*, trans. Lynn H. Nelson (Philadelphia, 1991), p. 71 (chap. 36).
254 Desclot, *Chronicle*, 1:3–7 (chap. 1–2).

come to an end. By treaty, Aragon was cut off from the conquest of any further Andalusian land.[255] This vast territory was reserved for a Castilian conquest that took almost two centuries to complete. Aragonese arms, diverted from the Iberian Peninsula, spilled over into north Africa and finally across the central Mediterranean. Tied by marriage to the Hohenstaufen heiress, Constanza, Pedro took on a new and powerful enemy in the person of the French prince, Charles of Anjou.[256] Winning Sicily in 1282, Aragonese kings engaged in a twenty-year war with the Angevins that made them the rulers of a central Mediterranean power with outposts stretching from Calgiari to Palermo to Athens.[257] The scope of these conquests was no accident, but is rather attributable to armies hardened in the throes of reconquest warfare.[258] This same phenomenon would recur after 1492 when the attitudes and techniques of the Castilian reconquest would underpin Iberian victories in the New World.[259] Like his Castilian counterparts, Fernando III (r.1217–52) and Alfonso XI (r.1312–50), Jaime I thus unleashed a flood tide of conquest that grew in magnitude with the Catholic Kings and carried Spain (unready as it was in many ways) into the modern world.

In military terms, Jaime I must be considered a full-fledged member of a crusading elite of the twelfth and thirteenth centuries which surely includes Richard I of England (r.1189–99), Saladin, caliph of Egypt (r.1173–93), Fernando III and Alfonso X of Castile, and Louis IX of France (r.1226–70). Like Saladin and Fernando, he seldom went on the defensive, but fought every campaign as a series of attacks that would build toward ultimate victory. Unlike Alfonso, Louis and Richard, his knowledge of war was almost entirely based on practical experience and was scarcely instructed by classical military models at all. Yet, like all of these contemporary figures, Jaime had experienced defeat, but had learned from his losses to attain one stunning success after another. These victories were accomplished in the face of a baronial and urban opposition that endured through all his great campaigns and eventually in his last decades brought a large portion of the Aragonese and Valencian population against his military enterprises. Like the other accomplished generals of his day, then, the

---

[255] For the treaty of Almizra which began this delineation in 1244, *DJI*, 2:176–77 (doc. 388).

[256] E. L. Miron, *The Queens of Aragon: Their Lives and Times* (London, 1913), pp. 111–37; Jean Dunbabin, *Charles I of Anjou: Power, Kingship and State-Making in Thirteenth-Century Europe* (London, 1998), pp. 99–101.

[257] The exact nature of Aragonese holdings has been a matter of some disagreement with J. Lee Shneiman declaring that the Aragonese kings established an "empire" in the Mediterranean and Jocelyn Hillgarth vehemently denying it. Shneiman, *Rise*, 2:354; Jocelyn N. Hillgarth, *The Problem of a Catalan Mediterranean Empire* (London, 1975).

[258] Roger Sablonier, *Krieg und Kriegertum in der Crónica des Ramon Muntaner: Eine Studie zum spätmittelalterlichen Kriegswesen aufgrund katalnischer Quellen* (Berne, 1971).

[259] Paul Stewart, "The Soldier, the Bureaucrat and Fiscal Records in the Army of Ferdinand and Isabella," *The Hispanic American Historical Review* 49 (1969), 292; Donald J. Kagay, "Columbus as Standardbearer and Mirror of the Spanish Reconquest," *American Neptune* 53 (1994), 254–60.

Aragonese king persisted to win most of his military objectives through skill, good fortune, and most of all, by unbending determination.

Appendix

Major Military Conflicts of Jaime I

Dates	Type of war/enemies	Outcome
1222–24	Domestic: Guillem de Montcada, Prince Fernando, Pedro Ahones	Peace settlement between Cabrera and Montcada
1225	Reconquest: siege of Peñiscola (Valencia)	Truce bought by tribute from Zeit Abuzeit
1228	Domestic: Guerau de Cabrera, Ramon Folç III de Cardona	Defeat of Cabrera
1229–32	Reconquest [crusade]: invasion of Balearic Islands	Conquest of Majorca and Minorca
1234–38	Reconquest [crusade]: invasion of Valencia	Conquest down to Valencia city
1244–45	Reconquest [crusade]: invasion of southern Valencia. Caused by Al-Azraq's revolt.	Conquest of Jativa and Biar. Al-Azraq undefeated
1259–62	Domestic: Aragonese nobility led by Cardona and Cabrera clans	Renewal of feudal ties between king and nobles
1264–66	Domestic: all Aragonese *ricoshombres*	General truce. Issuance of Fueros of Exea – 1265
1265–66	Reconquest: invasion with Castile of Kingdom of Murcia	Conquest of Murcia. Turned over to Alfonso X of Castile
1267	Domestic: Ferriz de Lizana	Capture of Lizana. Execution of Ferriz de Lizana
1268–72	Domestic: Benat III of Foix, Ramon Folç IV of Cardona	Peace treaty – 1272
1269	Projected Acre crusade	Jaime abandons project. Several small units of his retainers get to Acre

| 1272–75 | Domestic: Ferran Sanchis de Castro, Foix and Cardona, retainers | Death of Ferran Sanchis de Castro Peace treaty – 1275 |
| 1276–77 | Reconquest: uprising of Al-Azraq and Andalusian Muslims | Pedro III defeats Al-Azraq in 1277 |

4

Numbers in Mongol Warfare

Carl Sverdrup

The Mongols created the largest land empire known to history during the thirteenth century. It was an empire created by means of military conquest. The military successes of the Mongols are now generally seen as a result of superior weaponry, tactics, and organization. Historians have rejected the older view that the Mongols greatly outnumbered their foes, holding instead that the Mongols were in fact generally outnumbered.[1] The Mongol run of conquests took them all the way into Central Europe. At Mohi in 1241, they defeated a Hungarian army. It is not known how large the armies were at Mohi, but it has been estimated that each side had more than 50,000 men. Such numbers are hard to reconcile with the reality of the medieval world where the King of France and the Emperor of Germany, two of the most powerful men in Europe, each struggled to get more than 2,000 horsemen and 10,000 men in total on a single battlefield in 1214.[2] When Edward I of England, another powerful European ruler, invaded Scotland in 1300 he fielded 700 horsemen. He aimed to raise 16,000 infantry, but only managed to get 9,000 and this total quickly dropped to 6,000.[3] It seems unlikely Hungary could field an army many times larger than those fielded by the rulers of Germany, France, or England. It will be argued in this article that the Mongol forces were in fact much smaller than generally accepted, though they were larger on the battlefield than the enemy armies. To construct the argument, the numbers of the Mongol armies and their foes will be considered at the various stages of the Mongol westward advance. Finally, the numbers involved in the Chinese wars will also be considered.

The size of the Mongol armies is far from clear and has been the subject of intense scholarly debate, most notably between David Morgan and John Masson Smith. Morgan is not willing to accept that the Mongol field army which attacked Khwarizm in 1220 was up to 800,000 men strong, as some near contemporary sources have it. He uses logistical considerations to show that a high total is

---

1 Robert Cowley and Geoffrey Parker, eds., *The Osprey Companion to Military History* (London, 1996), pp. 308–09 and Ernest Dupuy and Trevor Dupuy, *The Harper Encyclopedia of Military History* (New York, 1993), pp. 367–73.
2 See J. F. Verbruggen, *The Art of Warfare in Western Europe during the Middle Ages* (Woodbridge, 1997), pp. 239–52.
3 Christopher Candy, *An Exercise in Frustration: The Scottish Campaign of Edward I, 1300* (Durham, 1999), pp. 20, 26, 44.

unlikely.[4] On the other hand Smith accepts high army totals, supporting his view with estimates of population size. He holds that: "The Mongol conquests were the product of the irresistible combination of skill and numbers."[5] Few scholars support the position of Smith, though they still consider high army totals likely. For example, Denis Sinor says that the Mongols were opposed by a Khwarizmian army of 400,000 men in 1220. He also says that 105,000 to 150,000 Mongols struck into Central Europe in 1241 where the central column fought against 65,000 Hungarians at Mohi.[6] The Hungarian historian Kosztolnyik estimated that the Mongols and Hungarians had both around 50,000 men in that battle.[7] Desmond Martin is one of a few Western authors to have dealt with the Mongol campaigns in China in detail. He credits the Mongols with 110,000 men when they first attacked central China in 1211 and says that in one battle they faced a Jin army with 300,000 men (including some non combatants).[8] It can be concluded that opinions vary about the size of Mongol armies and of those fielded by their enemies, but generally the armies are held to be very large.

Near-contemporary sources provide two good numbers for the size of the early Mongol army.[9] The *Secret History of the Mongols* records that Cinggis Qan had a total of 105,000 soldiers in 1206.[10] Rashid al-Din says he had 129,000 soldiers in 1227. The latter total excluded some distantly located units[11] and it included 27,000 men from units added after 1206, which came mainly from Liaodong (Manchuria).[12] Without the forces added later, Rashid al-Din has 102,000, or 3,000 less than the *Secret History*'s total. This difference could be explained by units left to guard the western regions.[13] It therefore seems that the total number of "Mongol" soldiers was quite constant from 1206 to 1227. Within the Mongol soldiers, 20,000 served with Muqali in China after 1217.[14] When Cinggis Qan marched against Mohammad II of Khwarizm in 1219, he

4   David Morgan, *The Mongols* (Oxford, 1986), p. 88.
5   John Masson Smith, "Mongol Manpower and the Persian Population," *Journal of the Economic and Social History of the Orient* 18 (1975), 272.
6   Denis Sinor, "The Mongols in the West," *Journal of Asian History* 33 (1999).
7   Z. J. Kosztolnyik, *Hungary in the Thirteenth Century* (Columbia, 1996), p. 155.
8   Desmond Martin, *The Rise of Chingis Khan and his Conquest of North China* (Baltimore, 1950), pp. 11–47. He credits the Mongols and Khwarizmians with respectively 150,000 and 400,000 men in 1220.
9   Both David Morgan (*Mongols*, pp. 86–87) and John Masson Smith ("Mongol Manpower," pp. 273–74) accept this.
10   *Secret History*, ed. Igor de Rachewiltz (Leiden, 2004), p. 202.
11   Rashid al-Din, *Rashiduddin Fazlullah's Jamiut-tawarikh (Compendium of Chronicles)*, ed. W. M. Thackston, 3 vols. (Cambridge, MA, 1998–99), 2:400–414. Hereafter cited as Rashid al-Din.
12   The units of Uyar Wanshai and Tughan Wanshai as well as the Qoshaqun and Oyirat tribes.
13   Alaq for example may have been at Khojend. See Igor de Rachewiltz, *In the Service of the Khan: Eminent Personalities of the Early Mongol-Yuan Period (1200–1300)* (Wiesbaden, 1992), p. 584.
14   Details on who served with Muqali are given by Rashid al-Din (1:333–34) and the *Sheng-wu Chin-cheng-lu* (3395), see Wang Guowei, *Meng-ku shih liao ssu chung* (Taipei, 1970).

left his brother Otchgin to look after Mongolian affairs. In addition his mother remained behind and Rashid al-Din notes that Udutai did not go on campaign. Consequently at least 9,000 soldiers should therefore have been left in Mongolia. Further, an officer called Qacin operated in Korea in 1218.[15] Allowing him no more than 3,000 Mongol soldiers means Cinggis Qan could have marched west with more than 75,000 men.[16] The subject tribes west of the Altai provided some additional forces, though hardly more than a few hundred men each.[17]

All the Mongol numbers so far given are totals formed by adding together units of 1,000 soldiers. These units were called *mingghans*. The nominal totals are unlikely to have been the same as actual or effective totals. Even if a unit had men on paper, some would have been sick or for some other reason unavailable during the campaigns. The effective total of the Mongol army was likely 70–80% of the nominal total.[18] The percentage of effectives should have been high when the army set out from home territory with a gradual decrease as time passed. In addition, the Mongols detached significant forces to guard their spare horses. When Wanyen Hota and the Jin officers discussed what to do in the wake of a battle against Toli and Sube'etei in January 1232, it was said: "The Mongol Army is known as [having] 30,000 soldiers, but their impedimenta [guard] take up one-third ..."[19] The camp guard and the horses were normally stationed in a position some distance behind the army. In 1221, for example, Sube'etei and Chepe "... secured their bags and baggage in the marshy, muddy place which lies between the cities of Bartaw and Belukan."[20] Consequently if Cinggis Qan had a nominal total of some 75,000 men in 1219, he had, after dispatching a part to guard the camp, and allowing for a lower effective total, 35,000 to 40,000 men ready for combat.

Once Cinggis Qan arrived close to Otrar on the Khwarizmian border in late 1219, he split his forces into four divisions. Joci, his oldest son, marched up along the Jaxartes River, while Ogedai and Ca'adai, the third and second sons, started to besiege Otrar. Presumably they operated with at least their own guard units. Alaq, Sogetu (Siktur?), and Taqai were sent towards Khojend, again prob-

15 William E. Henthorn, *Korea: The Mongol Invasions* (Leiden, 1963), pp. 32–33.
16 Including the Oyirats.
17 Idiqut supported Chepe with 300 men in 1217–18. See Ata-Malik Juvaini, *The History of the World Conqueror*, ed. John Andrew Boyle (Manchester, 1958), p. 46; hereafter cited as Juvaini. When a Mongol army marched into Persia in 1230, the western subjects provided 1 of the 3 or 4 total *tumens*. See Rashid al-Din, 1:54.
18 The sources do not give examples of actual number counts. A check of Chinese units in Mongol service in 1241 found these were 7.5% below the nominal strength. On active campaign this total should logically be lower. See Chi-ch'ing Hsiao, *The Military Establishment of the Yuan Dynasty* (London, 1978), p. 75. Smith estimates that the units on average had 70% of the nominal total. See John Masson Smith, "The Nomads' Armament: Home Made Weapons," in *Religion, Customary Law, and Nomadic Technology*, Toronto Studies in Central and Inner Asia, no. 4 (2000), ed. Michael Gervers and Wayne Schlepp (Toronto, 2000), p. 53.
19 Tuotuo, *Jin Shi* (Beijing, 1975), p. 112.
20 K. A. Melik'-Ohanjanyan, *Patmut'iwn Hayoc*, ed. Kirakos Ganjakec'i (Erevan, 1961), p. 202. Translated text: http://rbedrosian.com/kg7.htm

ably with their own units.[21] Cinggis Qan and the main column were therefore left with about 60,000 men as a nominal total and some 30,000 effectives ready for combat. Mohammad II was urged by his son Jalal al-Din to accept battle. Others favored avoiding battle.[22] What was in this situation the best strategy for the Shah to follow?

Mongol forces had operated in West Liao territory, just east of Khwarizm, since the winter of 1216–17. Mohammad II and Jalal al-Din assembled an army in early 1219 and marched against a Mongol army led by Joci, Sube'etei, Chepe, and Toquchar. A battle fought along the Irghiz River was indecisive. Sube'etei, Chepe, and Toquchar were later (in May 1220) sent across the Oxus with 10,000 men[23] while it is known that Joci had a 4,000-man personal guard. Therefore it may be estimated that Joci and the commanders with him had a nominal total of 14,000 in 1219. The Mongol base camp had actually been overrun by Mohammad before the battle[24] so on this occasion the camp guard might have fought with the main forces. If so, the Mongol could have fielded 10,000 or more effectives. The army of Mohammad was not a small one raised quickly either, for Mohammad specifically returned to Samarkand to gather more forces before setting out against the Mongols.[25] To reach the battlefield Mohammad had to march 1200 kilometers through the plains north of the Aral Lake. It is possible he only had cavalry. Mohammad is credited with 60,000 men,[26] but the battle between the two sides was a balanced parallel encounter and it therefore seems unlikely that Mohammad's army was many times larger than the Mongol one. In fact, it is likely that his soldiers were on average better armed than the Mongols and held an edge in man to man fighting.[27] If anything, he had 6,000 men rather than 60,000.

When Cinggis Qan struck towards Bokhara and Samarkand in 1220, he was this time getting closer to the home territory of Mohammad who therefore might have been able to field slightly larger forces than the year before. Even so, Cinggis Qan's army was far too large for Mohammad to contemplate a set-piece battle. Having been unable to defeat a smaller Mongol army in 1219, what could Mohammad do against an army many times stronger? Never before had such a massive army invaded Transoxiana from the north. Mohammad could not expect that Cinggis Qan was able to field such large forces so far from his homeland. Mohammad is generally censured for his inept conduct, but retreating into Iran while leaving the cities to hold out as best they could was a logical action. Even

---

[21] Estimated at 3,000 men. Juvaini, p. 91, credits them with 5,000.

[22] Juvaini, p. 376.

[23] *Yuan Shi*, ed. Sung Lien (Beijing, 1976), p. 121; see Jean-Pierre Abel-Remusat, *Nouveaux mélanges asiatiques*, vol. 2 (Paris, 1829), p. 91.

[24] Ibn al-Athir, *The Chronicle of Ibn al-Athir for the Crusading Period from al-Kamil fi'l-Ta'rikh*, ed. and trans. D. S. Richards, vol. 3 (Aldershot, 2008), p. 209.

[25] Juvaini, p. 370.

[26] Nasawi, *Histoire du Sultan Djelal el-Din Mankobirti*, ed. O. Houdas (Paris, 1895), p. 16.

[27] See Aresenio Martinez, "Some Notes on the Il-xanid Army," *Archivum Eurasiae Medii Aevi* 6 (1986), 144–45.

if he had concentrated his forces south of the Oxus, he would not have been able to hold the Mongols off. There was, however, no escape for Mohammad. Cinggis Qan sent forces to hunt him down. Five months later he was dead.

Contemporary Muslim historians say Cinggis Qan had 600,000 or 700,000 men while Mohammad II had 400,000.[28] The Mongol total is almost 10 times as high as the estimate arrived at above (using the nominal total). Possibly the total for the Khwarizmian army is exaggerated by the same magnitude. It seems indeed quite possible that Mohammad had 40,000 soldiers, though these were spread over a large area. It is certain that all sources considered the Mongol army to be significantly larger than the forces of Mohammad. The Muslim historians often get Mongol army totals wrong because they count a *tumen* as 10,000 men. A *tumen* is a larger unit containing several *mingghans*, but hardly 10. In Chinese "10,000" can simply mean a large number. It is quite clear that when Cinggis Qan detached an officer with several *mingghans*, he usually gave him 2, 3 or 4 *mingghans*. Toquchar was sent across the Altai Mountains with 2 *mingghans* in 1211,[29] Alaq had 3 in 1220,[30] Joci Qasar operated with 3 (in addition to his own guard unit) in 1215,[31] while Sube'edei, Chepe, and Toqachar had 10 together in 1220.[32]

When Cinggis Qan marched against Jelal al-Din during the second half of 1221, he had a nominal total of more than 50,000 men.[33] For the battle fought along the Indus, he probably had at least 25,000 effectives at his disposal. Jelal al-Din probably had about 3,000 horsemen and was therefore seriously outnumbered. The core of his forces consisted of a 700-man bodyguard unit.[34] Jelal al-Din could not hope to win this battle, and indeed the larger Mongol forces encircled him and attacked from all open sides. Jelal al-Din managed to escape, but lost most of his men.[35]

Joci, the eldest son of Cinggis Qan, died in 1227. Batu, Joci's second son, inherited his position as ruler of the western territory. He camped near the Aral Lake with the 4,000 men associated with his father plus additional local recruits (maybe 6,000).[36] Batu attempted to conquer the Bulgars in 1232, but his army was not strong enough to overcome them. He asked Ogedai for help.

---

[28] Minhaj al-din Juzjani, *Tabakat-i-Nasiri: A General History of the Muhammadan Dynasties of Asia*, ed. and trans. H. G. Raverty, vol. 2 (Calcutta, 1895), p. 968; Rashid al-Din, 2:346.

[29] Rashid al-Din, 1:320.

[30] Juvaini, p. 91.

[31] *Secret History*, p. 253.

[32] *Yuan Shi*, 121, p. 91. David Morgan also doubts a *tumen* consisted of 10,000 men, noting that in Yuan China the unit was between 3,000 and 7,000 men strong (*Mongols*, p. 72).

[33] Sube'etei was in Persia with 10,000 men and Joci remained in the north. Some additional forces had been left behind to guard Transoxiana.

[34] Juvaini, p. 410.

[35] Juvaini, p. 409.

[36] Vassaf says they increased their forces to 10,000, but as this means a *tumen* it cannot be taken as a secure number. See Thomas Allsen, "The Princes of the Left Hand," *Archivum Eurasiae Medi Aevi* 5 (1987), 10.

The *Qan* agreed to send Sube'etei. Ca'adai proposed that each son of Cinggis Qan provided two of their sons to support Sube'etei, meaning six grandsons. In addition Kolgan, a son of Cinggis Qan, came along. The princes brought with them 10,000 to 16,000 guard soldiers. In addition Sube'etei selected more than 17,000 other soldiers.[37] With the forces Batu already had, the full western army was therefore nominally at least 37,000 to 43,000 men strong. Sube'etei gained a quick victory over the Bulgars and had taken all their major cities by early 1237. The size of the Bulgar army is not known, but they are likely to have fielded much less cavalry than Sube'etei.[38]

The Mongols moved west from Bulgar territory into the Rus territory before the end of 1237. Individually the Rus states could probably only field a few thousand horsemen so they needed to unite in order to have a chance against the Mongols.[39] The Mongols, however, operated with three separate columns that threatened the states of Chernigov, Raizan, as well as Vladimir-Suzdal. The threatened states were reluctant to send forces to support their neighbors. Each Mongol column was much larger than any force fielded by a single Rus state outside the cities. At Yaroslavl, two Mongol columns converged on the largest of the Rus armies. The Mongols encircled and destroyed the outnumbered Rus.[40] Kolgan was killed during the operations against the Rus in early 1238. Guyuk and Mangku returned home in 1240. It is not known if Kolgan's guard was withdrawn, but Guyuk and Mangku certainly took a part of the army with them. On the other hand soldiers were recruited from the conquered tribes in Russia.[41] That could explain why Kolgan had 4,000 men in 1227 whereas his son Qucha inherited 6,000 in 1238.[42]

In total, Sube'etei and Batu's army could still have counted around 40,000 men when they struck into Central Europe in 1241. Of these a third were probably left behind somewhere close to the Dnjepr River to guard the main camp and the spare horses. The Mongols split their army into five columns. One of these struck into Poland. A near-contemporary source credits this column with 10,000 men,[43] meaning probably one *tumen*. As discussed earlier, a *tumen* did not need to be of 10,000 men. In Poland, Baidar had his own unit and Orda

---

[37] Including the units of Sube'etei, Koki, Mogatu, and Moqur Quaran, Rashid al-Din, 1:198, 2:152.

[38] The travelling priest Julianus credits the Bulgars with 50,000 fighting men. See Hansgerd Gockenjan and James R. Sweeney, *Der Mongolen-sturm* (Graz, 1985), p. 104. Such a high total is unlikely, though many men could be mobilized for the defence of cities.

[39] John Fennell, *The Crisis of Medieval Russia 1200–1304* (London, 1983), p. 85. He estimates the large cities could field 3,000 to 5,000 fighting men, but only a part of these were horsemen.

[40] The Novgorod Chronicle records: "... Yuri sent out Dorozh to scout ... and Dorozh came running, and said: 'They have already surrounded us ...'" *Novgorod Chronicle*, ed. and trans. Robert Mitchell and Nevill Forbes (London, 1914), p. 83.

[41] R. A. Skelton, Thomas E. Marston and George D. Painter, *The Vinland Map and the Tartar Relation* (New Haven, 1965), p. 80. Hereafter cited as *Tartar Relation*.

[42] Rashid al-Din, 2:411.

[43] *Tartar Relation*, p. 80.

commanded his share of his family's forces. With additional recruits from Russia, their *tumen* might have had somewhat more than 3,000 men, but not 10,000. The Mongols defeated the main Polish army at Legnica (9 April 1241). One modern historian estimates that the Poles had 2,000 men,[44] another puts the total higher at 7,000–8,000 men.[45] The lower total seems reasonable given the size of the Mongol army. Perhaps both sides had about 2,000 effectives on the battlefield. The Mongols prevailed after some hard fighting.[46] The aim of this Mongol column was to distract Poland and prevent the Polish lords from supporting Hungary, the main Mongol target. Poland was at this time split into four feuding principalities and struggled to respond effectively to the attack by a relatively small Mongol army.

Three of the five Mongol columns fought against the Hungarians at Mohi (11 April 1241). The Mongols probably had a nominal total of at least 30,000 men[47] with the personal units of Batu and Sube'etei forming the core of the army. The effective total could therefore be more than 15,000 men. Hungary was in theory able to field large cavalry forces, but King Bela IV of Hungary was on bad terms with his lords and the allied Kipchaqs refugee tribesmen left just before the Mongols struck. The Kipchaqs were angry after a riot by some Hungarian lords led to the death of their ruler. Two Hungarians lords blundered into the Mongol army on their way to join Bela and were overwhelmed. The Hungarian army was therefore smaller than it might have been. A near-contemporary source says the Hungarians lost 10,000 men in the Mohi battle.[48] This is no precise number, but as most of the army was lost it may be close to what the author believed the size of the whole army was. When Mongol officer Siban spied the Hungarian camp some weeks before the battle he counted 40 units.[49] In those days the Hungarian units, the so-called *banderias*, were usually between 50 and 400 men strong.[50] An average size of 250 would indeed give a total of 10,000 men. The Mongols outflanked the Hungarian position at the same time as attacking frontally. The Hungarian army was therefore driven back and encircled inside its camp. Subsequently the Mongols easily overcame the Hungarians.

The western campaigns of Cinggis Qan and Sube'etei were sideshows. The main Mongol effort was directed against the Xia, Jin and Song states in China. None of these states could field as many horsemen as the Mongols. Jin, the strongest of the three states, initially possessed Manchuria. Manchuria's mixed sedentary-nomad population was able to contribute more than 20,000

---

[44] Jerzy Maro , *Legnica 1241* (Warsaw, 1996), pp. 123–31.

[45] Labuda Gerard, *Zaginiona kronika w Rocznikach Jana Dlugosza* (Poznan, 1983), p. 231.

[46] *Tartar Relation*, p. 80.

[47] In addition to the *tumen* in Poland, 1 or 2 *tumens* operated in Transylvania. The rest of the Western Mongol forces were at Mohi.

[48] See Gustav Strakosch-Grassmann, *Der Einfall der Mongolen in Mitteleuropa in den Jahren 1241 und 1242* (Innsbruck, 1893), p. 183, citing the *Epternacher Notiz*.

[49] Rashid al-Din, 2:474.

[50] See Julius Bartl, *Slovak History: Chronology & Lexicon* (Bratislava, 2002), p. 191.

horsemen.[51] Additional horsemen were found in the interior Chinese districts, though these always struggled to raise and maintain sizable number of horses. The Jin lost control over Manchuria after a local Khitan lord rebelled there in 1212, just one year after the Mongols first attacked. As a consequence by 1232, the main Jin field army had only 20,000 horsemen left.[52] Attacked by the full Mongol army, complemented by Khitan and Chinese units now serving with the Mongols, they were hopelessly out-matched. The Jin could only rely on strong defensive positions and well fortified cities (and high technology weapons) in order to hold off the Mongols.

Looking back perhaps the best opportunity for the Jin would have been to defeat the Mongols when they first attacked in 1211, but then no reinforcements were sent to the border region and the forces stationed near the border allowed themselves to be defeated in detail. The border commanders even failed to call out the militia.[53] The Jin were heavily outnumbered in all three battles fought against the Mongols that year. A large Jin army moved against the Mongols the next year, but it had only 30,000 to 50,000 men (certainly rounded numbers) and only a part was cavalry. Cinggis Qan fell on the Jin with his full army, with a nominal total of more than 90,000 men, and gained a complete victory.[54] If there was a decisive battle in China, perhaps that was it.

The Mongols outnumbered the Khwarizmians, Bulgars, Rus, Hungarians, as well as the Jin in all important battles. They utilized their superior numbers in cavalry to encircle the enemy army along the Indus (except the section that was covered by the river), near Yaroslav, and at Mohi. In the more evenly contested battles fought along the Irghiz and at Legnica, only smaller Mongol forces were involved. Russia, Hungary, and Poland were easy targets because they were divided and lacked a strong centralized authority. This was typical for this period in Europe where no ruler could hope to be obeyed in the way the great Qans took for granted. Politically divided Europe was a stark contrast to the centrally controlled Mongolian Empire. The more centralized Jin state could field large armies, but they were nevertheless greatly outnumbered in the battles fought in 1211, and they were also outnumbered with regard to cavalry in 1212 even with a larger army.

It was held in Ancient Greece that whoever united the divided tribes of Thrace could conquer the world.[55] The Chinese could have said the same about whoever united the Inner Asian tribes. Cinggis Qan was a formidable political leader and a superb administrator who united and controlled the tribes to a

[51] This was the number of horsemen the Mongols added to their army after taking control over Manchuria. See note 12.
[52] Tuotuo, *Jin Shi*, 112, probably a rounded nominal total.
[53] Tuotuo, *Jin Shi*, 13 and 93. See also C. de Harlez, trans., *Histoire de L'Empire de Kin* (Louvain, 1887), pp. 208–09. The Jin Shi source is better than Yuan Shi 1, where very large numbers are given for the Jin army. See Friedrich E. A. Krause, *Cingis Han: Die Geschichte seines Lebens nach den chinesischen Reichannalen* (Heidelberg, 1922), p. 30.
[54] Krause, *Cingis Han*, p. 31; Tuotuo, *Jin Shi*, 101 and 102.
[55] Herodotus, *The Histories*, trans. Aubrey de Sélincourt (New York, 1972), pp. 341–42.

degree unmatched by any other leader known to history. Once he was master of the plains he was able to field a vast army. His neighbors could do nothing against such overwhelming numbers of mounted horsemen. The military operations of the Mongols must be understood within this context. The contemporary chroniclers can be faulted for giving too large numbers for all armies involved, but they were right to view the Mongols as fielding the largest battalions. It can be concluded from the survey that John Masson Smith is right to say that the Mongols conquered by means of skillful strategy as well as great numbers. However, David Morgan appears right to support lower army totals.

5

Battlefield Medicine in Wolfram's *Parzival*

Jolyon T. Hughes

Parzival is not the only hero in Wolfram von Eschenbach's narrative of the same name, which dates to around 1210–20. There is another feature woven into the text, in a section known as the Gawanbücher (Gawan books) using a "Doppelwegstruktur," or parallel narrative structure, in which Gawan is the focus of the author's narrative intent and not Parzival, the title character. Gawan embodies the virtues of knightly prowess and chivalric manners. While he is a physically gifted knight with the ability to outperform any knight except Parzival on the battlefield, he is also able to reason and use skills other than mere brute force to solve problems that arise in other areas.

In the Gawan books (VII–VIII, X–XIV) contained in the greater *Parzival* narrative[1] Gawan encounters a fallen knight, whom the reader/listener is later informed is named Uriens. Uriens is lying in Orgeluse's lap and is inwardly bleeding to death from a wound received to the chest in a joust:

dâ lac durchstochen ein man:	There lay a man pierced through,
dem gienc daz bluot in den lîp[2]	with his blood rushing inward.[3]

After inquiring whether the knight was still living and hearing Orgeluse's request that Gawan assist in dealing with this fallen knight, whose death is close at hand if he does not receive medical attention because he cannot breathe, Gawan replies:

disem ritter wolde ich sterben warn	"I could keep this knight from dying
ich trûwte in harte wol ernern,	and I feel sure I could save him
hete ich eine roeren:	if I had a reed (tube).
sehen unde hoeren	You would soon see him and hear
möhte ir in dicke noch gesunt.	him in health, because
wan er ist niht ze verhe wunt:	he is not mortally wounded.

---

[1] There are sixteen books in Wolfram von Eschenbach's *Parzival*.

[2] Karl Lachmann, ed., *Parzival / Wolfram von Eschenbach; mittelhochdeutscher Text nach der sechsten Ausgabe von Karl Lachmann*; Übersetzung von Peter Knecht; Einführung zum Text von Bernd Schirok (Berlin, 1998), pp. 505, 22–23.

[3] All English translations of *Parzival* are from Wolfram von Eschenbach, *Parzival*, trans. Helen Mustard and Charles Passage (New York, 1961). The stanza and line numbers match those of the Lachmann version of Parzival.

daz bluot ist sînes herzen last.
Er begreif der linden einen ast,
Er sliez ein louft drab als ein rôr
(er was zer wunden niht ein tôr)
den schoup er zer tjost in den lîp.
dô bat er sûgen daz wîp,
unz daz bluot gein ir vlôz.
des heldes craft sich ûf entslôz
daz er wol redte unde sprach.
(506, 5–18)

The blood is only pressing on his heart."
He grasped a branch of the linden tree,
slipped the bark off like a tube –
he was no fool in the matter of wounds –
and inserted it into the body through the wound.
Then he bade the woman suck on it
until the blood flowed toward her.
The hero's strength revived
so that he could speak and talk again.

That which is described in this section of book X in *Parzival* is Gawan's ability to administer battlefield medicine to a fellow knight who has lost a joust. Gawan is indeed "no fool in the matter of wounds" and knows exactly what to do to save the knight's life. Wolfram then describes the encounter so that the reader has a detailed account of how the injury was sustained; Uriens informs the reader about how he sustained his injury:

Lishoys Gwelljus
hât mich sere geletzet
und hinterz ors gesetzet
mit einer tjoste rîche:
diu ergienc sô hurtclîche
durch mînen schilt und durch den lîp.
(507, 2–7).

Lischois Gwelljus
injured me badly
and threw me off my horse
with a superb thrust.
It struck with terrific impact
through my shield and through me.

In this fairly detailed description, the reader or listener has enough information to diagnose the injuries sustained by Uriens and to know what kind of treatment he received at the hands of Gawan. It is here quite obvious that the lance did not impale Uriens or he would already be dead. Instead the lance went through the shield, past the arm into the armor smashing into the ribs, knocking him from his mount. Uriens has received a blow that has damaged his pleural space, and allowed blood to collect between the pleural linings, collapsing a lung and adding pressure to the heart. The blood collecting between the two pleural linings, the inner being right outside the lungs and the outer being just underneath the skin, is known as a pleural effusion, which is an accumulation of fluid in this space, and is more exactly diagnosed as a hemothorax, which entails blood accumulating in the pleural space.

Wolfram seems to describe this condition rather nonchalantly, not having Gawan become excited or nervous for the fallen combatant, showing his confidence in his abilities to heal the wound. However the results of this type of injury, if not treated, can lead to death. In today's modern hospital this is a common injury, which is most easily alleviated by a chest tube. A chest tube or Bülau drain, known as a tube thoracostomy in Great Britain, is a long hollow tube or needle of varying gauges, small and large bore, which a doctor or surgeon inserts through the side of the chest, sometimes through the spacing between the ribs, and into the pleural space. It is used to remove air, known as pneumothorax,[4] fluid (the aforementioned pleural effusion, most commonly consisting of blood or chyle), and lastly empyema, which is the accumulation of pus from the intrathoracic space. The complex operation of inserting a thoracic drain, or chest tube, to drain the blood from the pleural space is known as thoracentesis and must be kept separate from a similar, but much less complex procedure known as paracentesis, which is the removal of fluid from another cavity of the body, most frequently the abdomen.

The first question that first comes to mind is: how common was thoracentesis at the time of Wolfram? Are there prior records of this operation being done on the battlefield, or anywhere else for that matter? How would Wolfram have known about them? And are Wolfram's depictions of these injuries close enough to modern descriptions to warrant an investigation?

A similar, but much less complex operation using paracentesis for empyema, the accumulation of pus in the pleural space, comes from Hippocrates of Kos (c.460–370 B.C.E.), otherwise known as the father of medicine and for whom the Hippocratic oath is named. For empyema the treatment was:

> First, cut the skin between the ribs with a bellied scalpel; then wrap a lancet with a piece of cloth, leaving the point of the blade exposed a length equal to the nail of your thumb, and insert it. When you have removed as much pus as you think appropriate, plug the wound with a tent of raw linen, and tie it with a cord; draw off pus once a day; on the tenth day, draw all the pus, and plug the wound with linen. Then make an infusion of warm wine and oil with a tube, in order that the lung, accustomed to being soaked in pus, will not be suddenly dried out. When the pus is thin like water, sticky when touched with a finger, and small in amount, insert a hollow tin drainage tube. When the cavity is completely dried out, cut off the tube little by little, and let the ulcer unite before you remove the tube.[5]

Although the idea of inserting a knife only to the depth of a fingernail seems too little to pierce the three dermal layers, the layers of fat and finally the muscle in most individuals, this translation is the one most commonly used.[6] In order to drain the pus forming the empyema, there would indeed need to be an incision deep enough to perform a thoracic drain. Hippocrates was able to treat this inflammation successfully through his drain over many days, sometimes lasting up to two weeks.

A similar usage of paracentesis is also described by Galen (129–200 C.E.)[7] but there is no mention of hemothorax and therefore thoracentesis in the texts.

---

4   There are three forms of pneumothorax: spontaneous pneumothorax in which the cause is unknown; traumatic pneumothorax which is a direct trauma to the chest wall from either blunt or penetrating trauma; and disease-related pneumothorax.

5   Hippocrates, *On Diseases*, III, in Paul Potter, trans., *Hippocrates*, vol. 6 (Cambridge, MA, 1988), pp. 39–43.

6   See Raymond Hurt, J. E. Barry, A. P. Adams, and P. R. Fleming, "The Diagnosis and Treatment of Empyema," in *The History of Cardiothoracic Surgery from Early Times* (New York, 1996), pp. 153–58.

7   Galen, *On Anatomical Procedures*, trans. Charles Singer (London, 1956). Also see Galen, *On the Usefulness of the Parts of the Body*, trans. Margaret T. May (Ithaca, NY, 1968).

Galen took the technique of paracentesis from Hippocrates but, as he was not allowed to dissect the human body (he used animals instead) because it was illegal under Roman law, he made several errors in human anatomical judgment. He was also unable to distinguish between hydrops (swelling and inflammation) and hydatids (cyst or encrusted larvae from *Echinococcus granulosus*) and tried paracentesis to no avail.[8]

While the introduction of a tube in extreme cases might seem similar to the thoracentesis in Wolfram's text, there are wide ranging differences in technique and in difficulty. Another reason to doubt that Wolfram's description of thoracentesis derives from Hippocrates' text is that the Greek works were little known at the time, unless translated into Latin, and that Wolfram, in comparison to his contemporaries, claimed to be completely illiterate and not to have learned anything from books:

ichne kan deheinen buochstap.	I do not know a single letter of the alphabet.
dâ nement genuoge ir urhap:	Plenty of people get their material that way,
disiu âventiure	but this adventure
vert âne der buoche stiure.	steers without books.
ê man si hete vür ein buoch,	Rather than anybody think it is a book,
ich waere ê nacket âne touch,	I would sit naked without a towel,
sô ich in dem bade saeze,	the way I would sit in a bath –
ob ich des questen niht vergaeze.	if I didn't forget the bouquet of twigs.[9]
(115, 27 – 116, 4)	

Wolfram's source for his *Parzival* narrative is thought to be Chrétien de Troyes' *Le Roman de Perceval ou Le Conte Du Graal*.[10] The situation with the wounded knight is indeed a part of Chrétien's narrative (lines 6541–6651), but the section in which Gawan saves the knight's life is only in the German text. In the French text, Gawan merely wakes the sleeping knight very gently. Unlike Wolfram, who gives the reader/listener a description of the knight's injury from which one can begin to make a diagnosis, Chrétien describes only the external wounds:

Si voit le chevalier blechié	He saw that the knight had been hurt,
Qui le vi sot tot depechié,	his face cut to shreds,
Et o tune plaie [molt] grief	a great, deep sword wound
D'une espee parmi le chief	right in the middle of his head
Et d'ansdeus pars parmi les flans	and another along his side,
Li coroit a grans rais li sans.	and blood spurting all over.

---

8 Benjamin Lee Gordon, *Medieval and Renaissance Medicine* (New York, 1959), p. 339.

9 Mustard and Passage, *Parzival*, have a footnote for explanation here: "The bouquet of twigs used in steam baths to stimulate circulation. 'Fig leaf' would be the equivalent for Western readers."

10 See Sebastian Coxon, *The Presentation of Authorship in Medieval German Narrative Literature, 1220–1290* (Oxford, 2001) and Joachim Bumke, *Wolfram von Eschenbach* (Stuttgart, 1991).

Sovant del mal qu'il ot eü,	The wounded knight kept fainting,
Tant qu'en la fin se reposa.	again and again until he slept.[11]
(6552–6559)[12]	

As there is no evidence that this type of injury is even addressed in the supposed source material, which Wolfram in any case denies basing his work on (827, 1–4),[13] one must therefore posit that the injury and subsequent treatment must, at a minimum, be an addition in Wolfram's text. But to what purpose? For an author who claims to be illiterate, Wolfram seems quite willing to outdo his predecessors and, indeed, some noted physicians of the time as well, in order to show his skill in other areas.

According to Fielding H. Garrison's *An Introduction to the History of Medicine*, among the first persons to perform the operation of paracentesis of the thorax (thoracentesis), – the procedure to take out fluid that has collected in chest – was Alexander Monro, also known as Monro Secundus (1737–1817) in Edinburgh, Scotland.[14] Abdominal paracentensis may have been performed much earlier, however, since original descriptions of paracentesis are given by Paul of Ægina (625–90),[15] who was to have a great influence on El Zahrawi, Guy de Chauliac and others through the nineteenth century.[16]

El Zahrawi (936–1013), known in Europe as Albucasis, writer of the At-Tasrif, a massive medical encyclopedia of some thirty volumes, has sections devoted to the chest and chest wounds. There is, however, little new here in his description of treatment:

> On wounds in the chest and between the shoulders:
>
> If it be a piercing wound by a spear or knife, and you see that it is deep, examine if there be a passage of air out of it when the patient breathes; whence you may know that the injury is mortal. But if it is not deep and the haemorrhage is fresh, then do not straight away apply powder or bandage lest it keep the blood in the depths, so that it be returned to the heart and kill the patient; but apply to it a drawing ointment, apply carded cotton to the opening of the wound to soak up the humidities issuing from it.[17]

This type of treatment seems quite common. In subsequent medical texts Theodoric of Lucca (Teodorico Borgognoni 1205–96), for example, recom-

---

[11] Chrétien de Troyes, *Perceval: The Story of the Grail*, trans. Burton Raffel (New Haven, 1999).

[12] Chrétien de Troyes, *Le Roman de Perceval ou Le Conte Du Graal*, ed. William Roach (Paris, 1959).

[13] See Adrian Stevens' article "Wolfram's *Parzival* and its Narrative Sources," in Will Hasty, ed., *A Companion to Wolfram's Parzival* (Columbia, SC, 1999). Stevens discusses elements of Wolfram's free invention in a work of fiction and Wolfram's reasons for not acknowledging Chrétien as his source.

[14] Fielding H. Garrison, *An Introduction to the History of Medicine* (Philadelphia, 1929), p. 325.

[15] Ibid., 124.

[16] Peter Portmann, *The Oriental Tradition of Paul of Aegina's* Pragmateia (Leiden, 2004), pp. 312–13.

[17] Albucasis, *On Surgery and Instruments*, trans. Martin S. Spink and G. L. Lewis (Berkeley, 1973), p. 532.

mends soaking the wound in hot wine and binding with wide bandages.[18] Guy de Chauliac (1300–68) was aware that there were sucking chest wounds, that they were most often fatal and that non-punctured chests were treatable. He further asserts that some form of drainage was needed but he was not overly specific.[19] In 1316 Mondino de Luzzi, known as Mundinus of Bologna, completed his *Anothomia,* which would not be published until 1487 in Padua and again in 1493 in Leipzig, contains an incidental description of abdominal paracentesis.[20] Additionally, Hieronymus Braunschweig wrote on chest wounds in his *Liber de arte distillandi de compositis* in 1512.[21] However none of these describe hemo or tension pneumothorax in detail as Wolfram von Eschenbach did in his narrative fiction, *Parzival,* completed between the years 1210–1220. The lack of descriptions is not surprising according to Roy Porter, who states:

> Before 1850, however, serious surgical operations had to be short and sharp, although they were rarely sweet. Typically, they dealt with the exterior and the extremities while avoiding (except in the direst emergency, as with caesarian section) the abdomen and other body cavities and the central nervous system.[22]

While other surgeons, might describe or even operate on empyema or with an operation similar to paracentesis, a practical treatment for the real wound described in Wolfram's *Parzival,* known as hemothorax, is not described elsewhere. In the *Parzival* narrative the wound that is described comes from a lance piercing the thoracic cavity, but not through the lung. According to the University of Maryland Medical Center's reference guide for hemothorax: "In blunt chest trauma, a rib may lacerate lung tissue or an artery, causing blood to collect in the pleural space. In penetrating chest trauma, a weapon such as a knife or bullet lacerates the lung."[23] Or in this case from single combat with another knight, involving a lance, sword, mace or other such weapon.

The University of Maryland Medical Center also states that: "Depending on the amount of blood or air in the pleural cavity, a collapsed lung can lead to respiratory and hemodynamic failure, which is known as a tension pneumothorax." A tension pneumothorax is what is commonly referred to as a collapsed lung. A lung can be collapsed without being punctured, because it does not function like a balloon, by air being forced into it, but rather it inflates due to the pressure around it.

[18] See Theodoric, *The Surgery of Theodoric,* trans. Eldridge Campbell and James Colton, 2 vols. (New York, 1955), pp. 146–47.
[19] Guy de Chauliac, *The Cyrurgie of Guy de Chauliac,* ed. Margaret S. Ogden, vol. 1 (Oxford, 1971), pp. 260–66.
[20] Garrison, *Introduction,* p. 160.
[21] Hieronymus Brunschwig, *Liber de arte distillandi de compositis* (Strasbourg, 1512). The Goethe Institute has also digitalized Hieronymus's text: http://edocs.ub.uni-frankfurt.de/volltexte/2007/3982/
[22] Roy Porter, *The Cambridge History of Medicine* (New York, 2006), pp. 176–77.
[23] See Robert M. Zollinger, Jr., and Robert M. Zollinger, Sr., *Zollinger's Atlas of Surgical Operations* (London, 2003), p. 388.

All mammals breathe, but few of us ever think about the mechanism involved. The lungs are not like balloons that we actively inflate and deflate, but they actually function due to the air pressure being raised or lowered:

> Gas Exchange can only be take place effectively if fresh air is continually supplied to the blood-gas barrier. This is achieved through the repeated inflation and deflation of the lungs under the coordinated actions of the *respiratory muscles*, a process known as ventilation. The principal muscles of inspiration are the *diaphragm*, a sheet of muscle that separates the thorax from the abdomen, and the *intercostal muscles* that stabilize the ribcage. When activated, the diaphragm descends and, together with muscles of the thorax, creates a negative pressure (relative to atmospheric) around the lungs that acts to draw air into the airways. The region around the lungs in which this negative pressure acts is known as the *pleural space*, and is filled with a very thin layer of lubricating fluid that separates the outer surface of the lungs (the *visceral pleura*) from the inner surface of the rib cage (the *parietal pleura*).[24]

If the lungs have blood around them, filling the pleural space, then the diaphragm, lungs and ribs cannot produce the right circumstances in which a condition of lower pressure exists and oxygen can be inhaled. The fallen knight's inability to speak (506, 19) and his close proximity to death (505, 28) indicate hemothorax resulting in tension pneumothorax, which causes severe dysfunction in the cardiovascular system. In the case of the fallen knight, there is a build up of pressure in the lung cavity, which is slowing or stopping the blood from the veins back to the heart. The heart, therefore, has less blood that it can pump back into the main arteries. This lack of blood in the arteries causes the blood pressure to drop, which can quickly affect the knight's vital organs.[25] In this case the only solution is tube thoracostomy, or the insertion of a chest tube.

In a tube thoracostomy, the incision is made in the ribs and pushed through until it is in the pleural space. According to the *New England Journal of Medicine*, the incision for a chest tube should be in the triangle of safety along the ribs and under the armpit. The incision should be approximately 1.5 to 2.0 centimeters in length between two ribs. Once below the subcutaneous tissue the physician should then work diagonally upward, using the rib as the lower guide to help puncture the pleural lining and get into the correct intercostal space without puncturing the inner pleural lining.[26] Today this is a very involved operation and one done while the patient is under local anesthetic in hospitals. Zollinger states that: "All thoracotomies require endotracheal anesthesia. In cases of marked suppuration of one lung, the normal lung can be isolated by selective intubation with a Carlen endobroncial tube."[27] This is also not an undertaking that just anyone should embark on, or would even know how to successfully complete.

---

[24] Jason H. T. Bates, *Lung Mechanics: An Inductive Approach* (Cambridge, 2009), p. 4.
[25] For a view of a collapsed lung see: Sebastian Lange and Paul Stark, *Teaching Atlas of Thoracic Radiology* (New York, 1993), pp. 231–32.
[26] Zollinger and Zollinger, *Atlas of Surgical Operations*, p. 389.
[27] Ibid., p. 388.

The question of medieval anesthesia is also a problematic one. According to Leonard Rosenman, retired professor of Surgery at the University of California San Francisco and at Mount Zion Hospital, various forms of anesthesia were in use well before John Morton used ether poured on a sea sponge in 1846. There are descriptions of anesthesia in Theodoric's (1205–96) *Chirurgia*,[28] from Henri de Mondeville (1260–1320) and Guy de Chauliac (1300–68). All of these surgeons were influenced by Roger Frugard (1130?–1195) and his *Chirurgia*,[29] written around 1180 (between 1170 and 1230), which was widely used all over Europe and translated into many languages. While general anesthetics were attempted, local anesthesia was not possible. Typical anesthetics at the time were opium and mandragora. Theodoric definitely used early anesthesia, as did Henri and Guy, but Rosenman points out the likely reasons for these methods falling out of favor:

> Whoever did say it, whether Theodoric or Mondeville or Guy, the use of inhalation anaesthesia by medieval surgeons is written clear, for our eyes to read and for us to believe. I assume that it fell from favor because of toxic effects from some of the substances used for the compound, or because the successes with the method were not consistent.[30]

Once the chest tube is in place, according to the American Thoracic Society, an underwater seal is recommended to help with the drainage. In the case of Gawan and the wounded knight Uriens, Orgeluse is told to suck on the tube until blood comes out (506, 16–17): "dô bat er sûgen daz wîp, unz daz bluot gein ir vlôz". It is also important that other fluids or air do not find their way into the pleural space. Additionally, without anesthetic one would have to hold Uriens in place and his arm out of the way. It is doubtful that Orgeluse and Gawan alone could do this. Perhaps part of Gawan's unnamed retinue would be able to assist in this function. In such a case there would probably be a need for two or three strong men to hold Uriens' body still and his arm out of the way. As Wolfram makes no mention of anesthesia in the text, one must ask how a 1.5–2.0 cm incision could be made, the dermal layers, fat layers and muscle tissue cut through, the rib used as a guide to puncture the outer intercostal lining and a tube inserted through all of this while a patient, even if only semi–conscious, remains perfectly still and does not use any reflex to lower the arm to protect the ribs. One must also keep in mind that Wolfram indicated wood being used, not a flexible tube as is used today.

While the incision is a mere 1.5–2.0 cm in length the positioning of the cut, between the ribs, the depth of the incision and the insertion of the tube are

---

28 Theodoric, *Chirurgia*, 2:212–14.
29 See Tony Hunt, ed., *Anglo-Norman Medicine: Roger Frugard's "Chirurgia" the "Practica brevis" of Platerearius* (Rochester, NY, 1994).
30 Leonard Rosenman, *A Medieval Surgical Pharmacopoeia and Formulary: With a List of Simples and Compounds 1170–1325* (Philadelphia, 2006), p. 118.

extremely painful. There is a similar tale of Pero Niño,[31] in which the doctors prepared him a cauterizing iron, which he not only once, but twice uses on himself to cauterize a leg wound, which had been pierced by an arrow and had developed septicemia. Cauterization is known to cause extensive tissue damage and is best only used by experts. It is doubtful here that Pero Niño would be able to perform such a painful and dangerous operation on himself without some form of assistance, whether that be an anesthetic or holding him still, which is not named in this text either. It seems likely that in these cases only the action taken to heal the damage done is described by the author. The preparations and other information viewed as superfluous material, or even possibly material that a barber/surgeon would not want others to know, was left out.

An interesting note in this context is that Wolfram describes himself as a Franconian and a Bavarian in his narrative. Indeed, a town named Wolframseschenbach claims to be his hometown with the slogan "Stadt des Parzivaldichters."[32] Rosenman mentions the "Bamberg surgery," and Bamberg is a town not far from Wolframseschenbach, so it might be possible for Wolfram to know this procedure from Bamberg, although it is doubtful because he does not mention it. Wolfram is not one to hold back on information that he might have:

> References to the soporific sponge are found in pharmacopoeia of the classical and Arabic epochs. However, as Corner has shown, the first mention in a surgical source was in the "Bamberg surgery." That collection of materials copied mostly Arabic predecessors was used at Salerno perhaps a half of a century before Roger's more complete *Chirurgia*.[33]

Once a tube thoracostomy is properly in place and the blood has been drained the lung can re-inflate in as little as 15–30 seconds, which is why the fallen knight Uriens is able to speak so quickly after Gawan inserts the chest tube and Orgeluse drains the remaining blood from around his lung (506, 18). There are no long-term issues once a tension pneumothorax has been relieved. They are, however, more likely to reoccur once one has had an episode of a collapsed lung. Uriens is therefore at greater risk for suffering from a collapsed lung if he sustains a similar injury.

Wolfram wrote his masterpiece between 1210 and 1220. This is problematic when one looks at the description of Gawan's knowledge and successful execution of a chest tube thoracostomy, because the standard procedure for hemothorax was not in place until the mid to late eighteenth century. If this is the case, then Wolfram describes a medical procedure in battlefield medicine almost six hundred years before it becomes standard practice, although it had doubtless been performed earlier.

If one wishes to argue that Wolfram had read of similar treatments utilized by the Greeks, in the time of Hippocrates, then the question would have to be

---

[31] Díaz de Gamez, *The Unconquered Knight* (Cambridge, Ont., 2004), p. 40.
[32] http://www.wolframs-eschenbach.de/
[33] Rosenman, *Medieval Surgical Pharmacopoeia*, p. 119. Roger's *Chirurgia* dates to c.1230.

answered as to how he had access to these texts. While Wolfram takes the time to name the planets in Arabic[34] and gives Parzival a black and white checkered, Arabian half-brother, Feirefîz Anchevîn, does that mean he would have had access to the Arabic medical texts of the time, or have knowledge of the language beyond a certain, basic level? To be more precise, could he read and comprehend complex medical Greek or Arabic? This matter is further complicated by the fact that Wolfram claims to be illiterate, although this claim must also be called into question.

Arthur Groos discusses Wolfram's knowledge of medicine and states, that "Wolfram was clearly familiar with the massive influx of Arabic science into twelfth-century Latin culture."[35] It is clear from Groos' reading of the text that Wolfram mixed elements of astrology with medicine in the healing of Anfortas, the fisher king, that he received from Arabic sources in Toledo, Spain (Groos, 204). There is a major difference between these two situations however, namely Gawan's healing of Uriens and the healing of Anfortas. Uriens is injured in battle and healed with practical medicine that is consistent with today's standard medical procedures, and Anfortas is not. Anfortas' healing deals with the conjunction of Mars and Jupiter, causing a greater inflammation of the wound received during *Minnedienst*.[36]

The Arabs were the most skillful physicians of the time. It is, however, doubtful that Arabic medicine had gone much further than that of the Greeks. While the Arabs were careful to retain the information from the Greek sources[37] there was little official impetus to update or to change anything:

> Their [the Arabs'] reverence for the scientific works of ancient Greece was only second to their respect for the Koran. The greatest ambition of a student was to be able to understand the ancient masters in the original or translations. Few dared to question ancient Greek authority. The opinion of the Greek masters was considered law. The additions that Islamic physicians attempted to make to Greek medicine refer almost entirely to therapeutics. The theory and thought of the Greeks were left untouched. In such an atmosphere experimental medicine was practically impossible. Then too, since the Moslems were prohibited from performing any dissection on human bodies or on living animals, Galen's anatomical and physiological errors could not be corrected.[38]

The problem inherent in Benjamin Gordon's assumption in the passage just quoted is rather clear. Although he states what was law and common practice, it is difficult to believe a ban on dissection would actually keep practicing surgeons from trying the procedure. Just as a speed limit and fines do not keep

---

34 782, 6–12. He has Cundrîe la surziere name "Siben sterne" (782, 1) (seven stars) in the heathen tongue (heidensch): Zval (Saturn), Almustri (Jupiter), Almaret (Mars), Samsi (the sun), Allgafir (Venus), Alkiter (Mercury), Alkamer (the moon).

35 Arthur Groos, *Romancing the Grail* (Ithaca, NY, 1995), pp. 197–219.

36 Ibid., p. 203.

37 For information on Greek into Arabic translation see Portmann, *The Oriental Tradition of Paul of Aegina's Pragmateia*, pp. 239–58.

38 Gordon, *Medieval and Renaissance Medicine*, 149.

modern day motorists from surpassing the limit, a ban simply could not keep all Muslims from breaking the rules. Emilie Savage-Smith points out:

> There are two aspects to the problem, the legal status of dissection and the general intellectual acceptability of the practice, for a legal prohibition does not necessarily imply lack of practice, as demonstrated, for example, by divination or wine drinking, both of which continued to be practiced in Islam, though clearly prohibited.[39]

Ali ibn Abbas al-Majusi, also known as Masoudi, or under the Latinized name of Haly Abbas (910–92) wrote in his *Kitab Kamil as-Sina'a at-Tibbiyya* ("Complete Book of the Medical Art") later known as *The Complete Art of Medicine*, translated into Latin from Arabic around 1080 by Constantine the African (1015–87) as *Liber pantegni* (παντεχνη) that a physician should not rely solely on books for information, but must also practice the art of medicine. Haly Abbas used the work of Rhazes (860–923 or 932), who correctly identified small pox and measles, which Hippocrates had not described in his works, for his more complete *Kitab*. In the *Annals of Anatomy and Surgery* it is said, however, that Haly did not generally approve of paracentesis because of its potential for failure, but allows for the practice up to the age of seventy if the patient is considered to be of "vigorous constitution."[40]

In Piers Mitchell's *Medicine in the Crusades*, only one similar account of paracentesis can be found, but it deals with empyema not hemothorax. It is the account of Baldwin I of Jerusalem (c.1058–1118) by Albert of Aachen and was probably recounted by Guibert of Nogent; the case arose when Baldwin suffered a blow from a lance and then had a bear struck in a similar manner to see how to treat the wound. Pus had to be evacuated from wound for it to heal.[41] Likewise there is no other mention of a similar procedure, leading to the conclusion that it was either unimportant or not yet known.[42]

While there might be a lack of textual evidence exactly depicting the diagnosis and procedure for a chest tube thoracostomy to treat tension pneumothorax, there is an explanation for this apparent lack of knowledge. Thomas Morested illustrates a hidden surgical tradition of keeping the knowledge of important operations secret in his *Fair Book of Surgery*.[43] Most of Morested's techniques come from Galen and Guy de Chauliac and show that the art of surgery was lucrative and the need to keep certain things secret from a larger audience was in a surgeon's best (financial) interest. There certainly was knowledge of the chest tube and its use for chest wounds as Wolfram demonstrates. If

[39] Emilie Savage-Smith, "Attitudes toward Dissection in Medieval Islam," *Journal of the History of Medicine and Allied Sciences* 50 (1995), 67–8.
[40] George Jackson Fisher, *Annals of Anatomy and Surgery*, ed. Lewis Pilcher and Goerge Fowler (Brooklyn, 1883), p. 258.
[41] Piers Mitchell, *Medicine in the Crusades* (Cambridge, 2004), p. 160.
[42] See Stanley Rubin, *Medieval English Medicine* (London, 1974) and Richard Gabriel and Karen Metz, *A History of Military Medicine* (New York, 1992), vols. 1 and 2.
[43] See R. Theodore Beck, *The Cutting Edge: Early History of the Surgeons of London* (London, 1974).

this surgery was indeed one of those techniques known, but not written down, it will probably never be known.

The problem with using *Parzival* as a guide or a medical text is obvious at first glance. This text is fictional and is a combination of a story first written by Chrétien de Troyes and original material by Wolfram von Eschenbach. This text was never intended to be a medical text or have any other function than telling the story as Wolfram wished it to be told. This text was likely a vehicle of some criticism and is filled with various forms of information useful to historians, linguists and Germanists but up until now this text was not seen as useful for anyone in the medical field. In the field of historical medicine this text gives a very detailed description of the wound, how it was received and how it was treated, yielding a clue to what type of medicine was being practiced on the battlefield and beyond, even if Wolfram's contemporaneous medical specialists did not write it all down explicitly.

The only thing that is for certain is that Wolfram von Eschenbach clearly describes the procedure in a text, written and completed before 1220, that was not standard procedure in a hospital until the end of the eighteenth and beginning of the nineteenth century.[44] Wolfram says: "schildes ambet ist mîn art" (115, 11) meaning that he belonged to the rank of an un–free knight and that he was proud to be a part of the fighting class.[45] If Wolfram had knowledge of this medical procedure, and was a member of the *ritterliche ministerialis*,[46] then this would indicate some experience in having performed it on the battlefield (or perhaps on the tournament grounds) himself or having at least seen it performed.

This must be the case with Wolfram because "few traces of organized medical practice remained in the region which later developed into Germany."[47] In the early part of the thirteenth century in Germany at the time of Wolfram "the church placed a ban on priests who practiced surgery and as a further development this ban was later extended to include general medicine …"[48] The attitude of the Church stems from a biblical citation, "For your lifeblood I will surely require a reckoning; of every beast I will require it and of man; of every man's brother I will require the life of man. Whoever sheds the blood of man, by man shall his blood be shed; for God made man in his own image" (Gen. 9.5–6). The Church tended to view illnesses as punishments for sins committed against God and so superstition was an integral part of medicine.

Charles H. Talbot disagrees with Gordon on the issue of *why* a physician would not want to be involved in any kind of "manual operation." While Gordon

---

44 Duncan A. Killen and Walter G. Gobbel, *Spontaneous Pneumothorax* (London, 1968), p. 16.
45 For information on Wolfram von Eschenbach see Margaret Fitzgerald Richey, *Studies of Wolfram von Eschenbach* (London, 1957).
46 See Eduard Hartl, "Wolfram von Eschenbach," *Nachtrag von Walter Schröder und Werner Wolf* (Volume 5, 1955).
47 Gordon, *Medieval and Renaissance Medicine*, p. 384.
48 Ibid., p. 386.

states clearly his belief that the influence of the Church was the driving reason behind a ban on surgery, Talbot states that it is much more likely that there was a schism between physicians and surgeons that had been passed from Galen to the Arabs. Talbot says:

> The separation of surgery from medicine was not, therefore, an effect of ecclesiastical legislation: it was due not to the prohibition of medical practice to clerics, but to the influence of such texts as this which exalted the 'noble physician' to heights where any kind of operation was unthinkable. The physician's role, in Avenzoar's judgement, was to give consultants, advice, and instructions to his subordinates, but not to sully his hands.[49]

Wolfram adds this into the text to show that he is indeed knowledgeable of the tactics he describes in *Parzival*, referring here to not only battle tactics but medicinal as well. Clifford Rogers, in his *Soldier's Lives through History: The Middle Ages*, states that "Basic knowledge of practical wound treatment was widespread among medieval soldiers." Wolfram's claim to being an experienced knight would tend to lend credence to Rogers' statement and would go a long way in explaining how Wolfram knew of the techniques he so clearly describes in the text. This would also support Piers Mitchell's conclusion that battlefield medical care, even in European, Christian armies was more advanced than once previously thought and not as far behind the Islamic practitioners as is often thought.

Where Chrétien depicts a wounded knight about to die, Wolfram shows that he, unlike his predecessors, has an in-depth understanding of what these knights really do and that behind the fanciful descriptions are real actions with real consequences. He also shows that he alone of all the Arthurian authors can accurately show the full range of knightly combat, because he is familiar with the reality of battlefield medicine and the others are merely clerics, who can only depict the honor and glory of combat and not the inevitable consequence thereof: if there is a winner such as an Erec, Iwain, Parzival or Gawan, there must also be a loser such as Keie[50] or Uriens, and that loser can be wounded and must be cared for. Wolfram's ability or desire to contrast himself, also in the matter of injury and its healing process, with the clerical authors of the courtly epics further distinguishes his epic and endeavors to be more concerned with providing a critique of social mores, values and relations.

[49] Charles H. Talbot, *Medicine in Medieval England* (London, 1967), p. 54.
[50] Keie, Arthur's foster-brother, arrogantly rides against Parzival in a joust. When the two knights collide Keie is knocked off the horse with saddle and tack. Keie's right arm and left leg are broken and the horse is killed. For an in depth discussion of this section of *Parzival* see Joachim Bumke, *Die Blutstropfen im Schnee, Über Wahrnehmung und Erkenntnis im "Parzival" Wolframs von Eschenbach* (Tübingen, 2001).

6

Battle-Seeking, Battle-Avoiding or perhaps just Battle-Willing? Applying the Gillingham Paradigm to Enrique II of Castile

L. J. Andrew Villalon

On the night of 23 March 1369, just south of the city of Toledo in the central Iberian kingdom of Castile, one of the great medieval dramas played out as two bitter enemies faced each other for the first time in nearly fifteen years.[1] One of these men was the legitimate monarch of Castile, Pedro I (1350–66, 1367–69), better known to history as Pedro "the Cruel."[2] The other

[1] This paper is a follow-up to one presented at the 43rd International Congress on Medieval Studies that met at Western Michigan University in May 2008. In its preparation, I have used materials obtained from various libraries and archives, including (in the United States) the University of Cincinnati library system and the Perry-Castañeda Library at the University of Texas in Austin and (in Spain) the Archivo General de Simancas, the Archivo Histórico Nacional, the Biblioteca Nacional, and the Real Academia de la Historia. I would like to thank the following individuals (listed in alphabetical order) who have contributed over the years to the ideas contained in this article: Judith Daniels, Julian Deahl, Kelly DeVries, Mark DuPuy, Dan Gottlieb, Janine Hartman, Donald Kagay, Mark Lause, Sally Moffitt, Paul Moran (both the elder and younger), Marcella Mulder, Norman Murdoch, Clifford Rogers, Charles Seibert, Blasco Sobrinho, Ann Twinam, Theresa Vann, Thomas White, and several anonymous readers who have commented on related work. Finally, I am eternally grateful to two academic departments of which I have been a member: first, the University of Cincinnati's Department of Romance Languages and Literatures which afforded me a warm welcome during my last two years at that university and secondly, the University of Texas Department of History which was equally welcoming when my wife and I made the move to Texas.

[2] The monarch is also known, albeit less widely, as Pedro "the Just." The sobriquet one chooses depends largely upon how one views the sanguinary activities of this most controversial king who occupies a niche in Spanish history comparable to that reserved by the English for Richard III. The principal source for the reign of Pedro I is the king's chronicle written by the royal official, diplomat, military figure, and one of the foremost chroniclers of late medieval Europe, Pedro López de Ayala. The version cited in this paper is *Crónica del Rey Don Pedro Primero* [hereafter Ayala, *Pedro I*], in *Crónicas de los Reyes de Castilla*, 1, Biblioteca de Autores Españoles 66 (Madrid, 1953), pp. 393–614. For a more recent edition, see *Crónica del rey don Pedro*, ed. Constance L. Wilkins and Heanon M. Wilkins (Madison, 1985). Given his place in Spanish history, it is not surprising that there exists in that language a significant bibliography of the monarch. One quite useful book for the study of the reign is J. B. Sitges, *Las Mujeres del Rey Don Pedro I de Castilla* (Madrid, 1910) which despite its title is a scholarly work that reprints a number of key documents. The most important full-length account of the monarch's reign in English is Clara Estow's *Pedro the Cruel, 1350–1369* (Leiden, 1995). For my own

was his illegitimate half-brother and rival for the throne, Enrique II (1366–67, 1369–79).[3]

After suffering defeat in battle nine days earlier, Pedro had taken refuge in the nearby castle of Montiel, from which the encounter took its name.[4] While attempting to escape through the siege lines set up by his enemy, he and a few retainers were captured by French troops serving Enrique, one of whom took Pedro to his half-brother's tent. The scene that followed is recounted with certain key variations[5] by several contemporaries, including the most famous Spanish chronicler of the age, Pedro López de Ayala[6] (d.1407), and his even

assessment of Pedro and his highly impolitic policies, see: "Pedro the Cruel, Portrait of a Royal Failure," in Donald J. Kagay and Joseph Snow, eds., *Medieval Iberia: Essays on the History and Literature of Medieval Spain* (New York, 1997), pp. 201–16.

3   The principal source for this reign is the second of Ayala's four royal chronicles, the *Crónica del Rey Don Enrique Segundo de Castilla* [hereafter Ayala, *Enrique II*] in *Crónicas de los Reyes de Castilla*, 2, Biblioteca de Autores Españoles 68 (Madrid, 1953), pp. 1–64. While Enrique would have dated his reign from his coronation in Burgos in 1366, most historians place its beginning at Pedro's death three years later. Modern editions of Ayala's chronicle begin at that point.

4   The dramatic tale is told, with certain key variations, in a number of contemporary chronicles, including in particular the following: the anonymous *Chronique des quatre premiers Valois* (Paris, 1862), pp. 198–99; *Chroniques de J. Froissart*, ed. Siméon Luce (Paris, 1878), vol. 7 (*1367–1370*), pp. 81–82. Pedro López de Ayala, *Crónica del Rey Don Pedro Primero*, in *Crónicas de Castilla*, 1, Biblioteca de Autores Españoles 66 (Madrid, 1953), pp. 591–92. Pedro IV of Aragon (Pere III of Catalonia), *Chronicle*, 2 vols., trans. Mary Hillgarth (Toronto, 1980), 2:580–81.

5   The principal differences in how the event is portrayed center around two issues: (1) the role assigned to Bertrand du Guesclin, the Breton knight commanding Enrique's French auxiliaries (see footnote 67) who would become the constable of France and a French national hero, and (2) the unheroic performance of Enrique who could not have won without the intervention of his followers. While there is a distinct effort on the part of several chroniclers to soft-pedal du Guesclin's involvement, blaming the betrayal of Pedro on one of his subordinates, the chronicle of Pedro López de Ayala asserts that the future constable played a key part, first in luring Pedro out of the castle, then betraying him into the hands of his deadly enemy. By contrast, Ayala glosses over the intervention of others in the fight between the half-brothers that decided it in favor of Enrique. This aspect of the affair, we learn of from Froissart. Ayala, *Pedro I*, pp. 591–92; Froissart, *Chroniques*, 7:81–82.

6   The first biographical sketch of López de Ayala appears in Fernán Pérez de Guzmán's *Generaciones y Semblanzas*, an early fourteenth-century work in which the author provided sketches of his contemporaries. Guzmán states that the Ayala family had branched off from the older line of Haro. See Fernán Pérez de Guzmán, *Generaciones y Semblanzas*, ed. Jesus Dominguez Bodona (Madrid, 1965), pp. 37–39. For a modern, full-length account of the chronicler's life and work, see Michel Garcia, *Obra y personalidad del Canciller Ayala* (Madrid, 1983). This work appends several of the contemporary sources that supply our information concerning the author. Despite providing useful material on his political career, an earlier biography in Spanish by Luis Suárez Fernández, *El Chanciller Ayala y su Tiempo* (Vitoria, 1962), is seriously flawed. English readers should consult Helen Nader, *The Mendoza Family in the Spanish Renaissance 1350–1550* (Rutgers, 1979). Nader's third chapter, entitled "Pedro López de Ayala and the Formation of Mendoza Attitudes," provides a fine capsule biography of the great chronicler, a penetrating analysis of his chronicle of Pedro I, and valuable bibliography. See also Clara

more famous contemporary from the Low Countries, Jean Froissart (d. c.1405).[7] Enrique soon arrived fully armed and asked in a loud voice, "Where is the son of a Jewish whore who calls himself king of Castile?" Without hesitation, Pedro replied, "Thou art the son of a whore, I am the son of Alfonso."[8] Grappling, the two tumbled to the ground, but when the larger Pedro[9] appeared to gain an advantage others quickly intervened, ending any pretense of a fair fight by giving Enrique time to draw his dagger and use it.[10] Enrique's retainers then

Estow's article, "Royal Madness in the Crónica del Rey Don Pedro," *Mediterranean Studies* 6 (1996), 13–28.

[7] As the foremost chronicler of the age, Jean Froissart has generated a considerable bibliography. A popular account by a leading medievalist of the late nineteenth and early twentieth century is George G. Coulton, *The Chronicler of European Chivalry* (London, 1930). A highly valuable collection of essays written by major twentieth century historians who have made extensive use of the chronicle in their own work is *Froissart: Historian*, ed. J. J. N. Palmer (Woodbridge, Suffolk, 1981). The list of authors in Palmer's collection includes Richard Barber, John Bell Henneman, Michael Jones, P. E. Russell, and Philippe Contamine. Peter F. Ainsworth has wrestled with the question of historical truth in chronicle writing in *Jean Froissart and the Fabric of History: Truth, Myth, and Fiction in the Chroniques* (Oxford, 1990).

[8] Ayala's treatment of the incident is not as dramatic as that of Froissart. The Spanish chronicler indicates that upon his arrival at the tent, "he [Enrique] did not know him [Pedro] because it had been such a long time since he had seen him." Told by one of the Frenchmen "Behold your enemy," Enrique remained dubious until Pedro cried out several times, "I am. I am," at which point Enrique slashed him in the face, then wounded him severely when both men fell to the ground. By contrast, Froissart introduces the far more colorful exchange of insults, after which he tells of the intervention of Enrique's men on their master's behalf during his final tussle with Pedro. The precise wording of the insults has been taken from the English translation of Froissart which accurately reflects the text as edited by Simeon Luce. John Froissart, *Chronicles of England, France, and Spain and the Adjoining Countries from the Latter Part of the Reign of Edward II to the Coronation of Enrique IV*, trans. Thomas Johnes, 2 vols. (London, 1857), 1:388–89.

[9] In the final chapter of his chronicle of Pedro's reign, Ayala provides a physical description of his subject, referring to the king as "asaz grande de cuerpo." By contrast, in his chronicle of Enrique II, this same author speaks of the usurper as being "pequeño de cuerpo." For his part, Froissart clearly identifies Pedro as the stronger man: "et fu plus fors de li et l'abati desous lui." See: Ayala, *Pedro I*, p. 593; Ayala, *Enrique II*, p. 38; Froissart, *Chroniques*, 7:81; Froissart, *Chronicles*, 1:389.

[10] All of the chroniclers acknowledge that the struggle between the brothers was an uneven one, due to the intervention of Enrique's men. It is Froissart who provides the most vivid description of the unequal contest and how it was resolved in favor of the weaker man:

> Don Pedro ... caught hold of king Enrique in his arms, began to wrestle with him, and, being the strongest, threw him down under him. ... Placing his hand upon his poniard, he [Pedro] would infallibly have killed him [Enrique], if the viscount de Rocaberti had not been present who seizing don Pedro by the legs, turned him over, by which means king Enrique being uppermost, immediately drew a long poniard which he wore in his sash, and plunged it into his [Pedro's] body. His [Enrique's] attendants entered the tent, and helped to dispatch him.

The accounts convey the impression that most of those who had accompanied Pedro in his attempt to escape simply stood by and watched as he was killed. (In all fairness, they were decidedly outnumbered and may have been disarmed.) Only Froissart mentions an unsuccessful attempt to help the king: a pair of Englishmen, Raoul Helines [Ralph Holmes] and finished off the wounded man, afterwards tossing his body out of the tent where it lay for three days, exposed to the elements, the camp animals, and some of the king's former subjects, who took this last opportunity to avenge themselves on the corpse.[11]

In this way, Enrique II secured the crown of Castile and initiated a new dynasty – the house of Trastámara – that would rule that kingdom for the better part of two centuries. In 1412, a cadet branch of the Trastámaran dynasty extended its control over the neighboring crown of Aragon and in 1469 the heirs to these two branches of the family, Fernando II of Aragon and Isabel I of Castile, married one another, thereby bringing about a dynastic union that became the genesis of modern Spain.[12]

Throughout his long and ultimately successful military career, the bastard king whose descendants would later unify Spain spent most of his time fighting one opponent after another, including one who had formerly been a staunch ally. This lifetime of martial activity renders him an appropriate figure for analysis in light of what has become known as "the Gillingham paradigm."

*

In 2002, the opening issue of the *Journal of Medieval Military History* initiated a debate over the degree to which medieval commanders either sought battle or, conversely, sought to avoid it. In a thought-provoking essay entitled "The Vegetian 'Science of Warfare' in the Middle Ages,"[13] one of the disputants, Clifford Rogers of the United States Military Academy, challenged the view that in recent decades has increasingly assumed the mantle of conventional wisdom – the view that medieval commanders, fearing the wager of battle, more often than not launched campaigns consciously eschewing battlefield encounters while opting for other, less risky alternatives such as sieges or *chevauchées*. According to this view, the reticence to engage was a major factor if not the major factor accounting for a relative absence of battles in the medieval period.[14]

James Rowland, were cut down trying to shield Pedro's body from Enrique's retainers. A ballad included in the *Romancero General*, "The Death of Don Pedro," quoted by Cervantes and translated into English by Sir Walter Scott, alters the facts in order to make the intervention of Enrique's followers seem less unchivalrous. According to the ballad, Enrique's loyal young page becomes the "sole spectator of the struggle," and impulsively decided to intervene in order to save his liege lord. Froissart, *Chroniques*, 7:82; Froissart, *Chronicles*, 1:389; *Romancero General ó Coleccíon de Romances Castellanos anteriores al Siglo XVIII*, 2, in Biblioteca de Autores Españoles 16 (Madrid, 1921), p. 43; *The Spanish Ballads*, trans. John G. Lockhart (London, n.d. [1842]), pp. 85–86.

[11] Ayala, *Pedro I*, p. 592.
[12] See the genealogical chart of the Trastámaran dynasty (pp. 136–37 below).
[13] Clifford J. Rogers, "The Vegetian 'Science of Warfare' in the Middle Ages," *Journal of Medieval Military History* [*JMMH*] 1 (2002), 1–19.
[14] Rogers quotes a number of today's leading military historians who he indicates have largely if not entirely endorsed the view that medieval commanders were overwhelmingly "battle-avoiding." These include Matthew Strickland, Philippe Contamine, James Bradbury, Stephen Morillo, and Michael Prestwich. According to Strickland, this view had become "so common-

Rogers dubs this "new orthodoxy" of recent decades the "Gillingham Paradigm," in honor of John Gillingham of the London School of Economics who argued the position in his seminal article, "Richard I and the Science of War in the Middle Ages."[15] According to Gillingham and those who accept his views, when avoiding encounters, medieval commanders were acting (whether knowingly or not) in accordance with advice handed down in a highly influential treatise on military matters, *De re militari*, written by the late Roman author, Flavius Vegetius Renatus.[16] Traditionally thought (on no very strong evidence) to have been produced in the wake of the disastrous battle of Adrianople (378) and dedicated to Emperor Valentinian II,[17] the *De re militari* became one of the most popular classical works known to the medieval West.[18] Its more cautious passages definitely convey a reluctance to do battle.

In the words of Vegetius,

> Every plan ... is to be considered, every expedient tried and every method taken before matters are brought to this last extremity [referring to a battle]. Good officers decline general engagements where the odds are too great, and prefer the employment of stratagem and finesse to destroy the enemy as much as possible in detail and intimidate them without exposing their own forces ...[19]

place that it may safely be said to have moved from revisionism to orthodoxy" while Prestwich states "the new orthodoxy is that medieval commanders sought to avoid battle wherever possible, seeking instead to wear down their opponents by waging wars of devastation." See: Rogers, "Vegetian," pp. 3–4, especially nn. 6 and 8.

[15] The article appeared in 1984 in *War and Government: Essays in Honour of J. O. Prestwich*, ed. John Gillingham and J. C. Holt (Cambridge, 1984), pp. 194–207. It is reprinted in Matthew Strickland, *Anglo-Norman Warfare* (Woodbridge, 1992). The article is available on the website of De re militari: The Society for Medieval Military History, URL: www.deremilitari.org/resources/articles/gillingham.htm.

[16] The *De re militari* has been translated into a number of post-classical languages, including English. The English edition consulted during the writing of this article was Flavius Vegetius Renatus, *The Military Institutions of the Romans*, trans. John Clark (Harrisburg, 1944). This same translation is currently available on the web at a site entitled: Digital Attic – Warfare: "De Re Militari" by Flavius Vegetius Renatus, URL: http://www.pvv.ntnu.no/~madsb/home/war/vegetius/

[17] Although very little is known of the author or the facts surrounding the genesis of his work, historians have deduced from the dedication to Valentinian and certain facts mentioned in the text that its date of composition may be approximately A.D. 390, during the reign of the second emperor of that name. There has recently been renewed debate over the question of its date.

[18] The introduction to the Clark translation indicates that the treatise by Vegetius was widely known to military commanders throughout the Middle Ages, strongly suggesting that some may have shaped their strategy along the lines of its recommendations. In 1985, the dean of America's medieval military historians, Bernard Bachrach, excellently summarized the debate taking place since the 1880s over the possibility of Vegetius's writings having influenced the military strategy of medieval commanders, in particular, the eleventh-century count of Anjou, Fulk Nerra. While admitting that there is no direct evidence, Bachrach makes a strong circumstantial case for such influence having occurred in the count's case. See Bernard Bachrach, "The Practical Use of Vegetius' De Re Militari during the Middle Ages," *The Historian* 47 (1985), 239–55.

[19] Vegetius, *Military Institutions*, p. 85.

The Trastamaran Dynasty in Castile and Aragon

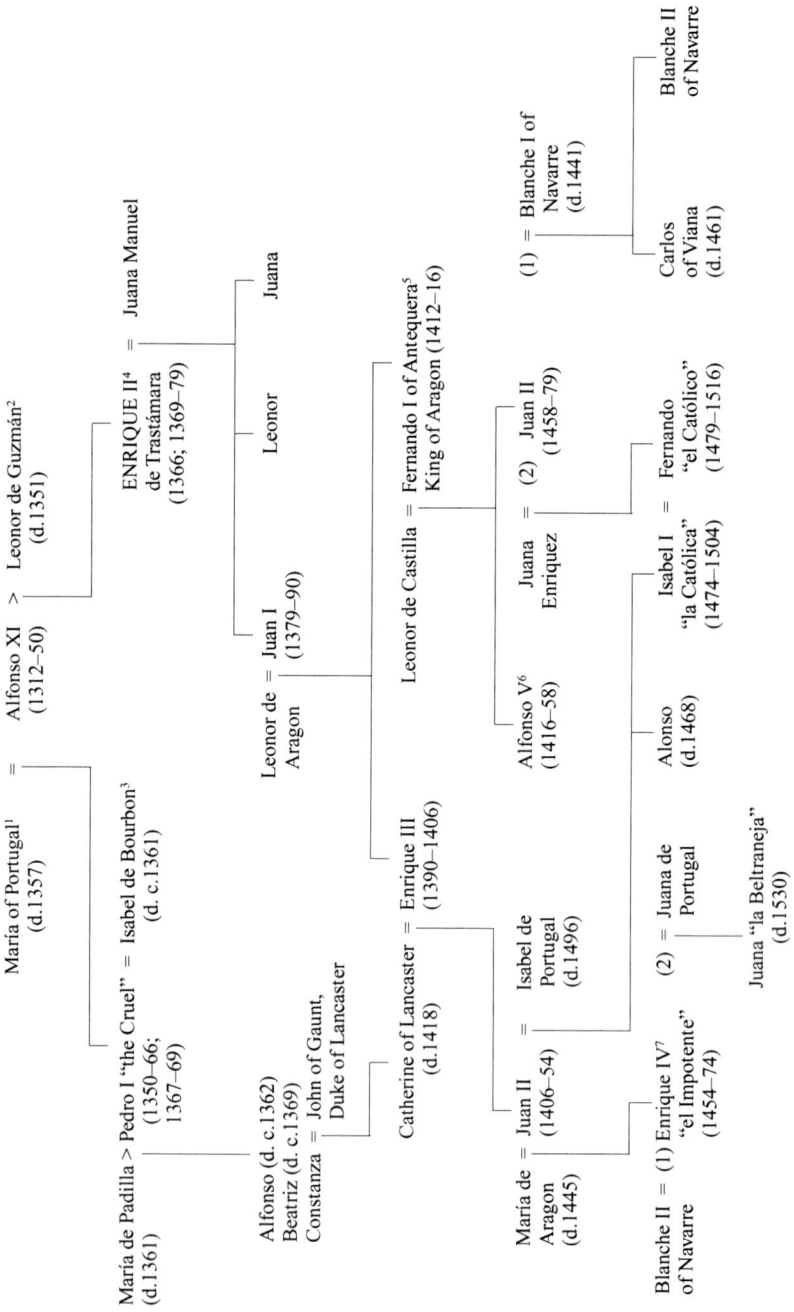

María of Portugal[1]
(d.1357)

=

Alfonso XI
(1312–50)

>

Leonor de Guzmán[2]
(d.1351)

María de Padilla > Pedro I "the Cruel" = Isabel de Bourbon[3]
(d.1361)   (1350–66; 1367–69)   (d. c.1361)

ENRIQUE II[4]
de Trastámara
(1366; 1369–79)

=

Juana Manuel

Alfonso (d. c.1362)
Beatriz (d. c.1369)
Constanza = John of Gaunt,
Duke of Lancaster

Leonor de = Juan I
Aragon   (1379–90)

Leonor

Juana

Leonor de Castilla = Fernando I of Antequera[5]
King of Aragon (1412–16)

Catherine of Lancaster = Enrique III
(d.1418)   (1390–1406)

Isabel de
Portugal
(d.1496)

=

Juan II
(1406–54)

Alfonso V[6]
(1416–58)

Juana
Enríquez

=

Juan II
(1458–79)

(1) = Blanche I of
Navarre
(d.1441)

María de = (1) Enrique IV[7]
Aragon   "el Impotente"
(d.1445)   (1454–74)

(2) = Juana de
Portugal

Alonso
(d.1468)

Isabel I
"la Católica"
(1474–1504)

=

Fernando
"el Católico"
(1479–1516)

Carlos
of Víana
(d.1461)

Blanche II
of Navarre

Blanche II
of Navarre

Juana "la Beltraneja"
(d.1530)

1 The queen's first son, Fernando, died in his first year, leaving only Pedro as her legitimate issue.

2 Leonor de Guzmán produced ten children by Alfonso XI, most of whom died before their brother, Enrique, became king. Enrique's major siblings were Fadrique, Master of Santiago, Tello, Count of Vizcaya, and Sancho, Count of Albuquerque.

3 Pedro I produced no heirs by his wife, Isabel de Bourbon, whom he deserted on their wedding day. In 1361, the king compelled the Castilian *cortes* to officially acknowledge as his legitimate heirs the children of his principal mistress, María de Padilla. His son, Alfonso, died shortly afterwards, leaving as his designated successors three daughters – Beatriz, Constanza, and Isabel. The duke of Lancaster claimed the Castilian throne on the basis of his marriage to the second, Constanza. The third daughter, Isabel, married Edmund Langley, duke of York.

4 Enrique also produced a number of illegitimate offspring including Alfonso Enríquez de Castilla, conde de Gijón y Noreña and Fadrique de Castilla, duque de Benavente.

5 In 1410, the death of Martín I, last in the ancient line of the counts of Barcelona, left the throne of Aragon vacant. In 1412, representatives of of the three realms that made up the crown of Aragon (Aragon, Cataluña, and Valencia) met at Caspe where they selected Fernando as the legitimate successor.

6 Alfonso failed to leave legitimate issue. His illegitimate son, Ferrante, inherited the realm of Naples which Alfonso had conquered during his lifetime.

7 Given the widespread belief that Enrique IV was impotent, there is considerable controversy over whether or not Juana "la Beltraneja" was really his daughter.

> Good officers never engage in general actions unless induced by opportunity or
> obliged by necessity. To distress the enemy more by famine than the sword is a mark
> of consummate skill.[20]

For his part, Rogers takes issue with the idea that most medieval commanders
were "battle-avoiding" most of the time. While eschewing the opposite extreme,
that medieval commanders were in general battle-seeking, he presents a nuanced
argument that most leaders were actually far readier not only to risk battle, but
even to seek it than the "Gillingham Paradigm" would have us believe – especially when they were on the offensive. In the course of his essay, he lays out
a variety of military circumstances that tended to promote such a readiness to
engage the enemy.

John Gillingham's lively rejoinder, entitled " 'Up With Orthodoxy': In Defense
of Vegetian Warfare"[21] and printed in the journal's second issue, contests many
of the counter-arguments raised by Rogers.[22] Quite early in his essay, he objects
to what he regards as imprecision on Rogers' part when characterizing the willingness of medieval commanders to engage in battle. Having quoted various
statements that appeared in Rogers' original essay,[23] he goes on to say

> What is striking about these passages is the use of such vague terms as "not all that
> rare," "quite common," "less common." If debates about patterns, Vegetian or other-

---

[20] Vegetius, *Military Institutions,* p. 113.
[21] John Gillingham, " 'Up with Orthodoxy!' In Defense of Vegetian Warfare," *JMMH* 2 (2003),
      149–64.
[22] Gillingham modestly disclaims the idea that he is responsible for the concepts contained in
      what Rogers has dubbed the Gillingham Paradigm:
> It is fair enough, of course, to say that I do think that in medieval warfare in
> the West both sides were, as a general rule, reluctant to risk battle. As is well
> known, this was orthodoxy long before I wrote the 1984 article "Richard I and
> the Science of War in the Middle Ages." ... But one reason that, regretfully, I
> think that "Smail paradigm" would be a better term than "Gillingham paradigm"
> is because when I wrote that I was "doing no more than transferring to a wider
> stage many of the insights contained in R. C. Smail's Crusading Warfare," I had
> in mind above all his analysis of defensive strategy.

      Gillingham, " 'Up with Orthodoxy!'," pp. 150, 153.
[23] Gillingham, " 'Up with Orthodoxy!'," p. 150:
> Battles, he [Rogers] says, were "actually not all that rare." "Certainly," he acknowl-
> edges, "there were some campaigns in which neither side wanted a battle, but,"
> he continues, "contrary to the current orthodoxy these were probably even less
> common than campaigns in which both sides were seeking battle." He notes that
> "it was quite common in medieval warfare that both sides were willing to offer
> [his italics] battle," and even though he explicitly accepts that often "neither side
> was willing to attack the enemy on ground of the defender's choosing," that this
> too he regards as being "contrary to the Gillingham school's thesis that medieval
> generals usually sought to avoid battle." On the same page Rogers states that
> campaigns without battle were "less common" in later centuries than they had
> been in the Middle Ages.

wise, in medieval warfare are to be fruitful, I think we have to look for less vague ways of measuring frequency.[24]

Having identified what he regards as a key problem in Rogers' attempt to rebut his thesis, Gillingham suggest a commonsense solution, one calling for "more studies of whole military careers in other centuries and in different parts of medieval Europe"[25] as the best means of testing the paradigm.

> In the context of a discussion of strategy and generalship, I suggest that there are two appropriate units of measurement. The first is the career of an individual commander. How many campaigns were there in his entire military career? The second unit is the campaign. What did each campaign comprise – sieges, battles, *chevauchées*, or what?[26]

The following essay is one such study. It will begin by summarizing the military career of Enrique II, a man who spent most of his adult life fighting first to gain a crown and then to hold it. Afterwards, it will focus in on his campaigns with an eye to determining whether he was "battle-seeking," "battle-avoiding" or perhaps something else not adequately accounted for in the current paradigm.

*

Born in Seville around 1332, Enrique II of Castile was the eldest surviving son of Alfonso XI (1312–1350) and his notorious mistress, Leonor de Guzmán.[27] The principal source for Alfonso's reign, the *Crónica del Rey Don Alfonso el Onceno*, supplies us with much of the information we have concerning Doña Leonor and her family during her lover's reign.[28] While all of the pair's illegitimate children were well-endowed by their father, as the eldest,[29] Enrique reaped the lion's share. Showered with properties by the crown, named heir to one of the realm's wealthiest, but childless nobles, and created count of Trastámara, he became a leading figure in Castile while still in his teens. In 1350, at age eighteen, Enrique participated in his father's ill-fated Gibraltar expedition, during which the king became Europe's highest-ranking victim of the Black Death.[30] The favoritism shown him by the crown ended abruptly with the succes-

---

[24] Ibid.
[25] Ibid.
[26] Ibid.
[27] There are a number of references to Doña Leonor and her family throughout the later sections of Alfonso XI's chronicle and in the early chapters of Pedro I's. According to Ayala, following Pedro's accession, she was murdered by her rival, Pedro's mother, the dowager queen, María of Portugal. *Crónica de Alfonso XI*, see esp. pp. 230–31; Ayala, *Pedro I*, p. 412.
[28] *Crónica del Rey Don Alfonso el Onceno* in *Crónicas de los Reyes de Castilla* 1, Biblioteca de Autores Españoles 66 (Madrid, 1953). While it is not stated specifically, the chronicle suggests that one of Enrique's siblings, Fadrique, was probably a younger twin. Fadrique numbered among the victims of their half-brother, Pedro I, who had him assassinated in 1358 while the pair were dining in the alcazar of Seville. His death ranks among the most vivid scenes in Ayala's chronicle of Pedro's reign. See: Ayala, *Pedro I*, pp. 481–83.
[29] Two sons, both older than Enrique, apparently died during their father's lifetime. *Crónica de Alfonso XI*, p. 230.
[30] *Crónica de Alfonso XI*, p. 390; Ayala, *Pedro I*, p. 403.

sion of his half-brother, Pedro I. The two soon became irreconcilably bitter enemies as Enrique helped establish an aristocratic coalition that tried to seize both the reins of power and the king's person. In 1354, when this attempt failed, Enrique was forced into exile, an exile that would endure for a dozen years.[31]

Fleeing from Castile, he first crossed the Pyrenees and for a time took service with the French crown as a mercenary captain.[32] Then, in 1356, Pedro I launched a war of conquest against his eastern neighbor, Aragon. As a result, Enrique returned to Spain, where he served the Aragonese monarch, Pere III "the Ceremonious" (1336–87),[33] against his own half-brother. In the process, he became Pere's closest ally during a decade-long conflict that historians call the War of the Two Pedros (1356–66), a conflict written about extensively by several Spanish historians, including Luis Suarez Fernández and María Teresa Ferrar i Mallol, but largely unknown outside of Spain.[34] As the years passed and the Castilian Pedro eliminated one after another of his potential successors, opposition to his rule came to center around the bastard son of the former monarch. In turn, Enrique used the growing band of exiles who rallied to his banner to launch significant raids into Castile in the midst of an otherwise defensive war being waged by the Aragonese. By 1363, Enrique had decided to challenge Pedro for the throne, a venture for which he received promises of Aragonese aid in the secret treaty of Monzón.[35]

Three years later, his plans came to fruition when he led an expedition against Castile that included not only his own followers, but also a force of Aragonese

---

[31] Ayala, *Pedro I*, p. 473. Although Enrique requested and received a royal license to leave the realm, Ayala indicates that Pedro tried to intercept him, but was unable to do so when Enrique chose to leave through Vizcaya, a region in which the crown's power was relatively weak.

[32] Ibid. At La Rochelle, Enrique took service in the army of King John II of France (*tomó sueldo dél*).

[33] The second Pedro was the Aragonese monarch, Pedro IV, known as Pere III in the county of Cataluña. To avoid confusion between the two, throughout this paper, the Aragonese monarch will be referred to as Pere.

[34] Very little of the work of Luis Suarez Fernández or María Teresa Ferrar i Mallol has been translated into English. However, readers can find one article by Ferrar i Mallol entitled "The Southern Valencian Frontier during the War of the Two Pedros," in L. J. Andrew Villalon and Donald J. Kagay, eds., *The Hundred Years War: A Wider Focus* (Leiden, 2005), pp. 75–115. My own publications that touch at some length on this conflict or its leading figures include: "Pedro the Cruel, Portrait of a Royal Failure"; "Seeking Castles in Spain: Sir Hugh Calveley and the Free Companies Intervention in Iberian Warfare (1366–1369)," in L. J. Andrew Villalon and Donald J. Kagay, eds., *Crusaders, Condotierri, and Cannon: Medieval Warfare in Societies around the Mediterranean* (Leiden, 2003), pp. 305–32; and "The Battle of Nájera and the Hundred Years War in Spain," in Villalon and Kagay, eds., *The Hundred Years War*, pp. 3–74.

[35] In March 1363, Pere and Enrique signed the secret treaty of Monzón in which the Aragonese king agreed to support his ally in a bid for the Castilian throne in return for extensive territorial concessions. While the agreement is not mentioned either in Ayala's chronicle or the *Memoirs of Pere III*, the great sixteenth-century Aragonese historian, Jerónimo Zurita, deals at some length with this and other secret negotiations between the two men in his *Anales de la Corona de Aragon*, 8 vols. (Zaragosa, 1973), 4:457. The Monzón agreement is printed in its entirety in Sitges, *Las Mujeres*, p. 81.

volunteers and, most significantly, thousands of out-of-work members of the Free Companies who had poured across the Pyrenees to take part in the invasion. With them came several of the leading captains of the Hundred Years War, including Bertrand du Guesclin (d.1380), the future constable of France, and Sir Hugh Calveley (d.1393), a renowned English knight and veteran of the famed Combat of the Thirty.[36] Pedro I's failure to meet the invaders followed by his precipitate flight southward led much of the realm to go over the Enrique. Having already proclaimed himself king upon entering Castile, he staged his formal coronation at Burgos several weeks later, after which he pursued his rival southward, a pursuit Pedro eluded only by fleeing into Portugal, then making his way to English territory in southern France. Here, the deposed monarch appealed to his English allies for help.[37]

In 1367, England mounted an expedition commanded by the Black Prince[38] to put Pedro back on the throne. Although Enrique and du Guesclin at first managed to block their way, the Castilian army was eventually routed at the battle of Nájera fought on April 3rd.[39] Although Aragon hurriedly withdrew its backing from Enrique, he escaped into France and with French aid, rebuilt his forces. Later that same year, he reentered Castile and initiated a civil war that would last until spring 1369, when he won the most significant battle of the war at Montiel in the wake of which came his deadly nocturnal encounter with Pedro.

---

[36] For more about this fascinating figure, see my article "Seeking Castles in Spain." For the Combat of the Thirty, see Steven Muhlberger, "The Combat of the Thirty against Thirty: An Example of Medieval Chivalry?" in L. J. Andrew Villalon and Donald J. Kagay, eds., *Hundred Years War (Part II): New Vistas* (Leiden, 2008), pp. 285–94.

[37] Ayala, *Pedro I*, pp. 545, 549.

[38] Most historians attribute this sobriquet, not mentioned in historical sources until long after Edward's death, to a penchant for wearing black armor. See, for example, Dwight Sedgwick, *The Life of Edward the Black Prince, 1330–1376* (New York, 1993), p. 27. The best medieval account of the prince's life is to be found in a lengthy poem by an anonymous author known only as the Chandos Herald, the most reliable surviving manuscript of which resides in Worcester College, Oxford. A critical edition from the turn of the century used in the preparation of this article contains not only the original text in meter, but also a useful prose paraphrase. While the introduction to that edition is overwhelmingly linguistic rather than historical in nature, the inclusion of voluminous endnotes, often cross-referencing to other chronicles, more than makes up for this. See *Life of the Black Prince by the Herald of Sir John Chandos* [hereafter Chandos Herald, *Life*], ed. Mildred K. Pope and Eleanor C. Lodge (Oxford, 1910). In addition, a somewhat freer English translation of the work can be found in Richard Barber, *The Life and Campaigns of the Black Prince* (London, 1979).

[39] For a summary account of the battle in English, see Charles Oman, *The History of the Art of War in the Middle Ages*, 2 vols. (New York, 1924), 2:179–90. My own treatment of the encounter comes in "The Battle of Nájera and the Hundred Years War in Spain." For a brief summary, see also my entry "Nájera, battle of" in the *Oxford Encyclopedia of Medieval Warfare and Military Technology*, ed. Clifford J. Rogers (Oxford, 2010).

Despite the king's assassination, the conflict did not end.[40] Enrique still had to face an array of enemies including not only Pedro's un-reconciled supporters, but also the kingdoms of Portugal, Aragon, and Granada, all of which sought to profit at the expense of their war-weary neighbor. He even faced the threat of a second English invasion, this one to vindicate the royal duke of Lancaster's claim to the Castilian throne acquired through a marriage to Pedro's daughter.[41]

To make good his claim, the usurper fought a drawn out and bloody border war against Granada,[42] twice invaded Portugal,[43] and sent an army into Navarre.[44] Despite the fact that Enrique's military activity abated somewhat after 1374, in the end, it took the better part of his reign to pacify the realm he had won at Montiel. At his death in 1379, he had just finished the latest round of fighting against his Navarrese counterpart, Charles the Bad (1349–87).[45]

While fighting to secure his crown, the first Trastámaran also brought his kingdom into the Hundred Years War on the side of France. An agreement to supply the French each year with a Castilian fleet helped set the stage for a critical French victory.[46] In 1372, Enrique's admiral, Ambrosio Bocanegra, smashed an English squadron at the battle of La Rochelle, a victory that led to England's loss of that important port city and the reestablishment of a significant French naval presence on the Bay of Biscay.[47] The following year, the king crossed the Pyrenees at the head of a Castilian army for the purpose of besieging English-held Bayonne.[48] Due to no fault of his, the campaign failed when Enrique's ally, the French royal duke of Anjou, brother of King Charles V, failed to show up as agreed, excusing himself on the grounds that he was fighting the English elsewhere.[49]

*

From his appearance at the siege of Gibraltar in 1350 at roughly the age of eighteen until his death twenty-nine years later, Enrique II pursued a career characterized by almost unceasing military activity. In this respect, it paralleled that

---

[40] According to Luis Suarez Fernandez "la muerte de Pedro el Cruel, lejos de ser la solución definitiva de la guera civil, la ampliaba." While this may be something of an overstatement, it is not all that far off the mark. Enrique II would have to undertake nearly five more years of military campaigning before managing to solidify his hold on the realm. Luis Suarez Fernandez, "Política Internacional de Enrique II," *Hispania* 16 (1956), 16–129.
[41] Ayala, *Enrique II*, p. 22.
[42] Ibid., pp. 2, 4.
[43] Ibid., pp. 3–4, 14–17.
[44] Ibid., pp. 33–34.
[45] Ibid., pp. 36–37.
[46] As part of Enrique's agreement with Portugal signed in 1373, the Portuguese king committed his country to contributing five galleys to the fleet Castile sent each year to aid the French. This presence of this clause clearly indicates that Castile's naval contribution to the French war effort was an annual one. Ibid., p. 16.
[47] Ibid., p. 12.
[48] Ibid., p. 23.
[49] Ibid.

of Richard the Lionheart some two centuries earlier. According to Gillingham, between 1173 and his death in 1199, Richard embarked on a military campaign during every year but two (one of which he spent in prison when seized by the archduke of Austria on his journey home from the Third Crusade). Yet in all that time, the English king fought only three battles, leading Gillingham to use him as the paradigmatic example of a warrior whose strategic outlook was "battle-avoiding." Can the same be said of the Spanish monarch? Can he be advanced as a "battle-avoiding" paragon in the midst of unceasing hostilities?

Before making any judgment, it would be useful to examine in a more detailed manner his military endeavors, beginning with his participation in the War of the Two Pedros.[50] Despite the bitter nature of this ten-year conflict, one of its major characteristics was an absence of battles. Both sides launched large scale incursions or "*calvagadas*",[51] aimed at devastating enemy territory. Both engaged in coastal raiding.[52] Several of the most successful actions during the war resulted from sneak attacks undertaken by Castile.[53] And of course, there were sieges, mostly directed against Aragonese holdings near the lengthy frontier.

Battles, however, were few and far between. On most occasions, when it looked as if the two sides might meet in the field, one or the other backed away. From the start, encounters that did take place tended to be small and indecisive. Even during the war's largest operation, the naval campaign of 1359, when the city of Barcelona was threatened and the fleets came within two leagues of one another, no engagement ensued.[54]

This may in large part have to do with the attitude of the royal antagonists for whom the conflict is named. Throughout the conflict, both men appeared reticent to face one another in the field, their rhetoric to the contrary not withstanding. On various occasions when his opponent seemed most likely to fight, each monarch chose to back away. The actions of both Pedros seemingly support the Gillingham paradigm. By contrast, Enrique de Trastámara, who emerges as the war's leading offensive figure, was habitually ready and willing to engage the enemy.

---

[50] For a more detailed summary of the conflict and its largely defensive nature, see my article " 'Cut off their Heads or I'll cut off Yours': The Strategy and Tactics of Castile in the War of the Two Pedros," in Villalon and Kagay, eds., *The Hundred Years War (Part II): Different Vistas*, pp. 153–82.

[51] The word "*calvagada*," comparable to the French "*chevauchée*" can be literally translated as "ride-abouts." The word is found in several Castilian documents generated during the conflict. The best-preserved such documents currently known and available to historians are preserved in the archives of Murcia. They are printed in a two-volume work composing part of the more extensive *Colección de Documentos para la Historia del Reino de Murcia* and are entitled *Documentos de Pedro I* [hereafter *Documentos*], ed. Angel Luis Molina Molina, 2 vols. (Murcia, 1978). For the use of the term "*calvagada*," see *Documentos*, 169–70 (letter 110).

[52] Ayala, *Pedro I*, p. 475.

[53] Ibid., pp. 478, 520–22.

[54] Ibid., pp. 494–98.

In September 1359, Enrique shared command of an Aragonese force that entered Castile. Many of the 800 who participated were, in fact, Castilian exiles owing him their allegiance. Although the expedition seems to have begun as a *calvagada*, when confronted by a larger force of some 1,500 assigned by Pedro I to guard the border, Enrique refused to run for cover. At a place called Araviana, he and his men fought one of the two major battles of the war, one in which Pedro's army was routed and several of his leading supporters were killed.[55]

A few months later, in spring 1360, Enrique led a second and even larger raid into Castile, supported by 1,500 cavalry and 2,000 infantry. On this occasion, Pedro himself rushed to the frontier with a force said to number 5,000 cavalry and 10,000 foot. When the two sides met in what some Spanish historians call the first battle of Nájera, once again, Enrique stood and fought, despite being badly outnumbered.[56] This time, the battle went against him. His force was roughly handled, his standard was lost to the enemy, and he was almost captured before he could regain the safety of the town. Nevertheless, according to the Spanish chronicler, Ayala, he was fully prepared to continue the fight on the following day. In the end, it would be Pedro who blinked. Despite victory on the first day, the king decided to break off the engagement. Only then did Enrique withdraw into Aragon.

Was Enrique actually seeking a battle on these two occasions? There is no way to answer this with any certainty. Both incursions seem to have started as *calvagadas* bent on devastating enemy territory. Most such ventures during the ten-year conflict did not give rise to anything more than minor skirmishing. On the other hand, both of these *calvagadas* were larger than the norm and in both cases their leader proved quite ready to accept battle, despite being outnumbered. Under any circumstances, by no stretch of the imagination could either event be categorized as "battle-avoiding."

In 1366, Enrique helped lead the invasion of Castile, a "battle-seeking" gambit that ultimately put an end to the War of the Two Pedros. At the beginning of the enterprise, he probably expected to face the Castilian king in battle, an eventuality forestalled only by Pedro's refusal to meet him in the field followed by the king's precipitate flight from the realm. On two of these occasions, at Araviana and "first Nájera," Enrique's willingness to fight involved him in a battle against superior forces serving a man who would not hesitate to put him to death if he were captured. On the third occasion, his active move to force an engagement was frustrated, due not to any reticence on his part, but to the flight of his enemy.

During the Castilian civil war (1366–69) that grew out of the War of the Two Pedros, several other clear examples of Enrique's battle readiness cropped up. In the spring of 1367, when the Black Prince led his Anglo-Gascon army into Castile, Enrique maneuvered to block the prince's entry. The expedition was

55 Ibid., p. 499.
56 Ibid., p. 505.

no mere *chevauchée*, but a thoroughly battle-seeking exercise, whose success depended upon rapid victory in the field before logistical considerations could shut it down. Under the circumstances, any attempt to actually block rather than merely harass the English could be expected to lead to a battle (as indeed it did.)

As the prince swung westward from Navarre into Castile, Enrique countered by marching north to Vitoria where he seized the heights around the city. Here, the two armies faced one another uneasily for several weeks in March.[57] The chronicler Ayala, who was present at these events, suggests that even then, Enrique was ready to fight; not surprisingly, however, he wished to do so on favorable terms. He refused to abandon a superior position on the high ground in order to face the English on an even field. And although Edward was even more desirous of a fight, he had no intention of attacking under such disadvantageous circumstances.[58] The fact that no confrontation occurred at Vitoria should not be taken to mean that the protagonists were "battle-avoiding"; on the contrary, here we find two "battle-seeking" commanders restrained by positional considerations.

But not entirely restrained. In the midst of the general stand-off, Enrique launched a surprise dawn attack against Edward's army, involving numbers that exceeded those he had had available at Araviana. Led by his volatile younger brother, Don Tello, several thousand Castilians quietly moved down off the heights and around breakfast caught the English vanguard unaware. The English began to flee, stopping only when the duke of Lancaster provided a rallying point by raising his standard on a nearby hill. Although the arrival of the prince with the main body of his army forced the now outnumbered Castilians to fall back, the fact remains, Enrique's men had sought out and confronted the English in a sharp encounter that he initiated and that led to the death or capture of a number of Englishmen.[59]

Soon afterwards, circumstances precipitated the general engagement both commanders either desired or were willing to accept. Stymied by stalemate, Edward made the best strategic move of the campaign. He retreated into Navarre, then swung southeastward through that kingdom, crossing the Ebro River and reentering Castile at the city of Logroño, after which he started to march westward along the main pilgrim route to Santiago de Compostela.[60]

---

[57] Among the chronicle accounts the 1367 campaign is best treated in Ayala, *Pedro I*, pp. 550–67. The most valuable account from the English side is that found in the Chandos Herald's lengthy poem on the life of the Black Prince.

[58] Ibid., p. 554.

[59] No single account adequately explains this event; it can only be reconstructed by drawing on material found in the three principal sources of information concerning the 1367 invasion. See: Ayala, *Pedro I*, pp. 553–54; Chandos Herald, *Life*, pp. 158–59; Froissart, *Chronicles*, 1:365–67.

[60] Chandos Herald, *Life*, p. 159. On 1 April 1367, Pedro wrote to the city council at Murcia informing it of his arrival in Logroño, extolling the people of Murcia for their loyalty, and commanding that they seize all followers of "the traitor" on whom they could lay their hands. The letter is reprinted in an editor's footnote to Ayala, *Pedro I*, p. 554.

Now, the Castilian army would either have to fight him on terrain which did not inordinately favor either side or let him pass unmolested.

A battle-seeking move by the prince earned a battle-seeking response by Enrique. Operating along interior lines, he and his principal adviser, du Guesclin, retraced their steps south from Vitoria, recrossed the Ebro well to the west of Logroño, then marched eastward to arrive at the town of Nájera, in plenty of time to block the main route along which the prince would have to advance. Originally, the Castilian army established a new camp west of the Rio Najerilla; thus, for a time, it still held a river line Edward would have to force in order to move farther into Castile.[61]

Throughout the campaign, Enrique's leading French advisers, in line with orders from their very "battle-avoiding" monarch, Charles V (1364–80), had urged caution on this French client, advising him to harass the English, interdict their supply lines, and cut off their retreat, rather than meet them in the field.[62] Enrique now not only overruled those advisers, he even abandoned the advantage of the river line by crossing over to fight on level ground east of the Najarilla. While this tactical decision may have reflected topographical realities – after all, the majority of Enrique's effective force consisted of cavalry, better suited to operate on an open plain than defend a river line[63] – the fact remains, it became a major reason that his army suffered one of the great defeats of the century.

According to Ayala, the decision to fight may have reflected at least in part Enrique's fear that his failure to do so would lead to another mass defection, this time to the other side. On the other hand, as Cliff Rogers has pointed out, the fact that such fears may have inspired or even necessitated battle-seeking behavior does not make it any less "battle-seeking."[64] The result of the two armies meeting on fairly equal ground was *the* battle of Nájera, fought on 3 April 1367, in which the army of one "battle-seeker" was virtually crushed by his even more "battle-seeking" opponent.

Contemporary accounts agree that among the Castilians on the field, Enrique made the best showing, several times rallying his cavalry for an assault on the longbow-studded English left. Only when the men he was commanding joined the general flight did he see to his own safety. Eluding the pursuit that followed his defeat, Enrique managed to escape into Aragon. Finding himself no longer

---

[61] Ayala, *Pedro I*, p. 554.

[62] Ibid., pp. 553, 556.

[63] In his treatment of the battle, Oman advances the argument that Enrique probably crossed the river to operate on the plain due to the fact that his army was principally made up of cavalry.

> He [Enrique] had now only to choose whether he would fight east or west of the Najarilla, and, as he placed his main confidence in his cavalry, he resolved to advance into he broad plain beyond the river, instead of staying on his own bank and waiting for the prince to attack him. Horsemen, as he perhaps reflected, are not suited to defend a position.

Oman, *History*, 2:185.

[64] Rogers, "Vegetian," p. 18.

welcome in the kingdom of his former ally, he retired to southern France where, with help from French crown in the person of the king's brother, Louis, duke of Anjou, he rebuilt his shattered army. Within months, Enrique led it back into Castile for another try. Fortunately for him, he now had only to face Pedro; his main battle-seeking opponent, the prince, having left the peninsula, disgusted at the conduct of the man he had put back on the throne, in particular his failure to pay the sums promised when the expedition was being put together.[65]

For the next eighteen months, fighting mostly took the form of sieges and skirmishes, centering around Enrique's siege of Toledo. That city's imminent surrender in spring, 1369, afforded him a chance to exhibit the "purest" battle-seeking behavior of his career. Learning that Pedro was moving north from Seville to relieve his beleaguered garrison, he and du Guesclin[66] split their army, leaving only a holding force to maintain the siege while rushing south with the remainder, including du Guesclin's Franco-Breton troops, to meet Pedro in the environs of Montiel.[67]

In the ten years that followed, as Enrique strove to solidify his hold on Castile, he continued to demonstrate the "will to combat" that had characterized him as both a mercenary captain and a challenger for the crown. Throughout these years, even when he was not actually "battle-seeking," he was willing to stand and fight when an opportunity arose. Once more, it would be his enemies, not he, who repeatedly backed away from potential conflict.

Castile's military interaction with Portugal during this period supplies the best example of the king's "battle willingness." Twice in the next five years, he entered the neighboring kingdom at the head of a large invasion force, challenging the Portuguese monarch to come out and fight. The first invasion came shortly after Pedro's death in 1369, when King Fernando claimed the Castilian throne based on his legitimate descent from the Castilian royal family. Almost immediately, much of northwestern Castile declared for Fernando, including the city of Zamora and the province of Galicia, both of them staunch supporters of Pedro in the past. In turn, the Portuguese monarch led a force into the region.

---

[65] Ayala indicates that the prince was also angered by Pedro's battlefield brutality. The Castilian king murdered one prisoner, his former supporter, Iñigo Lopez de Orozco, and apparently tried to "purchase" the other captives from the prince in order to execute them. Ayala, *Pedro I*, pp. 558, 562–63.

[66] Ransomed by the French monarch, Charles V, following his capture at the battle of Nájera, du Guesclin returned to Spain where he spent several more years in the service of Enrique II, until recalled to France early in the 1370s to assume the office of constable. Ayala supplies a colorful description of du Guesclin's strategem for convincing the prince to put him up for ransom. Ibid., pp. 561–62.

[67] The precise status of du Guesclin's force within Enrique's army presents something of a definitional problem. Although the men were foreigners for whose services Enrique paid dearly, simply to refer to them as "mercenaries" fails to take into account the fact that they were, in a sense, on loan from the French crown which was substantially aiding Enrique in his struggle for the Castilian crown. Perhaps they might better be referred to by the term Machiavelli used for such forces in *The Prince*, i.e. "auxiliaries." See Niccolò Machiavelli, *The Prince*, in Machiavelli, *The Chief Works and Others*, trans. Allan Gilbert, 3 vols. (Durham, 1989), 1:51–52.

Enrique responded without hesitation. Having gathered an army that included du Guesclin's mercenaries, he advanced first on Zamora, then entered Galicia, ready to all appearances to face the Portuguese monarch on a Castilian battle-field. It was the Portuguese king who hurriedly backed away from such a confrontation. Having placed a garrison in Galicia's leading port city of La Coruña, he took ship back to Portugal rather than accompany his army in its more dangerous land-bound retreat.

At this point, acting at the advice of his French captain and his most loyal sibling, Sancho, Enrique determined to advance across the border in an attempt to force the issue. Entering Portugal between the Duero and Miño rivers, he attacked and took Braga. Pushing deeper into the kingdom, he invested Braganza "devastating all of the surrounding territory."[68] Having learned that problems were arising in other parts of Castile that required his attention, he began plan-ning a withdrawal, plans he postponed after receiving letters from Fernando "that he wished to give battle if he [Enrique] would await him."[69] Having agreed to meet the Portuguese monarch, Enrique camped at a place called Tras los Montes not far from Braganza, to which he summoned military reinforcements from Castile for the upcoming battle. In the end, he left Portugal only when it became abundantly clear that the Fernando had no intention of following through on his bellicose challenge.

Four years later, Enrique launched a second and an even more impressive invasion, marching deep into Portugal and again summoning reinforcements from Castile when threatened with battle. When Fernando failed once more to meet him in the field, he briefly occupied and then burnt part of Lisbon. On this occasion, an encounter was averted only when a papal legate engaged in "shuttle diplomacy," fourteenth-century style, thus arranging a treaty that gave Enrique most of what he wanted.[70]

Even though he may well have preferred to reach such an agreement rather than fight a battle or face the possibility of a protracted siege, the fact remains that his actions in Portugal demonstrate an unmistakable willingness to follow through on his threat. After all, having placed himself deep in Portuguese terri-tory, he would have had little choice had Fernando accepted the wager of battle. The only alternative, a precipitate retreat into Castile, would have cost this newly installed usurper political capital he could not afford to lose.

Shortly after settling matters in the west, Enrique found himself once again facing the very real possibility of a battle along his eastern frontier. Here, a coalition had formed against him that included his former ally, Pere III of Aragon, and the Black Prince's younger brother, John of Gaunt, duke of Lancas-ter.[71] Lancaster, who had replaced the dying prince as English commander on

---

[68] Ayala, *Enrique II*, p. 4.
[69] Ibid., p. 4.
[70] Ibid., pp. 14–17.
[71] Lancaster had played a prominent role in the 1367 invasion. Having arrived on the continent just in time to join the expedition, through much of the campaign he had shared command of the

the continent, had begun as early as 1372 to entitle himself king of Castile and Leon, a claim he based on his marriage to Pedro I's eldest surviving daughter, Costanza.[72] Despite a renewal of the Hundred Years War north of the Pyrenees, the duke entered into lengthy negotiations with Enrique's neighbors in a search for allies who would support his claim. One such was the Aragonese monarch, Pere, who still hoped to acquire extensive lands along the border promised to him by Enrique when he had lent his support to the 1366 invasion of Castile.

Early in 1374, when Enrique learned of these machinations and the duke's efforts to gather a substantial force, his reaction was typical: he mustered at Burgos an army said to number 5,000 Castilian lances, 5,000 foot, and 1,200 light cavalry and advanced into the border province of Rioja to confront Lancaster if he entered Castile.[73] In the end, nothing came of the threat. Pere and his would-be English ally failed to reach an agreement on the timing of Aragonese intervention and the duke's current campaign against the French came off badly. Once again, however, Enrique appears to have been ready to fight had the need arisen.

With the English threat removed, the Castilian monarch now went on the offensive. Having negotiated with the duke of Anjou a joint attack on the English-held port city of Bayonne in southern Aquitaine, he marched an army across the Pyrenees and invested the place only to learn that his ally had withdrawn from the enterprise, due to his involvement elsewhere in fighting the English.[74]

Time and again, Enrique II took a highly aggressive stand that, had his opponents been willing, might well have led to a battlefield encounter. This was particularly so in respect to his invasion of English territory north of the Pyrenees since the English had a considerably better track record for joining battle than either the Portuguese or Aragonese whom Enrique threatened on other occasions.

*

The tenor of this essay should leave little doubt in the mind of the reader that I believe my subject to have been far more "battle-seeking" than "battle-avoiding." In fact, a close examination of Enrique's actions has turned up virtually no evidence to support the latter conclusion. Here, then, is a career contradicting the Gillingham Paradigm that medieval military commanders as a general rule sought to avoid fighting battles.

vanguard with Sir John Chandos. When a wasting disease felled the Black Prince in the wake of the Spanish expedition, Lancaster assumed command of English forces on the continent. Chandos Herald, *Life*, pp. 153, 158, 162; Froissart, *Chronicles*, 1:357, 365–66, 451–54. For a brief biography of this fascinating and controversial figure, see Norman F. Cantor, *The Last Knight: The Twilight of the Middle Ages and the Birth of the Modern Era* (New York, 2004).

72 Ayala, *Enrique II*, p. 22. One of the earliest examples of Lancaster signing a document *Dei gratia Rex Castellae et Legionis* appears in Rymer's *Foedera* dated 25 June 1372.

73 Ayala, *Enrique II*, pp. 22–23.

74 Ibid., p. 23.

On the other hand, is there any further light that Enrique II's military career might shed on the debate over the paradigm? To answer this question, we must examine more closely how that debate is currently framed.

While Rogers contested the idea that medieval commanders generally eschewed battle, he did not argue the opposite extreme, that they generally sought it. The farthest he has ventured in this direction has been to state that English armies of the fourteenth century were more often than not battle-seeking and that in the majority of medieval campaigns, the stronger side, especially when it assumed the role of invader, was more likely than not to be seeking an encounter. In short, he makes no attempt to establish a dichotomy between "battle-seeking" and "battle-avoiding" and fit all war leaders into one of the two categories.

Nevertheless, something of a dichotomy does seem to characterize the debate as developed in the *JMMH*. In both articles, only two categories are identified – "battle-seeking" and "battle-avoiding" – leading to an either-or framing of the debate. I would argue that a third category, situated between the other two, does exist, one that might be dubbed (in order to retain a certain verbal symmetry) "battle-willing."

The term "battle-willing" should encompass medieval commanders whose strategic plans, while not irrevocably committed to battle, clearly envisaged that possibility. If a battle offered itself under circumstances they could accept, they would engage the enemy. Realizing (perhaps even hoping) that their goals could be achieved short of the *ultima ratio*, they would nevertheless be ready to accept the wager. While commanders with such a strategic outlook cannot be said to have been "battle-seeking" in the strictest sense of the term, they were most certainly not "battle-avoiding."

To understand why this tripartite distinction provides a better means of characterizing the actions of medieval war leaders, it is helpful to analyze in somewhat greater detail what John Gillingham seems to be alleging in his rejoinder to Rogers. Several passages from Gillingham's article highlight the key problems that arise out of any either-or debate, problems that to my way of thinking load the dice against anyone trying to locate "battle-seeking" behavior in the Middle Ages.

To begin with, according to Gillingham

> Because tactically a commander was willing to risk battle, it does not follow that he was pursuing a strategy that was battle-seeking. As I made explicit at the beginning of my Richard I paper, in it I was concentrating "on one aspect of war only – strategy, the planning and conduct of campaigns," not on tactical opportunities that might occur at moments during those campaigns.[75]

The obvious problem here lies in determining just what was the strategic thinking behind any given medieval campaign. To put it another way, how can one really know (at least in most cases) if a medieval commander embarked on

---

[75] Gillingham, "'Up with Orthodoxy!'," p. 151.

the campaign determined to fight a battle? Does one accept the commander's post-facto rhetoric in order to decide? If so, then Enrique's Aragonese ally, Pere III, would have to be adjudged a major "battle-seeker" during the War of the Two Pedros, a conclusion his actual conduct firmly belies.

While this problem afflicts military historians studying many periods, it is particularly pronounced for an era like the Middle Ages where much or, in some cases, most of what we know about a battle or campaign may come from later accounts, often written years or decades after the event, sometimes by people far outside of the military loop.

A good example of the danger in Gillingham's approach can be seen when he applies his criteria for "battle-seeking" to one of the true turning point events of the Middle Ages – an event about which we know a fair amount since we have available more sources, some of them closer in time, than is usually the case – the battle of Hastings fought on 14 October 1066. Here, he states that

> A field army capable of giving battle is one thing: a field army seeking battle quite another. That Harold had an army capable of giving battle against William in October 1066 is beyond dispute; whether or not he actively sought to bring William to battle cannot be known for certain.[76]

According to Gillingham, we cannot be certain that one of the two antagonists, Harold Godwinson, had actually embraced as part of his strategic thinking a determination to seek battle; this despite the fact that two weeks earlier, after leading his army on a forced march northward, he had initiated a battle at Stamford Bridge, then pushed the remnants of his tired army on a second forced march south from York to London, and finally, rather than await the arrival of needed reinforcements, had hurried forward to take up his fateful position on Senlac Hill. It must have been clear to a talented military leader like Harold that his own actions, given William's precarious situation on the coast, made a battle virtually inevitable. Yet for all this, Gillingham is not willing to stipulate that the Anglo-Saxon leader was "battle-seeking."

What implications can be drawn from Gillingham's statement concerning Hastings? First of all, he has placed the bar for determining "battle-seeking" behavior very high indeed. Just what would be needed to label Harold "battle-seeking" on the eve of the encounter? A written, strategic plan setting forth how he intended to drive William's invading army back into the sea? Unfortunately, few if any, such "smoking gun" documents survive from the Middle Ages. In fact, in probability few, if any, ever existed.

Second, he has erected a substantial impediment to using the very procedure for determining "battle-seeking" behavior that he himself recommends earlier in the article. For how can the "studies of whole military careers" that he has called for truly establish the presence of "battle-seeking" behavior when the facts surrounding the battle of Hastings are not deemed sufficiently probative of Harold's strategy?

---

[76] Ibid., p. 153.

Presumably, the only warriors whom Gillingham *might* accept as having cleared his bar and thus be defined as "battle-seeking" would be men like William the Conqueror in 1066 or the Black Prince in 1367, men who led their armies deep into hostile territory with the very strong possibility that any retreat could be cut off, and for whom battle alone could bring success. But if one is limited to only a bipartite paradigm, then everyone else would have to be classified as "battle-avoiding" even when few if any of their actions show that to be the case.

In the face of such daunting problems, converting the paradigm from a bipartite to a tripartite one seems, at least to this observer, eminently logical. Adding the category of "battle-willing" cannot help but supply a more nuanced scale for evaluating the strategic stance adopted by medieval war leaders.

*

To conclude, this analysis of Enrique II's military career suggests several things:

First and foremost, throughout decades of campaigning as captain, usurper, and king, Enrique almost always appears to have been either "battle-seeking" or, at the very least, "battle-willing."

Admittedly, it is sometimes difficult to determine precisely into which of the two categories he falls. In the single most important campaign of his career, he and his principal subordinate, Bertrand du Guesclin's, launched a dawn attack on Pedro's forces, scattering them and eventually capturing and killing their leader. Even John Gillingham would be hard-put to say that Enrique action on this occasion failed to clear the "battle-seeking" bar, despite the absence of any pre-existing battle plan announcing an intention to provoke a battle.

On the other hand, in the case of Enrique's most famous campaign – the one ending in his disastrous defeat at Nájera – it is more difficult to determine his strategic intentions and therefore to decide whether he was "battle-seeking" or only "battle-willing." While he was clearly "battle-willing" from the start of the campaign his initial strategy may have been more focused on what Gillingham characterizes as "harassing" the attacker than it was on actively seeking an engagement. It was this more cautious course that his French advisers, du Guesclin and d'Audrehem, were urging on him.

On the other hand, there can be little doubt that a hardened campaigner like Enrique must have realized that attempts to harass the Black Prince would very likely end by forcing him onto the battlefield (as indeed they did). What is more, Enrique's actions strongly suggest that by the final days of the 1367 campaign, he had made the transition to a fully "battle-seeking" strategy, a transition signaled by his very questionable decision to cross the Rio Najerilla and face the Black Prince on the plain beyond.

And what of those two invasions of Portugal? If (as seems to be the case) Gillingham is willing to recognize William the Conqueror as "battle-seeking" when he flung himself across the Channel in 1066, then by rights he should concede that same distinction to Enrique. After all, the Castilian monarch had twice propelled himself deep into the heart of enemy territory, tempting the Portuguese king to come out and fight and waiting patiently for him to do so. Had Fernando risen to the bait on either occasion, a battle would undoubtedly have ensued, as it had on that October day in 1066 when Harold took William's bait. Indeed, just such a battle would occur a few years later when the Portuguese finally did come out to face a Castilian invader deep in their territory. On that occasion, they would smash a far larger army led by Enrique's son, Juan I (1379–90), at the decisive battle of Aljubarrota (1385), thereby securing Portuguese independence for centuries to come.[77] In short, had his opponent been willing to fight, Enrique would have accepted the wager of battle. What is true in the case of Portugal seems true for most of his career.

Another significant observation arising from the study of this military career: neither "battle-seeking" nor "battle-willing" behavior necessarily leads to battle. Not much is likely to happen unless both adversaries are at least battle-willing and conditions that both sides find suitable present themselves. Even when two battle-seekers faced one another, for an encounter to take place, one or both had to be willing to accept it under the conditions offered. For example, when Enrique and the Black Prince confronted one another at Vitoria, in 1367, the former was unwilling to sacrifice his positional advantage while the latter refused to attack in the face of that advantage. Hence no general engagement took place. Given this reality, to judge the commander's military mentalité on the basis of whether or not an engagement actually takes place seems fruitless.

On the other hand, under certain circumstances, a battle may occur despite the fact that only one side is actively seeking it; in other words, under what Steve Morillo has called "almost accidental circumstances."[78] In March, 1369, Pedro I led an army north toward the beleaguered city of Toledo. He may have intended to link up with his supporters in the city in order to break the siege, a move that would very likely have engendered a battle in the environs of Toledo. Alternatively, he may have simply been positioning himself to harass the besiegers to the point that they would be forced to abandon their siege. Clearly, however, he had no intention of fighting a battle on the plains around Montiel, well to the south of Toledo. Ironically, this most controversial of Spanish monarchs entered the final and decisive battle of his career with no intention of being there.

In the end, I would argue that "studying the whole military career" of the first Trastámaran monarch supplies evidence supporting Cliff Rogers' side of

---

[77] I am indebted to Cliff Rogers for having made me aware of the work of João Gouveia Monteiro, a Portuguese scholar at the University of Coimbra. His article, published in *JMMH* 7 (2009) is entitled "The Battle of Aljubarrota (1385): A Reassessment." This and Monteiro's publication in his native tongue ("Estratégia e risco em Aljubarrota: a decisão de dar batalha à luz do 'paradigma Gillingham'") indicate that others are heeding John Gillingham's call to examine the campaigns of medieval war leaders in light of the "battle-seeking" vs. "battle-avoiding" debate. An older account of Aljubarrota in English can also be found in Oman, *History of the Art of War*, 2:191–95. See also *The Oxford Encyclopedia of Medieval Warfare and Military Technology* (forthcoming).

[78] Stephen Morillo, *Warfare under the Anglo-Norman Kings* (Woodbridge, 1994), p. 2.

the debate. Enrique was without doubt a medieval commander consistently ready to risk the wager of battle under the right (and in one case, at least, the wrong) circumstances. In some of his campaigns he was clearly seeking battle. In the others, he was willing to risk battle if his goals could not be otherwise accomplished. Having said all this, one thing cannot be denied: whether "battle-seeking" or "battle-willing," Enrique's lifelong behavior belies the Gillingham Paradigm of a battle-avoiding medieval commander. My only disagreement with Cliff Rogers comes in respect to terminology. The concept of "battle-willing" that I have proposed here is inherent throughout his essay. However, he chooses to expand the term "battle-seeking" to subsume behavior that I would prefer to characterize under this alternate term. On the other hand, whatever term one uses to describe Enrique II, historical figures over the centuries who have advocated boldness in seizing one's opportunities – men such as Machiavelli, Danton, and G. W. Plunkitt[79] – would all see in the Castilian king a highly kindred spirit.

---

[79] George Washington Plunkitt, the Tammany Hall leader at the beginning of the twentieth century, was complimented by a contemporary as being "a straight organization man!" He is famous for his sayings, including the one that has placed him in the rather rarified company of the great Florentine and the French Revolutionary: "I seen my opportunities and I took 'em." See: *Plunkitt of Tammany Hall: A Series of Very Plain Talks on Very Practical Politics, Delivered by Ex-Senator, George Washington Plunkitt, the Tammany Philosopher, from his Rostrum – the New York County Court House Bootblack Stand*, ed. William L. Riordon in The Project Gutenberg, 2001.

7

Outrance and *Plaisance*

Will McLean

Modern writers on medieval deeds of arms often use the terms *à outrance* to describe combats fought "using the normal weapons of war" and *à plaisance* to describe combats using "specially modified weapons with sharp edges removed or blunted." The definitions quoted are from Richard Barber and Juliet Barker's 1989 *Tournaments: Jousts, Chivalry and Pageants in the Middle Ages*. Barker's earlier work, *The Tournament in England 1100–1400*, defines *outrance* and *plaisance* with almost identical terms, as do Maurice Keen's *Chivalry*, Richard Kaeuper's *Chivalry and Violence in Medieval Europe* and Katie Stevenson's *Chivalry and Knighthood in Scotland, 1424–1513*. This definition can be traced back at least as early as 1918, when Francis Henry Cripps-Day's *The History of the Tournament* defined combat with "arms of war" as *à outrance* and with blunted arms of courtesy as *à plaisance*.[1] However, during the fifteenth century, when the terms came into use to describe specific types of combat and were most often used to describe contemporary deeds of arms, writers in Burgundy, France, Spain and England used the terms very differently.

The use of sharp rather than blunted weapons was not the consideration that distinguished *outrance* from *plaisance*. Combats *à plaisance* could be fought with sharp weapons, and arms *à outrance* were sometimes fought with wooden clubs. Instead, deeds of arms *à outrance* were distinguished by the willingness of the combatants to fight until one side or the other was captured or killed, unless the judge or judges stopped the fight. More generally, in the fifteenth century *outrance* or *oultrance* in French or *outraunce*, *utteraunce* or *utterance* in English meant to the end, to the finish, or the utmost. Arms *à plaisance* were less extreme, and would typically end as soon as an agreed number of blows were struck, or as soon as a combatant was carried to the ground. They included a variety of combats with limits agreeable to the pleasure and will of the participants. In other contexts, *plaisance* in French and *plesaunce* in English

---

[1] Richard Barber and Juliet Barker, *Tournaments: Jousts, Chivalry and Pageants in the Middle Ages* (Woodbridge, 1989), p. 212; Juliet Barker, *The Tournament in England 1100–1400* (Woodbridge, 1986), p. 14; Maurice Keen, *Chivalry* (New Haven, 1984), p. 86; Richard Kaeuper, *Chivalry and Violence in Medieval Europe* (Oxford, 1999), p. 165; Katie Stevenson, *Chivalry and Knighthood in Scotland, 1424–1513* (Woodbridge, 2006), p. 74; and Francis Henry Cripps-Day, *The History of the Tournament in England* (London, 1918), p. 46.

meant pleasure, including the sense of will, desire and consent, as in "at your pleasure."[2]

The encounter between Lord Scales and the Bastard of Burgundy in 1467 was twice called an act of *plesaunce* in a contemporary account ascribed to Thomas Whiting, Chester Herald.[3] Jacques du Clercq, a contemporary Burgundian chronicler, also described the encounter as *"armes à plaisance."*[4] Blunted weapons, however, do not appear to have been on the agenda. After a course with sharp lances, run without tilt or barrier, the champions fought on horseback, cutting and thrusting with sharp swords.[5] The Utrecht MS, probably written by a member of the Bastard's party, records that the Bastard split Scales' visor with an edge blow, making a substantial opening in the metal: "en la visiere a cost sy auant fendu que de trois doigs de large et vng gran de bled pouoit passer parmy la fente dont lespee fut escardee en deux lieux."[6]

The next day they fought on foot armed with axes and daggers. The axes were equipped with points above the head and at the lower end of the haft, and both champions used them vigorously. Whiting reports that "Lord Scales at the recounter with the point of his axe struck thorugh oon of the ribbes of the Bastardes plates, as the seid Basterd shewid him aftir the field" and finally "Lord Scales stroke him in the side of the visern of his basenet."[7] The *Chronicle of London* claims that the fight ended with Scales having the advantage: "the poynte of axe in the vysour of his enemyes helmet, and by force thereof was lykly to have born hym ovyr."[8] The Burgundian chronicler Olivier de la Marche reports that the Bastard also fought well "and in truth I saw afterwards the harness of Lord Scales, where the Lord Bastard had done great damage with the lower point of his axe."[9]

At the end of the fight the king "comaundid them ych to take other by the handes, and love toogedirs as brethirs in armes; which they so did. And there they immediately yafe yche to other as courteis godely and frendely language as coude be thought; and went togidre into the middes of the field. And there departed iche man to his loggyng."[10]

---

[2]   *Middle English Dictionary*, ed. Robert E. Lewis (Ann Arbor, 1952–2001), *s. vv.* outraunce, plesaunce; Frédéric Godefroy, *Dictionnaire de l'ancienne langue française, et de tous ses dialectes du IXe au XVe siècle, composé d'aprè le dépouillement de tous les plus importants documents, manuscrits ou imprimés*, ed. F. Vieweg (Paris, 1881–1902), *s.vv.* outrance, plaisance.

[3]   Samuel Bentley, *Excerpta Historica* (London, 1831), pp. 200, 211; hereafter cited as Bentley.

[4]   Bentley, p. 174.

[5]   Bentley, p. 181.

[6]   Sydney Anglo, "Anglo-Burgundian Feats of Arms: Smithfield, June 1467," *Guildhall Miscellany* 2, no. 7 (September 1965), 278; hereafter cited as Anglo.

[7]   Bentley, p. 211.

[8]   Anglo, p. 280.

[9]   Olivier de la Marche, *Mémoires*, ed. H. Beaune and J. d'Arbaumont, 4 vols. (Paris, 1883–88), 3:54.

[10] Bentley, p. 212.

For de la Marche "the arms of plaisance are done to exercise in arms and to continue their mastery, to train the body and to learn valor for the defense of the public good." Fifteenth-century gentlemen like Lord Scales and the Bastard saw no contradiction between that intent and the use of sharp weapons: they used very similar terms in their letters describing their desire to perform their own combat. In spite of their willingness to use sharp weapons, they disavowed any wish to cause injury, let alone death. "yif any of us two be hurt (that God defend)"[11] reads one of the articles for their deed, and neither seems to have been injured in spite of significant damage to their harness.

Sharp weapons presented obvious risks, but Scales and the Bastard used several strategies to mitigate them, starting with wearing the highly efficient armor of the era. For the course with sharp lances they increased that already high level of protection with reinforcing pieces[12] that added protection but were so cumbersome that they were discarded for swordplay. Beyond that, the combat was strictly limited. It was not to be fought to the finish, but would be honorably accomplished as soon as any one of several conditions was met. The mounted combat would be accomplished after a set number of blows, or if either champion was carried to the ground without their horse failing, or so wounded that they were unable to continue, whichever came first. The foot combat would end as soon as either was carried to the ground or disarmed. In either case the judge, in this combat the king of England, could also end the combat at any time; in fact this is how both fights ended.

The terms *armes à plaisance* or an act of *plesaunce* were not restricted to combats with blunted weapons. They encompassed a broader range of contests where the combatants could try their skill and courage against each other with agreed limitations on how far they might go. The vast majority of consensual foot combats in the fourteenth and fifteenth centuries were not fights to the finish, but contests that ended, like the contest between Lord Scales and the Bastard, either once one side or the other had struck an agreed number of blows or when one combatant was disarmed or thrown or struck to the ground. In de la Marche's *Memoires* the *Pas de l'arbre de Charlemagne* of 1443, the challenge between Galiot de Baltasin and Phillipe de Ternant in 1446, the *Pas de la belle pelerine* and the *Pas de La Fountain des Pleurs of 1449* all followed this limited format, in addition to the contest between Lord Scales and the Bastard described earlier,[13] Sharp weapons seem to have been the norm even for the more limited combats on foot. Mounted combats were usually similarly limited, typically for a set number of courses and no more, and these jousts for an agreed number of courses could be run with either blunt or sharp spearheads. These forms of restricted and limited combats were in effect the default option and the alterna-

---

[11] Bentley, p. 182.
[12] Bentley, pp. 208–09.
[13] De la Marche, *Mémoires*, 1:290–335; 2:64–79, 118–23, 129–35, 142–202.

tive a rare exception.[14] Contemporary writers rarely felt the need for a special term to describe them, and so *plaisance* only rarely occurs in contemporary accounts of deeds of arms.

In fifteenth-century England, France and Burgundy, a combat *à outrance* was not simply a combat with sharp weapons. A combat *à outrance*, or to the *utterance* or *utterest* in fifteenth-century English, was something much more specific and rigorous. It was theoretically a combat to the finish, where both sides were prepared to fight until one or the other was totally defeated: either surrendered to the opposite side or dead. In practice, judges would often intervene to prevent such a combat from going to extremes, but a champion in a combat *à outrance* could have no assurance that the judge or judges would prevent the combat from going to its ultimate conclusion. The term appears in two related contexts: it can describe a "gage of battle" or judicial duel. Alternatively, it can describe a particularly high stakes combat by consent. Neither form was common, and the gage of battle was particularly rare. Olivier de la Marche wrote:

> few living men have seen the execution of a gage of battle, and for more than seventy years under the house of Burgundy such work has not been executed between two noble men. And I, who have remained in that noble house more than sixty years, have not seen such a gage of battle in my life, although I have seen thirty times arms of *plaisance* and combat in the lists in many countries and realms …[15]

He did witness one gage of battle between commoners in Valenciennes. The combatants fought to the death armed with clubs, and de la Marche described it as a *combat à outrance*[16] in his *Mémoires*.

De la Marche describes a gage of battle as follows:

> it is an offense that requires the offended, when it is not possible to achieve proof, except by their body only, that they come to demand their rights before the judge, and throw down as gage a glove or a hood. That gage is to stand as surety, by pledges sufficient, to come and appear on a day which will be ordained for the plaintiff, to produce the battle; and if the defendant lifts up the gage, he will likewise provide surety to appear on the day … that is why they call it the gage of battle, because in all other sorts of arms, either to the *outrance* or arms of *plaisance*, they do not throw down any sort of gage beyond the consent of the parties, if they wish, to advance their honor, to put themselves to the test, and to fight …[17]

De la Marche then defines what outrance means in the context of a gage of battle:

---

[14] All of the combats and jousts between men at arms witnessed and described by de la Marche in his *Mémoires* were limited combats rather than fights to the finish. He describes one *outrance* combat held between knights and squires in Scotland, but he was not present himself.

[15] Olivier de la Marche, Hardouin de la Jaille, Anthoine de la Sale, et al., *Traicte de la Forme et Devis Comme On Faict les Tourneys*, ed. Bernard Prost (Paris, 1878), p. 2.

[16] De la Marche, *Mémoires*, 2:402–06.

[17] De la Marche, *Traicte*, p. 23.

... if one of the two combatants does not surrender, and the constable and marshal have not spoken, the battle should not cease until they are certain of complete victory [*oultrance*] according to those that are expert in arms.

And when one is defeated [*oultre*] this defeat [*oultrance*] may come about in three ways, among others. The first case is when one confesses his guilt or surrenders. The second is when the enemy is put to death, and outside the lists before him [*et hors des lisses avant luy*].[18] The third is when the enemy is not slain, but put by force outside the park and the lists and remains there. In that case the requirements are not completely fulfilled, however, the body is delivered, as affected by the case, to the marshals to do justice.[19]

Jean Chartier's *Chronique de Charles VIII* also describes a gage of battle as one type of combat *à outrance*:

Around this time (c. 1432) a gage of battle to the *outrance* was done between Robin de Malaunay, a Frenchman, native of Maine and William Regnault, an Englishman, at Mayenne-la-Juhez, in the said country of Maine, and the Englishman was discomfited ...[20]

The Brut or Chronicles of England also describes a gage of battle in similar terms:

And in the same yere ther fil a discencion and a debate betwene the Duk of Herford & the Duke of Norfolke, in so moche that thay waged batayle & cast doun her glove ... and than these ij worthi lordes comyn in to the ffelde, clene armed and wel arayed with alle her wepon, and redy to do her batayle, and were in the place redy to fight at the vttrest.[21]

De la Marche disapproved of the gage of battle, and by the fifteenth century the custom was falling out of favor. Such combats had been fought in the past, and sometimes evidence surfaced later suggesting that God had perhaps, for his own mysterious reasons, let the innocent man lose.

The notorious and controversial gage of battle between Jean de Carrouges and Jacques Le Gris was set in motion when Carrouges accused Le Gris of raping Carrouges' wife, Marguerite. Le Gris provided several witnesses supporting his alibi, but Marguerite was firm in her testimony that Le Gris had raped her. The Parlement of Paris ruled that there was insufficient evidence to settle the matter without a trial by combat between Carrouges and Le Gris, which was to take place on 29 December 1386. In the judicial duel Carrouges eventually succeeded in throwing Le Gris to the ground and got on top of him, repeatedly

[18] In this passage, leaving the field of battle while one's opponent remained in the field was the third definition of utter defeat. Putting a slain enemy outside the field before his opponent left the field avoided a possible quibble over the victory.
[19] De la Marche, *Traicte*, p. 40.
[20] Jean Chartier, *Chronique de Charles VIII, roi de France*, ed. Vallet de Viriville, vol. 1 (Paris, 1858), p. 149
[21] *The Brut or Chronicles of England*, ed. Friedrich W. D. Brie (London, 1908), part 2, p. 355. Text lightly regularized.

demanding his confession. Le Gris vehemently refused and Carrouges killed him. At the time of the combat there was less than complete agreement that justice had been done, and according to the chronicles of the contemporary Religieux de Saint-Denys and Juvenal des Ursins, who wrote in the 1430s, some years later another man confessed to the crime. This would be the last time the Parlement of Paris would authorize a gage of battle.[22]

Further, basing a judicial process on direct divine intervention was seen as tempting God, abhorrent to contemporary theologians and sensible lay writers like de la Marche, Honore Bonet and Christine de Pisan.[23] Even so the practice was so entrenched in customary law that most medieval rulers were not ready to abolish it. However, they often halted the combat if the protracted preliminaries did not produce a retraction or confession from one side or the other. Richard II's last minute cancellation of the judicial duel between Bolingbroke and Mowbray was a particularly well known example of this sort of intervention.

In addition to gages of battle *Outrance* combats were also fought by mutual consent, "without defamatory quarrel, but to acquire honor."[24] As in gages of battle, the parties would undertake to fight until either one side or the other yielded or was slain, or until the judge or judges stopped the fight. Opponents could be killed if they refused to surrender or if it was tactically advantageous to do so, but unlike a gage of battle those that surrendered could expect to be freed after paying a substantial ransom. These combats *à outrance* by consent were also rare, more often proposed than accepted and more often begun than fought out to the bitter end.

Few fights by consent were fought out to the *outrance* or *ad interitum*, a Latin phrase with the same basic meaning. One combat between seven English and seven French in 1402 was celebrated in no less than three commemorative poems by Christine de Pisan, in one of which she recounts how the French "ont occis et mene à oultrance l'orgueil anglois." The Religieux de Saint-Denys, writing in Latin, describes the 1402 fight as a "fight to the finish" in the following account:

> Although every private combat which does not have the goal of the public interest may be accused of temerity, there are, however, men who engage in these sorts of enterprises, solely to make themselves a reputation for valor. There were these that did so: Sir Arnaud Guillaume, Sir du Chatel, Bataille, Archambaud de Villars, Clignet de Brabant, Jean called Champagne, and a certain Carius, all brave French gentlemen. Desiring to give splendor to their enterprise, they sent to England a herald of arms to

22 Eric Jager, *The Last Duel* (New York, 2004), pp. 112–14, 203; *Chronique du Religieux de Saint-Denys*, ed. M. L. Bellaguet, vol. 1 (Paris, 1839), pp. 462, 464, 466; Jean Juvenal des Ursins, *Histoire de Charles VI, Roy de France*, in *Nouvelle collection des mémoires pour servir à l'histoire de France*, vol. 2 (Paris, 1851), p. 371.

23 Honoré Bonet, *The Tree of Battles of Honoré Bonet*, trans. G. W. Coopland (Liverpool, 1949); de la Marche, *Traicte*; Christine de Pizan, *The Book of Deeds of Arms and of Chivalry*, trans. Sumner Willard, ed. Charity Cannon Willard (University Park, PA, 1999).

24 Enguerrand de Monstrelet *(La) Chronique d'Enguerran de Monstrelet*, ed. L. Douët d'Arcq, vol. 5 (Paris, 1861), chap. 181, p. 139; hereafter cited as Monstrelet.

courteously provoke an equal number of English to swordplay. The issue of this fight would be to establish, they said, the superiority of French knights over English knights and therefore show which of the two nations ought to be considered the bravest. The herald, admitted into the presence of the King of England, added that the French had chosen a closed field near the city of Bordeaux, where they proposed to fight to the finish [*ad interitum*] and that they would agree on each side that whoever admitted themselves vanquished would pay a diamond for their entire ransom.

This unlooked-for provocation stung the pride of the English. Whether from resentment, hate or from shame of refusing such combat, Lord Scales, Sir Aymant Chotet, John Heron, Richard Boutevale, John Fleury, Thomas Tile and Robert de Scales, all brave and valiant men, accepted the challenge with the consent of the king of England ...

... Although wise men disapproved of this combat as unreasonable, and justifying in the eyes of foreigners the proverb which accused the French of being the most presumptuous of all people, the matter ... turned out successfully in the end ...

I leave it to courtiers and captains to describe the address and the agility each displayed in this circumstance, the eagerness and valor with which they aided each other, and the fear that seized the spectators, as they saw the blood cover those on both sides and the victory indecisive. I will content myself with saying that the combat was long and fierce, and they each were mutually weighed down with injuries. The English, all striking redoubled strokes with the arm of Hector, sent the French back in need of a healing broth, and on their side the French reproached their adversaries with the ignominious end of their King Richard. Finally an English knight was killed, and the others, who were gravely injured, surrendered.

So, with victory complete, the Lord of Harpedanne, Breton, led the victors to Paris, where the lords of the court received them with all sorts of marks of friendship, and many presents, as they had sustained the dignity and honor of France. The others returned to England humbled and troubled. This reverse ought to have taught them to abstain from similar hazards. But they did not leave off, during the next two years, to attempt the same proceedings against new adversaries, sometimes of a greater number, sometimes of a lesser number, and, what merits amazement, with such eagerness, in spite of how the fight had gone against them. I remember that during that time many people sought to understand how the French showed such an extraordinary animosity. I apprehend that they had conceived an implacable hate against the English because of the horrible murder of their king and the injurious banishment of the queen, daughter of the king of France, and that they did not venture to rise up openly against them, or be seen as having violated the truce, and so they sought an honorable opportunity for revenging their intolerable injuries.[25]

Juvenal des Ursins reports how Arnaud Guillaume, Lord of Barbazan, "the chief of those seven French," exhorted his companions.

Grandly and notably the Lord de Barbazan exhorted them to do well, and to guard their welfare and honor. He showed them the true and reasonable quarrel which the king had against his ancient enemies of England, without having regard to fighting for the ladies nor to acquire the grace of the world, and only to defend themselves against the enterprise of their adversaries, with many other good teachings ...

---

[25] *Chronique du Religieux de Saint-Denys*, 3:30–35.

And because it seemed to the English, that if they were able to strike down Sir Guillaume de Chastel, who was large and strong, they would be more easily able to accomplish their intention, they decided to go with two against him. And because they did this, Archambaud found himself alone without anyone facing him, so that he came to the one who was having to do with Carouis, who was the first that he found, and gave him a stroke of the axe on the head so that he fell to earth. This was the said Robert de Scales, who died ... There were many fine arms done on side and the other, and at last the English surrendered.[26]

An account ascribed to a bourgeois of Paris recorded a similar *combat à outrance* of three against three at Paris in 1415:

But at this time there were also knights of Spain and Portugal. Of these three from Portugal well renowned for chivalry took, through I know not what mad enterprise, the field of battle to meet with three knights of France; that is to say, Francois de Grin-quos ... La Roque ... Morigon; and it was ordained to the outrance for the 23rd day of February, the vigil of St. Peter and St. Ouin, and it was before sunrise ... that they entered the field; but in God's good truth, it didn't take longer than it takes to go from the gate of St. Martin to that of St. Antoine[27] by horseback, before the Portuguese were discomfited by the three French of which La Roque was the best.[28]

Juvenal des Ursins gives a more detailed account. A preliminary debate shows the link between the consensual *outrance* combat and the judicial gage of battle:

There was one difficulty, who was to enter the field first. But it was said that the Portuguese should enter first, and that was reasonable, because in effect they were plaintiffs ...

It seems that each of the Portuguese chose a Frenchman. The knight, who was a valiant man, went and advanced and presented himself to Sir Francois. According to what they say, the most valiant of them all, and most renowned in war, addressed himself against la Roque, and the other to Maurignon. And when they came to their axes the one who fought la Roque pierced him beneath the top of his piece [*piece*[29]], and when he felt that the iron of his axe was taken within the harness, he began to push strongly, seeking to open up the harness. And when la Roque perceived this, he held himself firm, with the intention of doing what he would do next: when he perceived that the Portuguese leaned forward to push more strongly, all of a sudden with the swiftness of his body with which he was most skillful, he stepped back so that the Portuguese fell, carried away headlong. La Roque gave him two strokes with the axe on the head, so that he was thoroughly stunned, and drew his sword to thrust him in the behind: others said that he lifted his visor and that he wanted to strike him in the face.

Anyway, whatever he did, the Portuguese surrendered, and was discomfited, and taken by the guards. After this la Roque looked to his companions to see who had

[26] Juvenal des Ursins, *Histoire*, 2:421–23.
[27] About a mile and a half by road. At a walk, a horseman might cover the distance in half an hour.
[28] *Journal d'un Bourgeois de Paris*, in *Nouvelle collection des mémoires pour servir à l'histoire de France*, vol. 2 (Paris, 1851), p. 644.
[29] The largest plate of the shoulder armor.

the most to do, and he went with the full force of his axe, and gave such a blow to the one who was having to do with Maurignon that he staggered him, and Maurignon with another stroke made him fall to earth and surrender. And then the two, that is to say la Roque and Maurignon, went to help Grignaux who was badly worked over and wounded, particularly in the left hand, which was pierced through so that he was unable to use it. But when the knight saw the two others come against him he saw that he could no longer resist and said in a loud voice "I surrender to you three." And it was said that all had done very valiantly: The French went through Paris, trumpets sounding and the people were joyful that they had the honor.[30]

Jean Le Fèvre's account is similar to de Ursins'. He notes that the Portuguese wore the red cross of their English allies on their coats of arms. He states that that the conditions "would be to fight with axe, sword and dagger until each one or the other of them were surrendered to their companions or was carried to the ground" and that the last of the three Portuguese to surrender "acquired, in spite of his misfortune, great honor that day and many held him to be the bravest of the six."[31]

The 1402 and 1415 combats were rare examples of combats *à outrance* by mutual consent that were actually fought to the end without being halted by the judge. The end in both cases was the surrender or death of everyone on the losing side. The combats were clearly seen as notable and unusual events, and the reaction of the contemporary chroniclers ranged from admiration for the bravery and skill of the combatants to condemnation of their unreasonable rashness and temerity.

One can see why these combats were rare. Of the twenty men who entered the field in the the 1402 and 1415 combats, one died and many were seriously injured. This was a grim casualty rate considering the small number involved and the voluntary nature of the combats, worse than that of a WWII fighter pilot on an average combat mission. In addition the surviving losers had to pay a substantial ransom. It was also far more dangerous than the more typical deeds of arms on foot of the fifteenth century, which were also normally fought with sharp weapons. Dozens of such combats are recorded without a single fatality. The key distinction was that these less extreme combats were not fought out to the utmost. Like the contest between Scales and the Bastard, they would generally end honorably when an agreed number of blows had been struck on either side, or if a champion fell or was disarmed, or the judge intervened.

In addition to the small number of fights fought out to the bitter end, fifteenth-century chronicles describe several combats *à outrance* that were halted by the judge before either side was defeated.

Monstrelet describes *armes à outrance* halted by the king of Aragon at Valencia in 1403, between the seneschal of Hainault and three companions including Sir James de Montenay on one side and their Aragonese opponents Colemach de Sainte Coulonne, and three companions including Sir Pierre de

---

30 Juvenal des Ursins, *Histoire*, 2:503–04.
31 Jean le Fèvre, Seigneur de Saint-Remy, *Chronique*, vol. 1. (Paris, 1876), pp. 208–11.

Moncada on the other. Both groups arrived at the field but were kept waiting fully armed in their tents for five hours while the king tried to bring about an agreement without combat. The seneschal, however, insisted that "this enterprise had been undertaken at the request of Colemach, and that he and his companions had come from a far country, and at great trouble and expense, to accomplish his desire, which he and his companions were determined upon doing." and the fight was allowed to proceed.

> And each of the others came very valiantly against the opponent they had picked out. Then Sir James de Montenay threw down his axe, and with one hand seized Sir Pierre de Moncada by the lower edge of his lames. In the other he had a dagger with which he sought to wound him underneath. But, as both sides seemed to be getting thoroughly worked up, the king had them restrained.
>
> And in truth, it appeared that the Aragonese would have been in great peril of having the worst of it had the matter been pursued to the utmost [*outrance*]. The seneschal and those with him were all four very powerful and strong, very experienced in arms, and equal to the accomplishment of any enterprise that might be demanded from them.
>
> When the champions were retired to their tents, the king descended from his scaffold into the lists, and requested of the seneschal and Colemach, in a kind manner, that the remaining deeds of arms might be referred to him and his council, and he would so act that they should all be satisfied. The seneschal, then falling on one knee, humbly entreated the king that he would consent that the challenge should be completed according to the request of Colemach. The king replied, by again requiring that the completion of the combat should be referred to his judgment; which being granted, he took the seneschal by the hand. And placed him above himself, and Colemach on the other side. He thus led them out of the lists, when each returned to his hotel and disarmed. The king sent his principal knights to seek the seneschal and his companions, whom, for three days, he entertained at his palace, and paid them as much honor as if they had been his own brothers. When he had reconciled them with their opponents, he gave them gifts and fine presents. And they departed thence on their return to France, and the seneschal to Hainault.[32]

The strenuous seneschal of Hainault arranged another *outrance* combat with the noted English knight, Sir John of Cornwall, to be held before his lord the duke of Burgundy.[33] However, in 1409 the king of France required that the combat be held before him instead in Paris. Monstrelet reports:

> … they both prepared to joust together with sharp lances. But before they began their run it was cried by the king that they should cease and go no further in doing their arms and that none in the realm, under penalty of death, should challenge another in the field without reasonable cause.[34]

---

[32] Monstrelet, *Chronique*, chap. 14, pp. 1:76–80.
[33] George Frederick Beltz, *Memorials of the Most Noble Order of the Garter, from its Foundation to the Present Time. Including the History of the Order; Biographical Notices of the Knights in the Reigns of Edward III. and Richard II., the Chronological Succession of the Members* (London, 1841), p. 407.
[34] Monstrelet, *Chronique*, chap 52, 2:6.

As at Valencia, the seneschal and his opponent were then "grandly feasted and honored," giving them some consolation for the cancellation of their proposed combat.

Letting the combatants enter the field and halting the fight before it began was frustrating for the participants and spectators and expensive for the ruler, but it demonstrated his authority and brought the matter to a conclusion emphatically and very publicly. It also gave the combatants a chance to publicly demonstrate their courage and resolve if not their prowess.

Jean le Fèvre records another 1415 *outrance* combat in Paris halted by the judge:

> ... in the same place of Sainthouyne, in the month of February a Portuguese named Diego d'Ollumen did arms, meeting with a Breton named Guillame de la Haye. Their arms were done before the duke of Guienne; the Portuguese and Breton were taken[35] as they were fighting without either one of them being defeated [*sans oultrance de l'un ne de l'autre*][36]

Des Ursins tells the story in greater detail:

> These English that were in Paris had with them Portuguese, who had a great willingness to do arms for the love of their ladies. There was also the unspoken issue of the principal quarrel between France and England, as they were allied with the English ...
>
> The fight continued for some time, but he (the Breton) still remained on the defensive as he had been advised. Often the Portuguese lifted his visor, and made signs to the other that he should do likewise. When the fight had continued for some time in this way the Portuguese lifted his visor and Guillaume de la Haye, without lifting his, sought to present the point of his axe to his face. The Portuguese began at once to retreat, but when they saw how it was going they cried "Ho, ho, ho" and went diligently to take them ... Then both of them were given honor and good cheer.[37]

In this combat, threatening to thrust at the naked face of an opponent crossed a line the judges did not wish to let the combat go beyond regardless of the wishes of the combatants, just as James de Montenay crossed a similar line in Valencia when he tried to stab his opponent in the groin.

Olivier de la Marche records a combat *à outrance* performed by a party headed by Jacques de Lalaing in Scotland in 1449, also halted before victory was assured:

> ... he was accompanied by Simon de Lalaing, his uncle, and Herves de Meriadet and many other good people. And as I understand Sir James Douglas, brother of the Earl Douglas, and the said Sir Jacques de Lalaing had formerly agreed to do the will of one against the other and each sought each other to meet together, and so Sir James Douglas arranged that a battle would be done before the King between him and Sir Jacques de Lalaing. But the matter increased and multiplied so that a battle to the

---

[35] That is, separated by the guards and prevented from fighting further.
[36] Le Fèvre, *Chronique*, p. 211.
[37] Juvenal des Ursins, *Histoire*, p. 503.

outrance was concluded, for three noble Scotsmen to meet with Sir Simon de Lalaing, Sir Jacques de Lalaing and Herve de Meriadet, and that they would all do arms at one time for the King of Scotland ...

Before the combat Jaques de Lalaing asked that, whatever happened in the fight, his companions would not rescue him, as it would seem that they did not "hold or know me as a man to sustain the assault and the battle of a single knight, holding a low account of me and my chivalry." Both parties entered the field and all six fought simultaneously. Two of the pairs of champions fought without either side getting the upper hand but Meriadet had more success against his opponent:

> And on the other part came Herves de Meriadet and the Scotsman came to hit Meriadet with a push of the lance; but Meriadet turned aside the blow with the handle of his axe, so that the lance fell out of the hands of the Scotsman and Meriadet followed up so vigorously that before the Scotsman was able to unsling his axe [*destrousse sa hache*] he entered within, and with a throw carried him to earth. And Meriadet stepped back to let the Scotsman rise who was quick, light and of great courage, and he lifted himself quickly and ran under at the said Meriadet for the second time, and Meriadet who was a man who was one of the most redoubted squires of his time, strong, light, cool and dexterous in arms and in wrestling, received the Scotsman coolly and with great watchfulness and soon after made an entry on the Scotsman. And with that entry he gave such a great blow that he carried him to earth with a stroke of the axe, and quickly the Scotsman sought to lift himself, but Meriadet put his palm and knee against the back of the Scotsman, and again made him fall and kiss the sand. And despite the request that Sir Jacques de Lalaing had made of him, the said Meriadet, seeing the two knights wrestle together went to aid the said Sir Jacques, but the king of Scotland threw down his baton and had them parted with the said Meriadet free in his battle to rescue his companions at his pleasure.[38]

Georges Chastelain, Lalaing's biographer, adds that when Meriadet's opponent was on the ground:

> ... if he had strived to destroy his body, he could well have done so, and lightly done it, as the arms were *à outrance*, but he did not wish to hit him either of the times he saw him on the ground, which was nobly done, and he deserves a reputation of great honor.[39]

The contrast between the Lalaing-Douglas fight and the 1402 and 1415 contests demonstrates how strongly the outcome depended on the intentions of the champions and judge. Relations between Burgundy and Scotland were more friendly than otherwise in 1449, compared with the strong national enmity that colored the earlier combats. Jacques Lalaing's decision to emphasize personal renown over tactical advantage, Meriadet's generosity to a fallen opponent and

---

[38] De la Marche, *Mémoires*, 2:105–109.
[39] Georges Chastellain, *Chronique de J. de Lalain*, ed. J. A. Buchon (Paris, 1825), p. 205.

the king of Scotland's refusal to let the matter go to extremes all helped minimize the decisiveness and bloodiness of the combat. Given the same teams and judges as the 1402 encounter one can imagine the same tactical situation leading to a far deadlier conclusion.

Two items in Boucicaut's regulations for his Companions of the Green Shield of the White Lady shed light on how he viewed combats *à outrance*. The first stated that if the companions had previously accepted other deeds of arms, they could put them aside to answer a later challenge *à outrance*. Potentially more dangerous than any other combats by consent, combats *à outrance* offered correspondingly greater opportunity for fame, honor and renown. And as we have seen, opportunities to perform them were rare.

The second item contemplated the possibility that companions who were defeated in such a combat might be held prisoner by the victor or victors until they paid a previously agreed sum for their freedom, and that the company as a whole would pay half the ransom on behalf of the defeated companion. By implication, a serious amount of money might be required.

Combats *à outrance* were extraordinary events and their potential to end in legalized homicide presented the judges with a dilemma. Their response gives a measure of how extraordinary these combats were. While the participants sought to demonstrate their courage and skill while exalting their own faction and humbling their opponents, the judges for deeds of arms had their own priorities. By taking an active role, the ruler emphasized his own power and authority. When the king of France moved the seneschal of Hainault's combat from the duke of Burgundy's jurisdiction to his own, he emphasized his paramount authority at a time when his over-mighty dukes were all too willing to pursue their own ends. Granting a request from a powerful subject was also desirable, and to a lesser degree, so was granting a request from an important foreigner. Providing a striking spectacle for the general populace was also desirable. Allowing subjects or foreigners to be killed or injured while seeking their own personal glory or undergoing a dubious judicial procedure was not. A deed of arms gone wrong was an affront to good public order, and the expense of hosting such an event was significant. Rulers who allowed deeds of arms to proceed under their control struck a delicate balance. Suppressing them entirely was awkward, but so was allowing them to proceed without limit. The dignitaries that accepted the role of judges in deeds of arms weighed a delicate balance of interests. Their goal was to provide the greatest possible spectacle and affirmation of their authority while keeping inconvenient corpses to an irreducible minimum.

Several times potential combatants made well publicized offers to do combat *à outrance* that apparently never reached the field. This is probably the single largest category of *outrance* combats by consent in the historical record.

Shortly after 1387, Boucicaut and his companions offered to "*combattre à oultrance*" any number of English from two to twenty. The lord of Chastiauneuf accepted on the part of the English, but negotiations broke down when English refused to accept any of the judges offered by Boucicaut, either the duke of

Bourbon or others. Boucicaut then proposed the count of Foix, but the count refused to accept the role of judge.[40]

A judge who was disposed to favor one side over the other could have a powerful influence over the outcome of such a combat. A judge who favored the French could stop the fight if the French were losing, but let it continue if it were going the other way. Given these possibilities it is not surprising that the English were less than enthusiastic about accepting a deed of arms with Boucicaut with the duke of Bourbon as a judge. Nor is it surprising that the count of Foix, a more or less neutral power, preferred to avoid involvement entirely.

Partisan concerns could cut the other way as well. A judge who too obviously favored his own adherents would diminish his own reputation for justice and fairness. When the duke of Burgundy judged a combat between Jacques Lalaing and an Englishman, Olivier de la Marche believed that the duke bent over backwards to avoid favoring his own subject and servant. As a result, the combat continued in spite of Lalaing's punctured wrist, which would have been sufficient cause to end the fight if it had happened to the other side.

In 1406 a Burgundian knight wore "the White Lady embroidered on his apparel, and a golden bracelet, to despite the knights of my lord the duke of Orleans." He said he was willing to defend the device in the lists, seven against seven, to fight "to the very uttermost." The six surviving members of the 1402 combat against the English accepted, and "challenged the devices" of their rivals. As Guillaume du Chastel had been killed in battle, the Spanish knight Pero Nino agreed to be the seventh, to fight as the six had "done once already."

The challenge was a symptom of the increasingly bitter rivalry between the dukes of Orleans and Burgundy, which would lead to the murder of the duke of Orleans in 1407 and open civil war by 1411. The king of France had no desire for a combat that could only inflame "the discord which was already beginning; he had all the knights engaged in the affair brought before him, and took away their devices, and reconciled the dukes and knights." Later that day all the parties ate together. "This peace between the dukes was but feigned, as was manifest thereafter ..."[41]

Like Boucicaut, the duke of Bourbon himself conspicuously offered to do arms *à outrance* in 1414, apparently without result:

> ... desiring to put aside idleness and display our person, in advancing our honor by mastery of arms, thinking to acquire good renown, and the grace of the great beauty to which we are servant, have just sworn and undertaken that we, accompanied by sixteen other knights and squires of names and arms ... bearing on their left leg a prisoner's iron hanging from a chain which will be of gold for the knights and of silver for the squires, for every Sunday for the next two years, beginning with the next Sunday after

---

[40] Steven Muhlberger, *Deeds of Arms* (Highland Village, TX, 2004), p. 72; *Le Livre des fais du bon Messire Jehan le Maingre, dit Bouciquaut*, ed. Denis Lalande (Geneva, 1985), pp. 56–58.

[41] Gutierre Díaz de Gámez, *The Unconquered Knight: A Chronicle of the Deeds of Don Pero Niño*, trans. Joan Evans (Cambridge, Ontario, 2000), pp. 61–63.

the date of these presents until we are able to find an equal number of knights and squires of names and arms without reproach, who wish to fight with us all together on foot to the outrance, each one armed in such harness as pleases him, carrying lance, axe, sword and dagger or lesser weapons of such length as he wishes to have until each one is taken prisoner by the others, according to the condition that those of our side which are defeated will be released by each giving a prisoner's iron and chain equal to those which we carry. And those on the other side who are defeated will be released by a bracelet of gold for the knights and a bracelet of silver for the squires to give where it seems best.[42]

There is no evidence that this challenge was accepted. It does offer additional evidence that a combat *à outrance* was expected to end in the surrender of one side or the other, with a substantial payment for release.

Sir Gerarde Herbaumes made a similar offer, some time after early 1414, with fourteen companions "who have now late Challenged fifteen Englishmen to the *outrance* they bearing a plate of gold for their device."[43] Again, there is no evidence the challenge was consummated. Shortly afterwards Gerarde Herbaumes was dead at Agincourt. Conspicuous tokens like that worn by the duke of Bourbon, Gerard Herbaumes and their companions had the advantage of advertising the courage of the bearer even if no combat transpired. One suspects, given the small share of proffered combats *à outrance* that were actually fought to the uttermost, that there was an element of bluff and calculation to some of the challenges. Some of the challengers may have viewed gaining the reputation of a bold man at arms willing to undertake such risky combats without actually having to fight them to the finish as a reasonably desirable outcome.

These sources give a fairly consistent view of what arms *à outrance* meant to writers in fifteenth-century France, England and Burgundy. It was an unusual high stakes combat that would be fought out, unless the judge or judges intervened, until one side or the other had surrendered or been slain.

Although several modern writers repeat the definition of combats *à plaisance* as combats with blunted weapons, this does not seem to be the terminology used in medieval accounts. It seems likely that these post-medieval authors conflated *outrance* and *plaisance* with other categories recognized in medieval records: jousts of war with sharp lances and jousts of peace with blunted *armes courtoise*. However, for medieval writers these terms were not synonyms for *outrance* and *plaisance*. They applied only to mounted jousts, not the foot combats described earlier. In spite of their name jousts of war could be limited contests for a set number of courses, not fights to the uttermost. The combats explicitly described by Froissart as jousts of war at Saint-Inglevert in 1390 were for five passes only.

---

[42] Cripps-Day, *The History of the Tournament*, appendix 2, p. xiiii, citing *Mémoires de M. de Peiresc*.

[43] Ibid., appendix 5, p. xxxvii.

And as we have seen, while jousts of peace were distinguished by the use of blunt lances, combats *à plaisance* were not limited to blunted weapons.[44]

Understanding the medieval definition of *outrance* and *plaisance* gives a better understanding of what was at stake in particular combats. It also gives cause to be cautious in reading secondary sources. When a modern author says a particular combat was *à outrance*, was it because the original account described it that way, or is it because the combat conformed to a post-medieval definition of the term?

A more correct understanding of the medieval terms helps us to realize that even in arms *à plaisance*, the participants could use sharp weapons to create a highly realistic approximation of true mortal combat. Arms *à outrance* were even more dangerous, and when voluntarily undertaken allowed a small number of the bravest men at arms to win honor and renown by publicly demonstrating their courage and confidence in their own prowess, freely exposing themselves to risks and hazards that were deliberately extraordinary.

---

[44] Jean Froissart, *Oeuvres de Froissart: Chroniques*, ed. Kervyn de Lettenhove, 25 vols. (1867–77, repr. Osnabrück, 1967), 14:55–56; Cripps-Day, *History of the Tournament*, appendix 5, pp. xxxiii–xxxiv.

8

Guns and Goddams: was there a Military Revolution in Lancastrian Normandy 1415–50?[1]

Anne Curry

Historians like labels and categories. In part this has been driven by the needs of pedagogy. It cannot be a coincidence that an early use of the term "La Guerre de Cent Ans" was in Chrysanthe-Ovide Desmichels' *Tableau Chronologique de l'Histoire du Moyen Age* published in 1823. This work was symptomatic of the expansion of schooling in early nineteenth-century France in which competitive examinations stimulated publication of aides-mémoire.[2] Other nations followed suit. Even in the 1970s teachers in Britain were still using William Edwards' *Notes on British History* and *Notes on European History*, cribs published almost a century earlier, which crammed the heads of unsuspecting students with "the so-and-so system," "the age of whatsit," and "the thingummy 'revolution'" so that it could all be spewed out again in the examination room.

Such labels and categories can be valuable communication tools. They also give shape to our research and facilitate comparison and debate. But they can operate as straightjackets and encourage tunnel vision. Take the expression "Hundred Years War." At one level it is useful because it emphasizes the insoluble nature of Anglo-French conflict once an English king had claimed to be the rightful king of France. Yet it is also misleading since it gives the wars fought between the 1330s and 1450s an artificial unity, a problem which links to the topic of this essay. Then there is the expression, "the military revolution." The historiography is now so well established that it would be otiose to spend time going through it.[3] Yet the military revolution has been a moveable feast. Cynically speaking, it is to be found in the period in which the particular author considers him or herself to be expert. There is an element of "seek and ye shall

---

[1] This paper was first delivered as the Journal of Medieval Military History Lecture at the International Medieval Congress, Kalamazoo, in May 2008.

[2] The first book to bear the title *La Guerre de Cent Ans* was published by Jean-Louis-Théodore Bachelet in Rouen in 1852. For broader discussion see Anne Curry, "France and the Hundred Years War, 1337–1453," in *France in the Later Middle Ages*, ed. D. Potter (Oxford, 2003), pp. 90–93.

[3] *The Military Revolution Debate: Readings on the Military Transformation of Early Modern Europe*, ed. Clifford J. Rogers (Boulder, 1995). Note also Clifford J. Rogers, "The Idea of Military Revolutions in Eighteenth and Nineteenth Century Texts," *Revista de História das Ideias* 30 (2009), 395–415.

find" about it, in much the same way as "the rise of the gentry" or "the rise of the state" is found wherever a period specialist is looking.

The reason is that we have tended to define "the military revolution" in any way we wish. Therefore it can be whenever we want it to be. And we all desperately want it to be in our period. After all, it is not *a* military revolution, but *the* military revolution. Or for Clifford J. Rogers, in his highly important article of 1993, military revolution*s* – the infantry revolution of the fourteenth century, and the artillery revolution of the fifteenth.[4] In his article, Lancastrian Normandy – signifying the English occupation of the duchy by the English from Henry V's renewal of war in 1415 to the expulsion by the French in 1450 – features in both revolutions. In the infantry revolution it is by emphasis on the English archers, and also the archer/dismounted man-at-arms combination, at the battles of Agincourt (1415) and Verneuil (1424). In the artillery revolution it features in the use of guns by Henry V at the siege of Harfleur in 1415 (although Rogers argues that the "intention was ... to silence the guns and catapults with which the defenders harassed his army") and at Rouen and other sieges in the second campaign (1417–19). Rogers sees a turning point in the mid 1420s when garrisons began to surrender "because the besiegers' guns have rendered their position indefensible." Here he features particularly the conquest of Maine (which, I would add, was made possible by the victory at Verneuil since that battle enabled the garrisons in Normandy to be reduced in size and diverted to the campaign southwards) and the power of the French gunpowder artillery in the reconquest of Normandy in 1449–50. His conclusion is that "a revolution occurred in the art of war around the 1420s to 1430s, as gunpowder artillery overturned the centuries-old dominance of the defensive in siege warfare."[5]

Agincourt apart, the fifteenth-century phase of the war has not excited as much interest in Hundred Years War studies as the fourteenth century. The problem may be one of the accessibility of sources. English chronicling in the fifteenth century is thin save for the Latin narratives of the reign of Henry V.[6] There are few chronicles produced within Normandy itself, although the narratives of the French reconquest of 1449–50 are more rewarding.[7] In other words, we have accounts of the conquest of Normandy by the English and the loss of Normandy to the French, but little in between. Lancastrian Normandy (more properly, Lancastrian France since the English held other areas of northern France – Paris and the hinterland to the east from 1420 to 1435, and Maine

4   Clifford J. Rogers, "The Military Revolutions of the Hundred Years War," *Journal of Military History* 57 (1993), 241–78.
5   Ibid., p. 266.
6   Antonia Gransden, *Historical Writing in England II, c. 1307 to the Early Sixteenth Century* (London, 1982).
7   *Narratives of the Expulsion of the English from Normandy MCCCCXLIX–MCCCCL*, ed. J. Stevenson (London, 1863); *Chronique de Charles VII roi de France par Jean Chartier*, ed. Vallet de Viriville, 3 vols. (Paris, 1858). The handful of works covering the interim include *Chronique normande de Pierre Cochon*, ed. Charles de Robillard de Beaurepaire (Rouen, 1870), and *Croniques de Normendie (1223–1453)*, ed. Amédée Hellot (Rouen, 1881).

from the mid 1420s to its surrender in 1448) can claim to be a "missing link" in studies of the medieval military revolution.[8] In the 1410s it appears to be the English who carried the torch in both infantry and artillery developments with their archers and their bombardments of fortifications, yet by 1449–50 it was the French who did so, with their *francs archers* and their use of field as well as siege artillery in the expulsion of the English.[9] The question arises therefore – what happened in between?

We may not have many chronicles for Lancastrian Normandy but we have exceptionally abundant financial records for military administration on both sides of the Channel.[10] Expeditionary armies, sent almost annually from England, were raised through the indenture system. Even where we do not have surviving indentures, we can know the leadership, size, composition, and other conditions of service, through the payments recorded in the Issue Rolls. This information is virtually complete for the whole period and for some armies we also have details of soldiers' names through muster rolls. For the first conquest made in France – Harfleur – we have muster rolls but more importantly the account book of its treasurer. Although Henry began his second campaign using English administrative procedures, his success soon enabled him to take over French structures, and from his death, all of his conquests were absorbed within the French financial system of the *chambre des comptes* based at Paris and, when the French capital was recovered by Charles VII in 1436, at Rouen.[11] This archive is huge, enabling us to reconstruct the garrison establishment of around forty-five manned places in Normandy as well as the field activities which were conducted, and which combined detachments from the garrisons with troops raised by other means within English-held areas and also with expeditionary armies from England. Again we have many muster rolls, enabling us to probe deeply into the patterns of service of the soldiers themselves. All of this material

8   Christopher T. Allmand, *Lancastrian Normandy 1415–1450. The History of a Medieval Occupation* (Oxford, 1983); G. L. Thompson, *Paris and its People under English Rule: The Anglo-Burgundian Regime 1420–1436* (Oxford, 1991); A-M. Bouly de Lesdin, "Le Vexin français sous la domination anglaise (1419–1449)," *Mémoires de la société historique et archéologique de Pontoise, du Val-d'Oise et du Vexin* 62 (1969). As yet, there is no comprehensive study of Maine under English rule but useful is Robert Charles, "L'invasion anglaise dans le Maine de 1417 à 1428," *Revue historique et archéologique du Maine* 25 (1889).

9   Philippe Contamine, *Guerre, état et société à la fin du moyen âge. Études sur les armées des rois de France 1337–1494* (Paris, 1972), chap. 10; idem, "L'artillerie royale française à la veille des guerres d'Italie," *Annales de Bretagne* 71 (1964).

10 Anne Curry, "English Armies in the Fifteenth Century," in *Arms, Armies and Fortifications in the Hundred Years War*, ed. Anne Curry and Michael Hughes (Woodbridge, 1994), pp. 39–68.

11 Anne Curry, "L'administration financière de la Normandie anglaise: continuité ou changement," *La France des principautés. Les chambres des comptes xiv⁴ et xv⁴ siècles* (Paris, 1996), pp. 83–103; eadem, "Harfleur et les Anglais, 1415–1422," in *La Normandie et l'Angleterre au moyen âge*, ed. Véronique Gazeau (Paris, 2003), pp. 173–87.

is being fed into a database project to list all known soldiers in the service of the English crown between 1369 and 1453.[12]

These administrative sources are crucial to our evaluation of both the "software" (i.e. the soldiers) and the "hardware" of any prospective military revolution. On the latter they record purchase, repair and movement of guns as well as providing much on fortifications, and indeed on so many aspects of military activity. Furthermore, they enable a much greater degree of granularity, and in particular a much clearer impression of change over time, than do the chronicles. The purpose of this essay, therefore, is to make some general observations, first on the infantry revolution and secondly on the artillery revolution as it applies to Lancastrian Normandy, and then to reflect on what this suggests about "the military revolution."

Lancastrian Normandy and the Infantry Revolution

First, then, the software – the "goddams," the nickname applied to English soldiers by those in their French conquests on account of their propensity for swearing. Do the English armies of the period (expeditionary, garrison, and field) constitute a military revolution? How do they compare with the fourteenth-century armies which Rogers considers evidence of the infantry revolution? At first sight, the answer looks simple. From the first invasion of 1415 to the loss of the duchy, the most commonly found ratio is one man-at-arms to three archers. That conclusion applies equally to all kinds of armies. It is seen in expeditionary armies both in terms of totals and within individual retinues (Table 1). It also applied in the garrisons in the conquered territories. For instance, the garrison at Harfleur initially held 300 men-at-arms and 900 archers. In the year 1422–23 it contained 40 + 120, but after the victory at Verneuil in August 1424 it was reduced to 15 + 45. In 1433–34 it held 30 + 90, and in the 1440s 50 + 150.[13] Similarly, the escorts of the commanders in France were commonly 20 men-at-arms and 60 archers,[14] and when field armies were put together from time to time from garrison detachments and other retinues, they also usually had three times as many archers as men-at-arms.[15] The ratio of 1:3 was the intended and the expected norm. This is revealed by the fact that on some occasions, espe-

[12] This project, based at the Universities of Reading and Southampton, is funded by the Arts and Humanities Research Council, and can be found at www.medievalsoldier.org.

[13] Bibliothèque Nationale de France [hereafter BNF], manuscrit français 4485, pp. 213–15; *Letters and Papers Illustrative of the Wars of the English in France during the Reign of Henry the Sixth, King of England*, 2 vols. in 3 (London, 1861–64), vol. 2, part ii, pp. 540–46; BNF manuscrit français 26274/10.

[14] For one example, see Anthony J. Pollard, *John Talbot and the War in France 1427–1453* (London, 1983), pp. 69–70.

[15] Anne Curry, "The Organisation of Field Armies in Lancastrian Normandy," in *Armies, Chivalry and Warfare in Medieval Britain and France*, ed. M. Strickland (Stamford, 1998), pp. 207–31.

cially in the raising of field armies, only the number of men-at-arms was given followed by the expression "et les archers," or "et les archers à l'afferant."[16] Since we can know from the sources what the number of archers raised was, we can see that it was indeed three times the number of men-at-arms.

Table 1. Some examples of expeditionary armies, 1423–1431
(information taken from the Exchequer Issue Rolls, The National Archives E 403)

Date	Men-at-arms (mounted)	Archers (mounted)
1423	380	1140
1424	411	1230
1425	349	1047
1427	300	300
1430	1196	3596
1431	200	600

In making comparison with the fourteenth century, we can see therefore that the infantry revolution was by no means linear but rather fluctuated across the period of the Hundred Years War. In the expeditionary armies of the early years of the war, taking the other kinds of troops, in addition to archers, as infantry, the ratio was between 1:1.6 and 1:2 (Table 2).[17] In the second phase from 1369 to 1389, it was commonly 1:1 with a range up to 1:1.6 (Table 2).[18] In addition, there was a trend towards simplification. From 1369 onwards to the end of the Hundred Years War, troops for the expeditions to France were recruited in two categories, men-at-arms and archers, and almost all were mounted. Commanders and captains always mustered as men-at-arms and are counted in the numbers. In terms of ratios, therefore, the exceptions of the Crécy campaign of 1346, at 1:5, and the Reims campaign of 1359, at 1:2.5, are notable. Save for these exceptions, however, the fifteenth-century expeditions contained proportionately more infantry than those of the fourteenth.

---

[16] For instance, in reference to the troops ordered for the conquest of Maine between December 1424 and February 1425 (BNF manuscrit français 4491, fol. 26v).

[17] These figures are derived from a number of studies, including Albert E. Prince, "The Strength of English Armies in the Reign of Edward III," *English Historical Review* 46 (1931); Michael Prestwich, "English Armies in the Early Stages of the Hundred Years War," *Bulletin of the Institute of Historical Research* 56 (1983); Andrew Ayton, "English Armies in the Fourteenth Century," in *Arms, Armies and Fortifications*, ed. Anne Curry and Michael Hughes; Cifford J. Rogers, *War Cruel and Sharp: English Strategy under Edward III 1327–1360* (Woodbridge, 2000); Andrew Ayton and Philip Preston, *The Battle of Crécy* (Woodbridge, 2005).

[18] James Sherborne, "Indentured Retinues and English Expeditions to France, 1369–1380," *English Historical Review* 79 (1964), 718–46; Adrian R. Bell, *War and the Soldier in the Fourteenth Century* (Woodbridge, 2004), pp. 10–11, 56–57.

Table 2. Examples of fourteenth-century expeditionary armies

	Ratio	Men-at-arms	Mounted archers	Other infantry
1339	1:1.6	1800	1100	1700
1340	1:2	1300	1000	1600
1342	1:2	1800	1800	1700
1346	1:5	2800	2800	8000
1355	1:1.6	1000	1000	600
1359	1:2.5	3000	3000	4000
1369	1:1.6	1200	2200	400
1370	1:1	2000	2000	
1373	1:0.9	3032	2893	
1379	1:1	2000	2000	
1387	1:1.3	1107	1390	

Why precisely the 1:3 ratio developed needs further research, as does the whole issue of whether numbers in individual retinues were set by the crown or by the captain who recruited them.[19] Its first use for an expedition to France was in 1412 (under Thomas duke of Clarence) but it is seen from at least 1406 in English armies sent to subdue the Glyndŵr rising in Wales.[20] Since the future Henry V was in command, it is tempting to link him to the devising of the 1:3 ratio, and it is certainly a ratio which dominated military organisation in his French campaigns.

Rogers has suggested that structures were moulded by the various military actions anticipated. Arguably, therefore, the 1:1 ratio of the late fourteenth century was deemed appropriate for chevauchée-style campaigns. Interestingly, at the same time that the 1:3 ratio became the norm for land campaigns, a ratio of one man-at-arms to two archers was preferred for naval activity (as in 1416),[21] presumably because for naval warfare opportunities for arrow shot were more limited and most fighting was hand to hand. Rogers' argument on the infantry revolution in his 1993 article focuses on battle situations. Is the development of the 1:3 ratio linked to anticipation of set-piece battles? Its use in the particular circumstances of Wales would not support this interpretation since the army

---

[19] For discussion on this point relating to 1415, see Anne Curry, *Agincourt: A New History* (Stroud, 2005), pp. 57–58.

[20] John D. Milner, "The English Enterprise in France, 1412–13," in *Trade, Devotion and Governance. Papers in Later Medieval History*, ed. Dorothy J. Clayton, Richard G. Davies and Peter McNiven (Stroud, 1994), pp. 80–101. In April 1406 Prince Henry entered into indentures as royal lieutenant in Wales with 500 men-at-arms and 1,500 archers (*Calendar of Patent Rolls 1405–1408*, p. 215). We also know that the prince was assigned 120 + 360 additional troops (The National Archives, London [hereafter TNA], E 404/21/310).

[21] Anne Curry, "After Agincourt, What Next? Henry V and the Campaign of 1416," *The Fifteenth Century* 7 (2007), 23–51.

of 1406 was intended largely to enable Prince Henry to establish garrisons. It is dubious whether battle was in mind in the 1412 expedition. Most of the expeditionary armies raised in the reigns of Henry V and VI were explicitly for conquest of places and territory. Indeed, it is important to remember that they provided garrisons for the places captured (as in the case of Harfleur in 1415 where, as we have seen, a garrison of 1:3 was installed). For Henry V's first campaign, however, it is significant that additional archer companies totalling 1650 men were raised from Lancashire, Cheshire and South Wales, taking the proportion of bowmen higher.[22] Even if Henry's march from Harfleur to Calais was undertaken in the hope of avoiding battle, it is difficult to deny that at the point he had raised his army, he had reckoned the French might attempt to meet him the field, and that a large number of archers would be useful, as they had been at the engagements of the fourteenth century. This was less of a concern in later campaigns, although Henry was astute enough to realise that different troops might suit different purposes, as when, during the siege of Rouen, he had a company of lightly armed and mounted Irish sent to Normandy to act effectively as cattle rustlers to stop food reaching the French but to take it instead for the English army.[23]

Military considerations surely played a role in establishing the 1:3 ratio, but none the less we need to see it in other contexts. The first was the perennial problem for English kings in their campaigns in France – their shortage of men-at-arms in comparison to their enemy. In the early campaigns Edward III sought to remedy this by using mercenary troops provided by his continental allies. In order to launch his great campaign of 1346 (if 14,000 strong, then the largest army ever sent to France), he had to make a huge effort to raise men-at-arms (about 2,800) as well as other kinds of troops. A similar effort is seen in 1415 in order to exceed 2,000 men-at-arms and to produce an army of around 12,000 men. Later in the reign Henry commissioned enquiries in the shires of England to try to find esquires who would be suitable for service in France and who had not yet served.[24] The database project will help us understand the size and nature of the military elite in England, and also why there was such a dramatic decline of knights in the fifteenth century. We can already conclude that in order to raise large armies to make an impact in France (such as Henry intended in 1415, and as Edward had intended in 1346 and 1359), the only possibility was to raise larger proportions of archers.

Save for the expeditions of 1415 and 1417, English armies sent to France under Henry V and VI were generally smaller than those of the fourteenth century. The largest after these was the army of just under 5,000 which crossed

---

[22] Curry, *Agincourt*, pp. 60–61.

[23] James H. Wylie and William T. Waugh, *The Reign of Henry the Fifth*, 3 vols. (Cambridge, 1914–29), 3:131–32.

[24] Anthony E. Goodman, "Reponses to Requests in Yorkshire for Military Service under Henry V," *Northern History* 17 (1981).

with Henry VI in 1430 on the coronation campaign.[25] But what we must not forget is the intensity of effort, which was much greater than in the preceding century. Expeditionary armies were sent every year until the truce of 1444, and often more than one per annum. The sustaining of this effort has implications for the composition of armies and for the infantry revolution. An intended ratio of 1:3 remained in place throughout the first half of the fifteenth century for armies raised in England for service in northern France but proved increasingly difficult to achieve. The first "chink" in the armor shows in the army raised by the earl of Salisbury in the summer of 1428 and which ended up at the siege of Orleans in the autumn. This was supposed to contain 600 men-at-arms and 1800 archers, but the earl could find only 444 men-at-arms and so compensated, as his indenture permitted him to do, by raising more archers (2,250 at the finish), so that the ratio moved to 1:5.[26] There are examples of similarly intentional higher ratios in the years which followed. Indeed, many expeditions after 1428 followed a 1:4 ratio, such as that sent under the earl of Arundel in the summer of 1434 (234 men-at-arms and 934 archers). Some went even higher on purpose, with 1:20 in a force sent under John Beaufort in February 1440, 1:11.5 in the army taken by John Talbot, earl of Shrewsbury, in 1442 with the hope of recovering Dieppe, and 1:8.8 in the force sent in March 1450. But in other cases the ratio was higher than intended. The army sent under John Beaufort in 1443, for instance, ended up with 6.6 archers to every man-at-arms instead of the intended 4.25.

Where the ratio was set deliberately high, we can suggest a financial imperative since archers had a daily wage of half of that of the men-at-arms (6d. as opposed to one shilling). Henry V had been able to raise massive and regular taxation to support his armies at the 1:3 ratio. The government of the early years of the minority kept this up since the relatively strong position of the English in France required the sending of relatively small, although regular, armies. The crisis of 1429 changed this situation, requiring more troops to be sent more frequently. This was not popular in England. It is not surprising that in August 1429 there should have been a request that those who had been granted lands in Normandy should return there to defend them.[27] Remember too that these land grants often included a requirement to provide troops for the royal host – intriguingly the ratio set by Henry V for this had been 1:2, perhaps more reflective of the situation in the duchy where there was a relative lack of archers in comparison to England.[28] Taxation was hard to prise out of the commons in

---

[25] Anne Curry, "The 'Coronation Expedition' and Henry VI's Court in France, 1430–32," in *The Lancastrian Court*, ed. Jenny Stratford (Stamford, 2003), pp. 30–54.

[26] Curry, "English Armies," p. 46. The following discussion is based on detailed study of the financing of expeditionary armies, as evidenced in the Issue Rolls (TNA E 403).

[27] *Proceedings and Ordinances of the Privy Council of England 1386–1542* [hereafter *PPC*], ed. Harris Nicolas, 7 vols. (London, 1834–37), 3:349.

[28] Anne Curry, "Le service féodal en Normandie pendant l'occupation anglaise, 1417–50," in *La France anglaise au moyen âge*, ed. Philippe Contamine (Paris, 1988), pp. 233–57.

the 1430s and 40s. It is also striking, as the years passed, how few members of parliament had experience of service in France. This phenomenon ties in with other indications of an increasing divide between the English in France and the English in Normandy especially after the king's coming of age and his own lack of interest in overseas interests. It was proving increasingly difficult to persuade the military elite to serve, as revealed not only by the declining participation of the nobility, knights and gentry but also the planned and unplanned fall in the proportion of men-at-arms in the expeditionary armies. At the moment of crisis in 1449–50 it even proved impossible to recruit the right number of archers. For the army of March 1450, the last real attempt to relieve the English position in the face of Charles VII's reconquest, recruitment of men-at-arms fell 60 short, and of archers 400 short.[29]

Some conclusions can therefore be suggested. The first is that the composition and size of armies was much affected by political will and financial resources. Henry V had been able to sustain his military effort; his successors could not do so. The second is that if there was an English infantry revolution, it was more sustained in the fifteenth century than the fourteenth. This has been shown to be true for the expeditionary armies. A few additional comments need to be made for the garrisons and other troops within Normandy. Whilst maintaining an overall ratio of 1:3, the garrisons increasingly had their men-at-arms in two groups: mounted and foot. In reality, therefore, the proportion of infantry in the duchy was greater than 75%. In the example of Harfleur, for instance, in 1422 the 40 men-at-arms were composed of 16 mounted men-at-arms and 24 foot. In 1424, the 15 men-at-arms were six mounted and nine foot. The 50 of the 1440s were between two and eight mounted with the rest unmounted. Commonly the composition of archers in the garrisons followed the same patterns. It is easy to understand why foot men-at-arms and archers should have been deemed adequate for garrison defence, especially where places were not deemed to be in much danger. The largest proportions of foot therefore tend to be found well away from the frontiers. Indeed, on the frontiers garrisons were either fully mounted, or else they had an ordinary garrison with a mixture of foot and mounted, and a mounted patrol of men-at-arms and archers specifically said to be "pour les champs."[30]

There was therefore flexibility and response to particular circumstances. This can be seen in other ways. For instance, it was common for the *baillis* and other administrative officials in Lancastrian Normandy to have retinues composed almost exclusively of mounted archers. The master of the ordnance commonly had a retinue of 14 mounted archers, but this could be boosted when a larger protective force was needed.[31] Archers were clearly seen as extremely useful

[29] Curry, "English Armies," p. 47.
[30] Reforms of the duke of Bedford in October 1434 put this on a regular footing, as the garrison indentures show (BNF manuscrit français 26058/2370–2385).
[31] Christopher T. Allmand, "L'artillerie de l'armée anglaise et son organisation à l'époque de Jeanne d'Arc," in *Jeanne d'Arc. Une Époque, un rayonnement* (Paris, 1982), pp. 76–77.

and adaptable. This is not surprising, since they were required to be armed with swords and daggers as well as their archery equipment. Although with less in the way of protective armor, in battle situations they could be involved in hand to hand fighting: at Agincourt, for instance, they came in with hammers and knives to finish off the French man-at-arms. The fact that so many were mounted enabled them to participate in raids, patrols and skirmishes, moving as quickly as their men-at-arms. Contingents sent out against brigands or for other policing actions were regularly made up of mixed retinues of men-at-arms and archers, as were the garrison detachments sent to sieges. Even if the mounted archers were not expected to fight from horseback, they performed some of the other functions of a mounted force: fast movement, harassment, pursuit.

We must remember too that in Lancastrian Normandy much military action was policing a civilian population, collecting victuals, maintaining a controlling and defending presence. In this respect infantry was just as useful as cavalry, archers as men-at-arms. At sieges it often proved difficult to maintain large numbers of horses because of shortage of victuals (as is well known, feeding a besieging army was as difficult as feeding one within a besieged place.) This caused a further blurring. On raids and in sorties from siege camps, much activity was in the form of skirmishing where battle-type positions would not be drawn up in advance with a delay before engagement. Whilst mounted men-at-arms would be essential for true cavalry charges against similar troops (for instance, when cavalry made a sortie from a besieged town), these engagements were few and far between. We can note here the actions of soldiers from the coastal garrisons who also patrolled the sea. To cite only one example: three foot men-at-arms and 53 archers of the garrison of Harfleur were in a boat capturing ships off the coast and sailing up to Calais to sell their booty from 1 November to 22 December 1441, but returning to their home garrison in time for Christmas.[32]

What we see most of all in Lancastrian Normandy is how men-at-arms and archers were integrated. They regularly operated in tandem in the mixed retinue, which also formed the basis of recruitment. Those mustering as mounted men-at-arms no doubt had more and better horses (trained for combat situations – the difference therefore is in the schooling of the horse) and superior personal arms. It was from their ranks that the commanders of units, captains, lieutenants, constables, marshals, *chefs des montres* came – a list which reflects the different levels of command needed in an army, especially one of occupation. Men-at-arms were commonly placed in command of groups of archers (in some muster rolls the archers are placed under a man-at-arms as their *maître*, often in the 1:3 ratio), and mounted men-at-arms are often seen in command of foot men-at-arms as well as archers. The distinction between the various kinds of troops is therefore as much one of social status as military function. Only men from a certain social status trained from their youth with the lance, whether for use on horseback or on foot. Only they participated in that upper class sport, the tournament. There may also be an age element here, with young men of status beginning their careers as archers. An occupation which lasted for thirty-five years was bound to have a major impact on soldiering as a career, stimulating the rise of professionalism for soldiers of all kinds, and also affecting patterns and trends in command (not least as the participation of the highest echelons diminished in the reign of Henry VI). It is perhaps this which is the real contribution of the period to a military revolution, especially for the infantry. However, there is emerging evidence from our database that from 1429 onwards, a good number of the archers of the garrisons, and even some of the men-at-arms, were not English at all but were locally recruited. If there was an infantry revolution in Lancastrian Normandy, we must ask whose it was – the English or the French – and also how it may link to the reforms which Charles VII made to his army in the mid 1440s which contributed to his success in the Reconquest of 1449–50. This issue will be returned to in the conclusion, but now let us turn to the second element in Rogers' medieval military revolution – the question of gunpowder artillery.

Lancastrian Normandy and the Artillery Revolution

The use of gunpowder artillery by the English predates the conquest of Normandy. Henry V as prince certainly used sizeable pieces in the Welsh wars, most notably in the siege of Aberystwyth in 1407 where there is reference to a piece weighing over 4,000 pounds, over ten times the weight of the majority of cannon in royal hands in 1382.[33] Was it this experience which encouraged Henry to a siege-based strategy in his invasions of Normandy? We know that he took gunpowder artillery with him in 1415. The bombardment of Harfleur is emphasised in the *Gesta Henrici Quinti*. Although to date I have not been able to find administrative sources which tell us more about the artillery pieces themselves, we do know the names of the gunners he took, and that they did not accompany him on his march northwards, the implication being that neither did the guns, which were left in Harfleur for the defence of the place. During the siege of Rouen the king ordered that the guns at Harfleur should be brought up the river to the siege. Yet there is little evidence of much bombardment either at Rouen or at earlier sieges of the second campaign.[34] Henry had learned an expensive lesson at the siege of Harfleur, that excessive damage to the fortifications of a place which then fell to him could make its defence expensive and problematic. Large sums had to be spent on the rebuilding of Harfleur's defences in the 1420s.

---

[33] Michael Prestwich, *Armies and Warfare*, p. 293.
[34] Anne Curry, "Henry V's Conquest of Normandy 1417–1419: The Siege of Rouen in Context," *Guerra y diplomacia en la Europa Occidental 1280–1480. XXXI Semana de Estudios Medievales. Estella 19–23 de julio 2004* (Pamplona, 2005), pp. 237–54.

We can trace the provision of gunpowder artillery for other expeditionary armies, most notably that of the earl of Salisbury in 1428 which was intended as a major push towards the Loire and beyond.[35] There is therefore some irony that the earl was the most famous victim of gunshot at the siege of Orleans. In addition to what was brought over from England, however, we must not overlook two other forms of supply. When the English captured places in France, they also captured the defensive and offensive weaponry within them, and compositions for surrender required that there should be no damage to *material de guerre* by those evacuating the place. Secondly, once in control, the English could commission the construction of artillery pieces. In theory therefore there is no reason to suppose the English lacked means of provision. The financial records of Lancastrian Normandy are not lacking in references to castles, towns and other fortifications housing guns, powder and other necessaries. At Pont de l'Arche in 1423, for instance, there was a *gros canon* "en la basse court dudit chastel aupres de l'entrée de la porte."[36] We can also trace *cannoniers* present in such places, as well as administrators responsible: take for example Jean Holland "garde des canons, artillerie et habillemens de guerre de monsieur le roy" in the town of Harfleur in September 1427, where he also held the office of grenetier.[37] Purchases of the ingredients for gunpowder are also evidenced.[38]

Christopher Allmand has already alerted us to the masters of ordnance and artillery, and their retinues.[39] The financial records also demonstrate how the masters were commonly given a sum of money to spend at the outset of a campaign or action, in addition to their regular annual payment. During the siege of Mont-Saint-Michel in 1426, Lord Scales as captain of one of the bastides built for the blockade by land was provided by the master of ordnance with seven "wuglaires" and three "menus bombardes" as well as powder. In June 1431 twenty cartloads of cannon, ribaudequins and culverins were taken to the siege of Louviers.[40] At the point in October 1431 when it was expected that Louviers would be taken by assault or would surrender, Philibert de Moulant, "maitre et visiteur de notre artillerie en France," ordered a quarry master to prepare and shape into rounds 100 balls from the quarries at Vernon at "vingt six poulces selon le kalibre sur ce lui bailla." These were to be delivered to the "cour de l'escurie" near the Seine at Rouen for transportation by river to the army around Louviers.[41] Eleven years later, masons from the vicomté of Alençon were paid five *sous tournois* per day for serving at the siege of Saint-Ceneri to make

---

35 For lists of equipment procured by John Parker, who was appointed the earl's master of ordnance, see TNA E 101/51/27/18 and E 101/51/30/4.

36 BNF manuscrit français 26046/62.

37 BNF manuscrit français 26050/771.

38 See, for instance, a reward made by the English government in 1450, when Cherbourg was under threat, to a local priest who had spent eleven weeks locating and purchasing powder and saltpetre (TNA E 28/79/72).

39 Allmand, "L'artillerie de l'armée anglaise."

40 Paris, Archives Nationales [hereafter AN], K 63/13/15.

41 AN K 63/13/27.

"pierres à bombardes, canons et culverins."[42] Add to this the ample examples of the hiring of carts for the transportation of guns and materials both between English-held places and from such places to sieges and back again, the presence of heavy guns being suggested by the use of 80 "grans beufs" for the movement of cannon to the siege of Le Mans in 1425.[43] We even know that gunpowder was used to blow up fortifications where it was decided not to man them but to disable them for fear of their falling into the hands of the enemy.[44]

I could go on providing examples. On the face of it, then, we have the men, the machines and the wherewithal. But do we have the artillery revolution? The presence of gunpowder artillery at sieges was certainly no guarantee of success even in the period which Rogers suggests began to see the triumph of artillery. The English did manage to recapture Harfleur in 1440 but only by a combination of actions against the place itself and by mobile actions within the vicinity. They never managed to retake Dieppe despite use of gunpowder artillery. Furthermore, in some cases, most notably that of Louviers in 1430–31, the scale of investment required in order to enforce a surrender was immense.

If there is one overriding point which emerges from a study of the financial material it is the huge cost of gunpowder artillery. This is not simply limited to the production of the guns themselves but also to their repair, their transportation, the provision of powder, and their manning. The wage levels paid to all groups involved – cannoniers, carpenters, voicturiers – were much higher than military wages. Admittedly they were paid only for short periods, but, combined with the other costs, it seems to me to provide a considerable constraint on the use of gunpowder artillery by the English. There are other caveats. First, there was a limited supply of weaponry, especially when war was being conducted on several fronts at once. This may be a result of costs but there were other factors. There was the fragility of the artillery pieces themselves. In September 1427 attempts to recover Montargis were held up by the fact that many cannon had been broken by use in sieges in the campaigns into Maine and Anjou, and others had been dispersed to different places.[45] Whilst it was possible to find some spares in Harfleur, they needed to be transported by boat to Paris and then overland to Montargis, not only a costly venture but a slow one. Furthermore, when guns were moved around, they needed to have substantial military escorts for fear of enemy capture. Guns were never in the place you needed them, and therefore they had less impact in emergency situations than in planned actions. Powder and stones could run out. Men could easily be moved, hardware could not.

I cannot claim to have exhausted all possible avenues of enquiry but my researches to date have suggested that there was little manufacture of guns within Normandy and that even repairs could be problematic. In October 1435

---

[42] BNF manuscrit français 26070/4623.
[43] BNF manuscrit français 26048/433.
[44] BNF nouvelles acquisitions françaises 1482/91 (concerning Vaudreuil, June 1430).
[45] BNF manuscrit français 26050/771.

the cannon in the castle of Rouen were "tournes a ruyne et empirance," but they could not be repaired on site because the forge did not have the right equipment. If they were removed for repair elsewhere, that would place the castle in danger (this was after all a very tense time for the English following the defection of the duke of Burgundy). The solution was to order the necessary equipment for the castle forge to be delivered to the *cannonier*, but alas we do not know the outcome of the case.[46] The continuing provision of artillery pieces from England would suggest that supply within Normandy was not possible.

Access to other sources was dependent upon the fortunes of war. The French successes of 1429–30 cut off Normandy from Paris and what was left of its hinterland (although so far I have not found evidence of the use of material in Normandy from a Paris arsenal before this time anyway). To redress this situation, and also to accompany the young king who was crossing in person, a large army was despatched from England, landing in Calais in late April 1430. Much attention had been given to ordnance. John Hampton, master of the ordnance, not only had a huge train of 89 men but was also given over £2,200 to make purchases. On 16 April, the lieutenant of Harfleur and the treasurer of Calais were ordered to deliver guns and equipment to him. Hampton also purchased two large guns in Calais, weighing 6,780 pounds and 7,022 pounds, the smaller being named "the Henry," no doubt in deference to the king's presence.[47] The suggestion is therefore that an arsenal was kept in Harfleur (the only place in Normandy to be "anglicised" as an intentional policy) and that Calais was a place of manufacture or of marketing. Alas, I have not been able to trace any further references to "the Henry," but perhaps it was one of the guns ordered later to be brought to the siege of Louviers. A further point to bear in mind is that the English position had been relatively secure until the reverse at Orleans. There had therefore been little incentive for major arsenals or centres of production to be developed in the duchy, hence the need not only for the greater provision from England and Calais for the royal expedition, but also in June 1431 the appointment of a "controlleur sur le fait des ordonnances de Normandie" with the specific charge of finding out what materials the English had in the duchy, where, and in what state.[48]

The defection of the duke of Burgundy and the loss of much of upper Normandy at the turn of 1435–36 was a disaster, not simply because it made overland communications between Calais and the rest of the English possessions impossible but also because it involved the loss of Harfleur where it appears that some kind of arsenal was kept. In May 1436 Paris was lost and Calais was itself threatened. Fear of further French penetration seems to have stimulated provision of (or at least movement of) guns to those places deemed to be most vulnerable, such as Rouen.[49] The knock-on effect was the need to

---

[46] BNF manuscrit français 26060/2643.
[47] *PPC*, 4:31, 33; TNA E 101/52/22.
[48] AN Collection Dom Lenoir [microfilm 104] 22, fol. 197.
[49] BNF manuscrit français 26060/2696, 2768; 26062/3016.

provide expeditionary forces with guns in England. The duke of York's anxiety over this point when he agreed to serve a second term in 1440 is seen in the terms he demanded, that he should be supplied with six great guns and four dozen stones for each of them "seying and consyderyng that in all Normandie is none or righte little neither for the stuff of garrison ner for the field." He also requested 26 gunners accompany his army.[50] When the earl of Shrewsbury set sail for France in May 1442 a large quantity of "instruments and hablements" were prepared for his expedition "withouten the whiche our said cousins entent may not be executed nor putte in euce." Arrangements were also made for the "artillerers" to cross with the army.[51] Similar arrangements were made for the expedition sent under the earl of Somerset in the following year.

These moves suggest that there was little spare artillery in what was left of Lancastrian Normandy and that what was there was being kept for defensive use.[52] The truce of 1444 served as another disincentive to increase local provision. Although the duke of Suffolk later claimed that the cessation had been intended to serve as a period of rebuilding the English position towards the reopening of hostilities, this did not happen. When Charles was poised to invade the duchy in the early summer of 1449, the duke of Somerset sent an urgent message to the parliament. He specifically mentioned that "there is no place in the kings obeissaunce there purveied nother in reparations, ordenaunce ne in eny maner artillerie," and that to remedy this "wold drawe to inestimable costs," costs which the local population could not sustain.[53] The problem was not solved by the time Charles invaded the duchy. Even where there were guns there was a shortage of powder.[54] Frantic efforts were made to send material across from England, not only for the defence of fortifications but also for use in the field against the French. In June 1450 the master of ordnance reported that he had supplied two serpentines, one culverin with nine chambers, 200 shots of lead, five great ribaudequins with 10 chambers, four greater ribaudequins with four chambers, as well as two carts and 30 carpenters, gunners, smiths and

---

[50] *Letters and Papers Illustrative of the Wars of the English in France during the Reign of Henry VI, King of England*, ed. Joseph Stevenson, 2 vols. in 3 (London, 1861–64), vol. 2, part ii, p. 587. See also TNA E 404/57/263. He also requested 1,000 spear shafts, 4,000 bows, 12,000 sheaves of arrows and some bowstrings.

[51] TNA E 404/58/92.

[52] An interesting insight is provided by André de Laval's receipt for the equipment at Valognes which its English captain, Thomas Chiseval, handed over at the surrender in 1450. This included two serpentines made of brass (*cuivre*), one with three chambers, the other with two; also a brass culverin without a chamber; an iron culverin; two "roundels" of sulphur; a half roundel of "poudre"; a half roundel of saltpetre; nine barrels of "charbon a faire poudre" (BNF pièces originales 1668 de Laval 56).

[53] *Parliament Rolls of Medieval England 1272–1509*, vol. 12 (1447–60), ed. Anne Curry and Rosemary Horrox (Woodbridge, 2005), pp. 56–57.

[54] TNA E 28/79/72, payment to a priest of Cherbourg for his efforts, over the space of eleven weeks, to provide "gunnepowder, saltpetre and other divers stuff" at his own expense (December 1449).

masons, along with powder for both guns and culverins.[55] This suggests that the English intended to have guns with them at any engagement with Cade's rebels, and indeed guns may have been used at Formigny. The list suggests a reasonably up-to-date provision but in England rather than within Normandy, another example of the problems of having artillery in the right place at the right time.

All in all, therefore, the evidence from Lancastrian Normandy is not supportive of an artillery revolution on the part of the English. A further observation can be made from study of the names of the gunners taken over at least in the early expeditions, and also of the members of the retinue of the masters of the ordnance in Normandy. Although the masters were English on the whole (save for Philibert de Moulant serving 1425–31), most of the gunners serving under them were foreign. Henry V had taken a company of German gunners in 1415. German and Spanish names are seen in the retinues of the masters, as well as large numbers of French.[56] The retinue always had a "clerc français," reflective of the linguistic needs not only within the retinue but also to assist the master in negotiating provision of guns, powder, etc. with *marchant artillerers* (evidenced in Rouen and Paris) and transport with local *voicturiers*, often arranged through the *vicomtes* who were all local men. In other words, the English in Normandy had developed little of their own expertise either in production or in manning gunpowder artillery. There was no real incentive to do so given the circumstances of the occupation. Not only did they hope for "integration" but also for much of the time their possessions were safe from attack, especially in Lower Normandy. The records show us that efforts were made to build anti-artillery defences such as boulevards, and to mount guns on towers and walls, but we must bear in mind that, with so many garrisoned places, it was extremely difficult to effect a consistent defence. The building of fortifications was as expensive, if not more so, than the provision of gunpowder artillery, and reliant on local taxation. It was therefore not surprising that in the Reconquest Mantes should surrender to Charles VII to avoid damage to the walls which the townspeople had spent money on.[57]

It is doubtful whether an artillery revolution could have helped the English in 1449. They had been taken by surprise. From the truce of Tours onwards, they had undertaken what we now call defence cuts, reducing the garrison establishment to no more than 2,500 men, thereby putting perhaps 2,000 out of employment, a figure increased by the abandonment of Maine in 1448. Many veterans, reluctant to accept their loss of employment, took to living off the land, causing relations with the local population to deteriorate. Various means were deployed to solve the problem. Soldiers of English birth were rounded up and frogmarched to Cherbourg and Barfleur to be shipped home. But can it be a coincidence that Charles was able to create his *francs archers* at the very

---

[55] TNA E 28/80/65.
[56] Allmand, "L'artillerie de l'armée anglaise," p. 77.
[57] Anne Curry, "Towns at War: Norman Towns under English Rule, 1417–1450," in *Towns and Townspeople in the Fifteenth Century*, ed. John A. F. Thomson (Gloucester, 1988), pp. 149–50.

point that the English were releasing large numbers of troops from their service? Remember the earlier point that many Frenchmen had joined the English garrisons. Shortly after the truce soldiers no longer needed in Lancastrian Normandy were detailed, as part of a bipartite agreement, to join the Dauphin in military action on the eastern frontier of France. The reforms follow the return of this force to Nancy, and were reminiscent of many aspects of English organization in Lancastrian Normandy, not simply in the use of archers alongside men-at-arms, the structures of command, and in the deployment of garrison troops for field service in the flexible English model.

Charles VII invaded Normandy with a huge army, certainly as large as that with which Henry V had conquered the duchy in 1417–19. On both occasions, there were few examples of actual bombardment as the significant factor. More commonly in the Reconquest, the French *preparations* for bombardment and assault, rather than actual bombardment, were enough to prompt surrender, much as they had been in Henry V's conquest. That does not deny that the guns used in 1449–50 were more powerful than those in 1417–19, as Rogers and others have shown. Furthermore, many surrenders were forced on the English by the local populations. That was certainly what happened at Rouen, which explains why there was no siege as there had been in 1418–19. Each place was picked off, one by one, but the fall of the major places led to a domino effect. As we have seen, the English had denuded their garrisons. There was little chance of raising a field army large enough to give battle within the duchy, unlike the situation in 1418–19 when Henry knew that the French had enough resources to attempt a relief. As we have seen, the troops which were finally sent from England were too few, too late, and with an imbalance between archers and men-at-arms. When forced to engage at Formigny, the English were very easily defeated, and with that defeat came the inevitable loss of the remaining places under English control.

Behind the English success in earlier decades, and the French success in 1449–50, was political will and also resources. Henry V had only achieved his conquest through the raising of, for England, exceptionally large armies. Behind these lay huge levies of taxation. His reign is one of the most heavily taxed of the whole of English history. In the 1420s it proved possible to sustain actions in Normandy and elsewhere in northern France through taxation levied in France itself. But once the French had rallied in 1429 and Charles had been crowned, it proved increasingly difficult for Henry VI's government to raise funds either in England or France. The political will diminished and the resource base with it, with the opposite trend occurring in France, although it took another twenty years for the "balance" between the two powers to be reversed. It also needed the English to lose their ally (France was too large a theatre to be controlled without internal assistance), and to reduce their manpower following a truce, and for Charles to increase both his political support (as for instance in his Breton alliance) and his manpower.

A military revolution needs a strong, well resourced government to produce it. Historians therefore need to look at the prerequisites rather than the effects of it. England had the prerequisites in the earlier part of the century, the French by the middle of it. In a sense this is Rogers' punctuated equilibrium but it is linked primarily to the balance of power between states and the relative standing of central control and resource provision. These condition the kinds of armies and weapons which states can deploy, not the other way around. The infantry revolution of the later Middle Ages was the product of monarchical power and resource (with the advantage lying with the English at first, and then the French). The artillery revolution was even more the product of such control and resource since, unlike provision of troops, it could not be provided by any other organisation than the state, or at least not at the level required to make an impact.

In no period can we understand military activity without understanding the political and resource context which produced and conditioned it. The real leap forward is therefore when states can support both an artillery revolution and an infantry revolution. This was beginning to happen in France in the mid fifteenth century, but it did not happen in England until well into the reign of Henry VIII, when it was linked to changes in the methods of taxation and revenue raising. Even so, it was not until there was permanent taxation, as opposed to one-off grants, on a large scale that there was the real development of standing armies of markedly larger sizes than those of the Middle Ages. This was a development of the seventeenth century in both countries. In terms of gunpowder, the breakthrough was the development of handguns. These required much less training "for life" than had been needed by late medieval archers or even men-at-arms, and therefore encouraged and made possible mass armies. But as mechanical instruments, they were also flawed, as were many of the larger pieces of the fourteenth and fifteenth centuries, and required a much larger number of men to fire them to have a real effect. Was this progress at all?

NOTE

The Name of the Siege Engine *trebuchet*: Etymology and History in Medieval France and Britain

William Sayers

It is now generally agreed that traction and counterweight trebuchets were developed in China centuries before the Christian era and reached the Middle East and Central Europe through such intermediaries as the Mongols, Arabs, Avars and their Slav armies.[1] Our most extensive description is found in Yusuf ibn Arunbughâ al-Zaradkâsh's *An Elegant Book on Trebuchets* (*al-Anîq fî al-manajanîq*) from about 1462, although as early as the 1180s Saladin's advisor Mardi bin Alî al-Târsûsi describes a hybrid trebuchet and shows an awareness of the foreign provenance of the engine.[2] Al-Zaradkâsh's key word, *manajinîq*, is

---

[1] Essential studies and accounts of construction of and experimentation with trebuchets include the following: Roland Bechmann, *Villard de Honnecourt: la pensée technique au XIIIe siècle et sa communication* (Paris, 1991), now discredited in the matter of trebuchet design; P. E. Chevedden, "Black Camels and Blazing Bolts: The Bolt-Projecting Trebuchet in the Mamluk Army," *Mamluk Studies Review* 8 (2004), 227–77; P. E. Chevedden, "Fortifications and the Development of Defensive Planning during the Crusader Period," in *The Circle of War in the Middle Ages: Essays on Medieval Military and Naval History*, ed. Donald J. Kagay and L. J. Andrew Villalon (Woodbridge, Suffolk, 1999), pp. 33–43; P. E. Chevedden, L. Eigenbrod, V. Foley, and W. Soedel, "The Trebuchet," *Scientific American* 273 (1995), 58–63; D. R Hill, "Trebuchets," in *Medieval Warfare 1000–1300*, ed. John France, The International Library of Essays on Military History (Aldershot, 2006), pp. 271–88, reprinted from *Viator* 4 (1973), 99–114; P. V. Hansen, "Experimental Reconstruction of the Medieval Trebuchet," *Acta Archaeologica* 63 (1992), 189–208; M. Kirchschlager and T. Stolle, "Das teuflische Werkzeug – Entstehung und Geschichte der Weißenseer Steinschleuder," in *"Wurfen hin in steine / grôze und niht kleine ..."*: *Belagerungen und Belagerungsanlagen im Mittelalter*, ed. Olaf Wagener and Heiko Lass, Beihefte zur Mediaevistik: Monographien, Editionen, Sammelbände 7 (Frankfurt am Main, 2006), pp. 27–46; Tanel Saimre, "Trebuchet – A Gravity-Operated Siege Engine," *Eesti Arheoloogia Ajakiri: Journal of Estonian Archaeology* 10 (2006), 61–80; W. T. S. Tarver, "The Traction Trebuchet: A Reconstruction of an Early Medieval Siege Engine," *Technology and Culture: The International Quarterly of the Society for the History of Technology* 36 (1995), 136–39. Particularly pertinent to the present study is D. Bachrach, "English Artillery 1189–1307: The Implications of Terminology," *English Historical Review* 121 (2006), 1408–30. Additional relevant studies will be noted below.

[2] Yusuf ibn Arunbughâ al-Zaradkâsh, *al-Anîq fî al-manajanîq*, ed. Ihsân Hindî (Aleppo, 1985); Mardi bin Alî al-Tarsûsî, *Instruction of the Masters on the Means of Deliverance from Disasters in Wars*, Oxford, Bodleian Library, MS Hunt. 264, ed. C. Cahen as "Un traité d'armurerie composé pour Saladin," *Bulletin d'études orientales* 12 (1947–48), 103–63. An important new

among possible sources for the term *mangonel*, a catapult employing the torsion method of propulsion (twisted ropes), but we have no comparable early eastern source, whether Islamic, Greek, or more distant, for a term designating the counterweight trebuchet that might have prompted a loan or calque in western European languages.[3] Unlike the smaller traction trebuchet, called *perrier* or "stone(-thrower)" in medieval French, for which projectile power was generated by a group of men pulling sharply down on ropes attached to one end of a rotary beam, the counterweight or counterpoise trebuchet was a large siege engine with a very substantial counterweight attached or hinged to the shorter end of the rotary beam, and a long rope and sling for the missile at the end of the much longer section of the beam past the pivot. Prior to firing, the sling and missile lay in a trough under the machine. When fired, the beam drew the sling into a great arc behind the machine, with the missile released at the top of the arc.

The present study is devoted to the origin of the name *trebuchet* and its subsequent absorption into the French and English of Britain. A sampling of European terminology displays great variation in orthography but a clearly recognizable semantic core. We find Old French *trebuchet, trebuket, trebusket, trebuchel*, Provençal *trabuquet*, Catalan *trabuco, trabuquet*, Spanish *trabuquete*, Italian *trabocchetto*, Medieval Latin *tra-, trebuchetum*, and Middle English forms, the earliest from the thirteenth century, reflecting, at some distance, the French term: *trepeget, trepgette, trebgot, tripgette, treget*, and the like.[4]

As concerns the etymology of *trebuchet*, a first consideration must be the Old French verb *trebuchier* "to stumble, trip." The larger semantic field of which *trebuchier* is a part includes *trebuc*, both "fall" and "trap," *trebuchage, trebuchement, trebucherie* "act of reversing, causing to fall," and *trebuchet* in the distinct sense of "tripping (a person) up." Old French *trebuc* "fall" and related words often occur in a homiletic, moral, or ethical context, where a fall is contrasted

---

English-language resource for descriptions of siege engines in action is *The Chronicle of Ibn al-Atīr for the Crusading Period from al-Kāmil fi'l-Ta'rīkh. Part 3, The Years 589–629/1193–1231: The Ayyūbids after Saladin and the Mongol Menace*, trans. D. S. Richards (Aldershot, England, and Burlington, VT, 2008).

3   Anglo-Norman *mangonel, mangunel, magnel*, Old French, Middle French *mangonel*, attested in many variant spellings from the twelfth century onward in British and continental sources. A source in Greek is less likely. The engine was called *onager* by the Romans, who also knew the *ballista*, a torsion machine that threw bolts or darts.

4   For the Middle English evidence, see *Middle English Dictionary*, ed. R. E. Lewis et al. (Ann Arbor, 1959–2002), to which I return below. For related terms in the French of Britain, see *Anglo-Norman Dictionary*, ed. W. Rothwell et al. (London, 1992), Anglo-Norman On-Line Hub, http://www.anglo-norman.net/. The vocabulary of siege engines everywhere in Europe was extremely entangled. After listing six different types of Aragonese engines, P. D. Humphries remarks, "That these words all describe siege engines is clear, but their exact meanings, which would accurately classify these machines, remain obscure": "'Of Arms and Men': Siege and Battle Tactics in the Catalan Grand Chronicles (1208–1387)," *Military Affairs* 49 (1985), 173–78. Meaning as a guide to classification may be an illusory goal. I hope to return to this Catalan word set in a future study.

with some prior state of ascendancy, security, pride, or power.[5] Its use might be thought a recasting of the popular wheel of fortune motif as a see-saw, a device employing the same principle as the siege engine.

Little recognized from the vantage point of military history is the fact that the earliest attestations of the noun *trebuchet* in Old French refer not only to siege engines but to animal and bird traps. In the late twelfth- to early thirteenth-century *Renart* corpus (the "beast epic" about Reynard the Fox) the trebuchet is listed with various other devices, snares and mechanical traps that a villein sets for Renart. At its simplest the trebuchet could have been a beam or plank pivoting on a fulcrum, sending its unwary victim tumbling into a pit.[6] *Trebuchet* was used of a cucking-stool, in which malefactors were dunked,[7] and of simple sets of scales with a weigh beam. First attestations of the use of *trebuchet* to designate siege engines are from about 1200.[8] Like much of medieval military reality, siege engines were so little exceptional that they were not singled out for special literary treatment as a motif or described in detail. A passage from one of the earliest preserved Old French works to name the machines, the *chanson de geste Ogier le danois*, illustrates how the term is, for this author as for many others, chroniclers included, part of a larger word set for siege engines. Ogier the Dane (Danish *Holger*) invests his fortresses against the attacks of Charlemagne's grandson, here called Kalles (Carloman).

> Li bons Danois ne s'i valt atargier;
> De Chastel Fort fist les murs esforcier
> Et Mont Quevrel qi est sus le rochier:
> Mult ricement les a fait batillier
> Et trebuquiaus e periere drechier;
> Tant furent fort, con j'oï tesmognier,
> Assalt ne crement de traite ne de lanchier;
> Ne doctent siege de duc ne de princier.[9]

---

5 Amply illustrated in *Altfranzösisches Wörterbuch*, ed. A. Tobler and E. Lommatzsch (Stuttgart, 1925–2001), s.v. *trebuc*.

6 *Le Roman de Renart*, ed. M. Roques (Paris, 1948–66), VII b, 6437.

7 *The Chronicle of Jocelin of Brakelond*, ed. H. E. Butter (London and New York, 1949), p. 3: "Levaverunt homines de Illegga quoddam trebuchet, ad faciendam justiciam pro falsis mensuris panis vel bladi mensurandi." The "cucking stool" or "ducking stool" was (OED) "An instrument of punishment formerly in use for scolds, disorderly women, fraudulent tradespeople, etc., consisting of a chair (sometimes in the form of a close-stool), in which the offender was fastened and exposed to the jeers of the bystanders, or conveyed to a pond or river and ducked."

8 For example, *Le roman de Renart*, ed. E. Martin (Strasbourg, 1882–87), XI, 2545; because of its satirical realism, the Raynard works are a treasure-trove of technical vocabulary. See further examples in *Altfranzösisches Wörterbuch*. Jean de Meun, in his translation of Vegetius's *De re militari* as *L'Art de Chevalerie*, complements the listing of catapults with an anachronistic reference to the trebuchet; *Li abregemenz noble honme Vegesce Flave René des establissemenz apartenanz a chevalerie*, traduction par Jean de Meun de Flavii Vegeti Renati Viri Illustris *Epitoma Institutorum Rei Militaris*, ed. L. Löfsted (Helsinki, 1977), book 4, p. 178.

9 *La Chevalerie d'Ogier de Danemarche*, ed. M. Eusebi (Milano, 1963), vv. 3435–42.

[The worthy Dane had no cause for delay. He had the walls strengthened at
Chastel Fort and Mont Quevrel, which is situated atop a rock. He had them
densely fortified and had counter-weight and traction trebuchets installed. The
castles were so strong, according to the testimony I have heard, that they feared
attack neither with shot nor projectiles, nor had they cause to fear any siege that
might be laid by a duke or princely lord.]

The authoritative lexicographical work on the etymology of the French
language is *Französisches etymologisches Wörterbuch (FEW)*.[10] It is organized
by etyma or root words, although the work is now complemented by an alphabetical index of all words treated. Thus, it is under the Frankish or Old Low
Franconian head word *bûk* "belly" that we find the discussion of *trebuchet* and
related words.[11] This term is seen to have evolved in Old French as *bu, buc*, with
the meaning "trunk (of a tree or body)." Writing of the derivatives *trebuchier*,
trebuc, and *trebuchet*, the editors state that these occupy a "special position" in
the history of this word cluster. The first element would reflect the Latin prepo-
sition *trans* "through, across," seen in Old French as *tres* or *tre-*. The editors
judge fortuitous any resemblance to Latin *trabs, trabis* "beam." The use of this
and related terms for animal and bird traps is explained as these latter having
first consisted of simple pits into which the prey fell, and only later of more
elaborate arrangements with a triggering device. Omitted from this explanation
is any discussion of the weigh-beam of a set of scales.

The *FEW* explanation of *trebuchet* may be judged plausible as concerns the
Gallo-Romance prefix *tre-*, which took on a reinforcing and perfective sense
("thoroughly") as well as denoting both lateral and vertical movement, but the
simple appeal to Old Low Franconian *bûk* "belly" does little to explain core
semantics.

A more plausible origin for Old French *buc, bu* is in Gaulish *bagos* "beech"
(or possibly originally another tree) or cognate Germanic *bōkō* "beech" (cf.
German *Buche*, English *beech*). The smooth bole of the beech may have facili-
tated the transfer of the term to the human body. This does not directly assist
in understanding the formation *trebuchier* or *trebuchet* but does at a minimum
dispose of the awkward "belly" association. Let us assume that the original
meaning of *trebuc* was something like "trunk down."[12]

---

10 *Französisches etymologisches Wörterbuch*, ed. W. von Wartburg (Bonn, 1928–); *Dictionnaire
    étymologique de l'ancien français*, ed. K. Baldinger, J. D. Gendron, and G. Straka (Quebec,
    Tübingen, and Paris, 1974–), has not yet treated *trebuchet* or its possible constituent elements.
11 *FEW, Germanische Elemente*, vol. 15.2, 3–7, s.v. *bûk*.
12 Another hitherto unexplored avenue toward a more satisfactory explanation of the term *trebu-
    chet* and related reflexes may be considered. From northern France and its Picard dialect we
    note the verb *buskier, buquier* "to strike," still seen in regional French and dialects as "to knock,
    bang." *FEW* postulates a connection with *bûcher* "to cut wood" (cf. *bûche* "log"), which would
    prompt an association with Old French *buc* (seen above) or a Germanic **buskan* "to beat." But
    there is little true beating or striking action seen in the kinetics associated with the various
    meanings of *trebuchet*, and Picard *buskier* seems a separate development.

Siege engines were often given familiar names, an element of psychological warfare that bonded the troops using them and also served to demoralize those against whom they were used, if they were unfortunate enough to learn of the names. Examples are Richard the Lionheart's *Male Voisine* "Bad (Female) Neighbor," the duke of Burgundy's *Periere Deu* "The Catapult of God," Edward I's *Warwolf* "Tight-Rigged Wolf," and Charles VI of France's *Coyllar* (standard orthography *coillart*) "Big Balled," a reference to sexual dominance and to the 800-kilo stone the commissioned engine was to be capable of firing.[13] Old French forms such as *trebuchet* and *trebuchel* are, however, unlikely to be hypocorisms or nicknames but are simply the unmarked names for a specific kind of siege engine, as are *mangonel* and *perrier*.

Because of widespread misunderstandings, both medieval and modern, it has been assumed that trebuchets were capable of firing arrows or darts. This capability was reserved for the ballista and it is clear the basic design of the trebuchet would not have permitted loading such missiles. Yet the *MED* is explicit: "A siege weapon designed to cast stones, darts, etc." In support, it adduces this pairing in an anachronistic bible translation from about 1425: "Thei maden arblastis ether trepeiettis, that is, an instrument for to caste schaftis and stoonys" ("they constructed arbalests or trebuchets, that is, an instrument for casting bolts and stones").[14] The modern translation of a commentary in Villard de Honnecourt's sketchbook from about the 1230s also clouds the waters. Villard's text reads:

> Se vos voles faire le fort engieng c'on apiele trebucet prendes ci garde. Ves ent ci les soles si com il siet sor tierre. Ves la devant les .II. windas et le corde ploie a coi on ravale le verge. Veir le poes en cele autre pagene. Il i a grant fais al ravaler, car li contrepois est mout pezans. Car il i a une huge plainne de tierre, ki .II. grans toizes a de lone et .VIIII. pies de le, et .XII. pies de parfont. Et al descocier de le fleke penses et si vos en dones garde. Car ille doit estre atenue a eel estancon la devant.[15]

Philippe Contamine's *War in the Middle Ages* (1984) offers this rendering:

> If you want to make the strong engine which is called a trebuchet, pay close attention here. Here is the base as it rests on the ground. Here in front are the two windlasses and the double rope with which one draws back the beam as you can see on the other

---

[13] On the first two names, see Ambroise, *L'estoire de la guerre sainte*, ed. G. Paris (Paris, 1897), vv. 4745, 4760. The *war-* element of *Warwolf* is found in compounds indicating tightening, e.g. ship's ropes, and the name means neither "werewolf" nor "war-wolf."

[14] *The Holy Bible ... by John Wycliffe and His Followers*, ed. J. Forshall and F. Madden, 4 vols. (London, 1850), 1 Mac. 6.20.

[15] *The Portfolio of Villard de Honnecourt (Paris, Bibliothèque nationale de France, MS Fr 19093): A New Critical Edition and Colour Facsimile*, ed. C. F. Barnes (Burlington, 2009). Meanwhile, the illustration may be consulted as plate 59 in *Carnet de Villard de Honnecourt: d'après le manuscrit conservé à la Bibliothèque nationale de Paris (no 19093)*, ed. A. Erlande-Brandenburg et al. (Paris, 1986). Villard's language has not been the object of exclusive study since F. E. Schneegans, "Ueber die Sprache des Skizzenbuches von Villard de Honnecourt," *Zeitschrift für romanische Philologie* 25 (1901), 45–70.

page. There is a great weight to pull back, for the counter-poise is very heavy, being a hopper full of earth which is two large toises [12 feet] long and nine feet across and twelve feet deep. Remember the arc of the arrow when discharged and take great care, because it must be placed against the stanchion in front.[16]

Villard's account is not highly technical in nature. He names some few principal parts but the text is clearly secondary to the illustration(s), the second of which has not been preserved. The greatest problem is the word *fleke – flèche* in Modern French. This has often been understood, as by Contamine, as a term for a projectile that, *grosso modo*, resembled an arrow or bolt. The reality is a good deal simpler. *Fleche* had a number of technical senses in medieval French: the fulcrum point of a crane beam; the vertical distance from the ground to the top of an arc or arch; the vertical measurement from the ground to the highest point of the trajectory of a projectile. None of these is applicable in this context, not even the last, since the moment of risk for bystanders would be long past, after the sling and missile had snaked out of the trough and risen to the top of their arc. Rather, Villard advises paying attention to the *tip* of the rotary beam, where it was locked down and the firing or tripping device would seem to have been located.[17] A more accurate rendering of the text is then:

If you want to construct the powerful engine that is called a trebuchet, pay attention to this. Here you see the base beams and how the engine is seated on the ground. In front, you see the two windlasses and the double-pulleyed rope with which the beam is pulled back and down. See further on the next page. It is very hard work to pull it back, because the counterweight is very heavy. For there is a bin, filled with earth, two good *toises* (more than 12 feet) long and eight feet wide and twelve feet deep. And, when the tip of the rotating beam is released, remember to be careful. For it will have been locked down on the stanchion at the front.

Trebuchets were employed by British lords, both those who spoke Anglo-Norman French as a first language, such as Richard I, and their successors, whose tongue we call Middle English. Written reference to the engines is first found in inventories of the materials of war, at times in conjunction with the gear for ship's castles, so that we must imagine some version of the machine being operated from a fighting castle at the mast head.[18] In literary works, the term is not isolated in a paratactic list but is grouped with comparable machines of war.

Þan ser Balaan ... Buskes him in breneis with big men of armes, With traumes & with tribochetis þe tild to asaile [Then Sir Balan ... arms himself in a coat of mail

16 P. Contamine, *War in the Middle Ages*, trans. Michael Jones (New York, 1984), 103.
17 More detailed discussion is in W. Sayers, "Villard de Honnecourt on the Counterweight Trebuchet," *AVISTA Forum Journal* 19 (2009), 46–48.
18 "iij toppelynes, v twystlyne, vj tregetrop..vj trusses, ij tregett, ij Cranelynes, et j toppelyne"; from an inventory of nautical gear from 1359–59, given in B. Sandahl, *Middle English Sea Terms* (Uppsala and Boston, 1951–82), 3:150.

with powerful men at arms, with siege towers and with trebuchets in order to attack the siege works.][19]

A somewhat more graphic account is found in an English translation of the Bible.

Then lete Vaspasian avale the laddirs and lete cast stones an high on eche side of the wallis and made shote tribgettis and engynes and quarellis [Then Vespasian had ladders raised and had stones cast aloft on both sides of the walls and fired with trebuchets and other siege engines and with arbalests.][20]

A last example will illustrate the same sense of wonder that we experience at the range of the trebuchet.

An hundrid gynnys þey were vpset, Of Maungeneles and Treybochet; The leste of hem, the sothe to seye, Myght castyn a large myle of þe way [A hundred siege engines were erected, mangonels and trebuchets; the least of them, to tell the truth, could cast a full mile of the way.][21]

The orthographies for the English name of the trebuchet and related instruments (trap, scales) that are recorded from trilingual medieval Britain vary quite considerably. The Middle English forms *trepeget, trepgette, trebgot, tripgette, treget* suggest that some recollection of the French verb *jeter* "to throw, cast" may have been discerned in the second element. English *trap* may also have been in play, blurring the phonic and semantic boundary of the French compound *trebuchet*.[22] To return to an even earlier stage, it cannot be ruled out that Old French *tref* "beam" may also have continued to resonate in the name of the siege engine in both France and Britain. In all of this, the mechanical structure and kinetic progression would have been preserved: TRAP – TRIP – JETTING. Although the borrowed term is not fully recontoured in English in the way that French *girasol* ("turning with the sun" = "sunflower") is recast as *Jerusalem (artichoke)*, this overall development – from French *trebuchet* to the many Middle English forms – may be put under the rubric of folk etymology.

As the siege engine became obsolete after the introduction of gunpowder, a written orthographical standard imposed itself – *trebuchet* – modeled on then current French spelling, although the original significance of the name was doubtless obscured. Today, when historical and antiquarian interest has replaced military applications, siege engines and their names have again stimulated widespread interest. In discrete lexicographical terms we may close by saying that English *trebuchet* and its medieval variants may be seen as loan words possibly affected by folk etymologizing, after being, in France and elsewhere, a

[19] *The Wars of Alexander, an Alliterative Romance*, ed. W. W. Skeat, Early English Text Society, extra series 47 (London, 1886; repr. 1973), 1296.
[20] *The ME Prose Translation of Roger D'Argenteuil's Bible en François, ed. from Cleveland Public Library MS W q 091.92–C468*, ed. P. Moe (Heidelberg, 1977), 84/13.
[21] *The Seege or Batayle of Troye*, ed. M. E. Barnicle, Early English Text Society 172 (London, 1927; repr. 1971), 1065b.
[22] *Trap* is attested from the Old English period as *treppe, træppe*.

quite accurate *terminus technicus* (basic signification "beam down") for several devices that could be cocked and then tripped, and for a siege machine whose fundamental mechanics were a short but heavily weighted arm rotating downward around a pivot in order to generate projectile force at the other end, to which were attached the rope, sling, and destructive missile.

Journal of Medieval Military History
1477–545X

Volume I

Volume II

Volume III

Volume VI

Volume VII

CPSIA information can be obtained at www.ICGtesting.com
Printed in the USA
BVOW022323181211

278635BV00003B/6/P